Book gathers im _____ naissance
meanderingly amon _____ points
Pastoro to make _____
Paradise must h _____ peac
paradise must be let _____ will have
we here is to know that will have
no abiding peace.
Is a poet and quoting Baltisows
comment on Housemans teen scip aptly
" I know fewer ~~the~~ neater then the
g the difference between a poets
ready and a scholars ready
" Terse packed language full of subtle
and significant thought"
" News degenerates into jargon or
degenerates into that species of Literary
outspun cliche which althf there are cocoon
g it can mar so much American and
english criticism"
feels Keats Ode to Maia" the most
perfect pastoral poem Ever written   see pg
219.
gerard de Nerval and the Return of the
gods — where th will be taken not as
literally "true" but metaphors as a language
g the heart
would have been enriched by a deeper
study g Jung, Blake and other pro
Platonic writers
Christianity now being replaced by
Reason, I gnore its buckling up with
Reason my theologians like Tillich and de Chardin

THE USES OF NOSTALGIA

THE USES OF NOSTALGIA

Studies in Pastoral Poetry

By

LAURENCE LERNER

1972

CHATTO & WINDUS

LONDON

Published by
Chatto & Windus Ltd
42 William IV Street
London WC2N 4DF

★

Clarke, Irwin & Co. Ltd
Toronto

ISBN 0 7011 1826 1

© Laurence David Lerner 1972

Printed in Great Britain by
T. & A. Constable Ltd,
Hopetoun Street, Edinburgh

CONTENTS

PART I: A MAP OF ARCADIA

PART II: SOME ARCADIANS

Acknowledgements

Many audiences have listened to parts of this book, and have helped me by discussing and demolishing what they have heard. Individual chapters, usually in an earlier form, were delivered to groups of students or teachers at various universities: Oxford, Cambridge, Kent, Newcastle, the North-West London Polytechnic, Strasbourg, Munich, Aachen, and my own ruthless colleagues in the University of Sussex Renaissance seminar; also to the invisible audience of the BBC; and a version of the whole was given to the members of my seminar on Pastoral at the University of New Mexico, and (later) to my students at Munich. It is said that nothing concentrates the mind better than impending execution, and I suppose, if one were a fast enough writer, the best time to write a book would be between the sentence and the guillotine. Failing this drastic method, I find that nothing concentrates the mind like an audience; and the impending execution of having to say what you think helps wonderfully in deciding whether you really believe it. To all these executioners, therefore, my lasting thanks.

Some chapters (often in slightly abridged form) have appeared in print: Chapter I, as 'An Essay on Pastoral', in *Essays in Criticism*, July 1970; Chapter IV in *Dylan Thomas: New Critical Essays*, edited by Walford Davies and published by J. M. Dent; Chapter VII in *English Studies in Africa*, September 1970; Chapter IX in *The Journal of English and Germanic Philology*, October 1971; and Chapter X in *Seven Studies in English*, a symposium by former students of the University of Cape Town, 1971.

I have the usual debt to those friends and colleagues who allowed me to pick their brains, or read some or all of my manuscript, and added comments of varying severity—Peter Burke, Gabriel Josipovici, Nick Osmond, Gamini Salgado, Werner von Koppenfels, and above all Tony Nuttall.

Finally, I must mention what is always (in such a work) the greatest debt, which is to those I know only through their books. In what follows, I have not written about the critics and scholars of pastoral, and I must therefore say in advance what will be clear to the well-informed reader, that this book could never have come about without the labours of those better read and more learned than I. Debts of detail are too numerous to mention; the following brief list includes only those whom I have read with steady admiration and far-reaching profit: W. H. Auden ('Vespers'; 'Dingley Dell and the Fleet'), Mircea Eliade (*The Myth of the Eternal Return*), William Empson (*Some Versions of Pastoral*), W. W. Greg (*Pastoral Poetry and Pastoral Drama*), Lovejoy and Boas (*Primitivism and Related Ideas in Antiquity*), Renato Poggioli (especially for 'The Oaten Flute' in the *Harvard Library Bulletin*, 1957), Jean Seznec (*The Survival of the Pagan Gods*) and Ernest Tuveson (*Millenium & Utopia*).

April 1971   L. D. L.

PART I

A MAP OF ARCADIA

I

WHAT PASTORAL IS

W<small>E</small> will begin with a country walk; and for a companion, who better than Robert Frost? His poems are full of walks in the New England woods or fields or swamps, telling us of what he saw there—steps in the snow, or snow without steps; the shapes of trees, the activity of birds; the occasional traces of man. One such trace was a pile of logs, and it provides the title of its poem:

The Woodpile

Out walking in the frozen swamp one gray day,
I paused and said, 'I will turn back from here.
No, I will go on farther—and we shall see.'
The hard snow held me, save where now and then
One foot went through. The view was all in lines
Straight up and down of tall slim trees
Too much alike to mark or name a place by
So as to say for certain I was here
Or somewhere else: I was just far from home.
A small bird flew before me. He was careful
To put a tree between us when he lighted,
And say no word to tell me who he was
Who was so foolish as to think what he thought.
He thought that I was after him for a feather—
The white one, in his tail; like one who takes
Everything said as personal to himself.
One flight out sideways would have undeceived him.
And then there was a pile of wood for which
I forgot him and let his little fear
Carry him off the way I might have gone,
Without so much as wishing him goodnight.
He went behind it to make his last stand.
It was a cord of maple, cut and split
And piled—and measured, four by four by eight.
And not another like it could I see.
No runner tracks in this year's snow looped near it.
And it was older sure than this year's cutting,
Or even last year's or the year's before.

The wood was gray and the bark warping off it
And the pile somewhat sunken. Clematis
Had wound strings round and round it like a bundle.
What held it though on one side was a tree
Still growing, and on one a stake and prop,
These latter about to fall. I thought that only
Someone who lived in turning to fresh tasks.
Could so forget his handiwork on which
He spent himself, the labour of his axe,
And leave it here far from a useful fireplace
To warm the frozen swamp as best it could
With the slow smokeless burning of decay.

What is this poem about? In a way, its subject never appears. Just as van Gogh's chair, thrusting on us the fact that someone made it, made it crudely but with gusto, is indirectly about that someone; just as his picture of his room is indirectly a portrait of the painter himself who was there so recently; so this poem is about the man who never appears, but is brought gradually to the forefront of attention. We are half-way through before the poem notices the pile of logs; and from this we move gradually to the fascinating conclusion that it must have been cut by someone so vigorous, so dedicated to work, that he never got round to fetching it. Ironically, it is the pile of logs that suffers, left 'to warm the frozen swamp as best it could', denied even a proper consummation on the hearth, treated like trees that had merely fallen down. It is a neat irony: the neglect of the logs converts the poem into a hymn of praise, for it is a neglect that shows strength, not weakness. I know few poems which jump more outrageously to a conclusion: on the basis of this cord of maple, the man's whole character is deduced. If we are to take so bold a deduction seriously, we have got to trust the narrator.

So, with another kind of indirection, the poem is about the narrator too. Hence the slow leisured introduction, gradually persuading us that he is a man with his eyes open, that he knows what he is talking about. It is an actual walk he is telling us about, described in matter-of-fact terms and the voice of reminiscence ('And then there was a pile of wood . . .'). Details are mentioned as they come to mind: 'What held it though on one side was a tree' (here the voice of actuality appears in the 'though'). It is clear that he noticed things, like the state of the snow; as he walks, he looks automatically for landmarks. He can judge the age of the cord of maple.

Almost everything in this poem is devoted to assuring us, unobtrusively but cumulatively, that we are listening to a countryman. In a way, it is a long cool boast: look, it says, you can trust me, I show you the countryside as it is. Frost loved to show off in this way, and it was not always so successful artistically as here. Here it is needed for the poem's sake, since we have to be coaxed into trusting what it says in the second half. And there is something attractive, too, in such cool self-assurance. We are going for a walk with an expert: he is good company in the woods, and knows it.

Let us now turn to another poet, also in the country, also concerned to see things as they are. This time the human being who forms the subject is very much present: he fills the poem, in fact, and there is nothing about the landscape:

The Labourer

There he goes, tacking against the fields'
Uneasy tides. What have the centuries done
To change him? The same garments, frayed with light
Or seamed with rain, cling to the wind-scoured bones
And shame him in the eyes of the spruce birds.
Once it was ignorance, then need, but now
Habit that drapes him on a bush of cloud
For life to mock at, while the noisy surf
Of people dins far off at the world's rim.
He has been here since life began, a vague
Movement among the roots of the young grass.
Bend down and peer beneath the twigs of hair,
And look into the hard eyes, flecked with care;
What do you see? Notice the twitching hands,
Veined like a leaf, and tough bark of the limbs,
Wrinkled and gnarled, and tell me what you think.
A wild tree still, whose seasons are not yours,
The slow heart beating to the hidden pulse
Of the strong sap, the feet firm in the soil?
No, no, a man like you, but blind with tears
Of sweat to the bright star that draws you on.

What is this poem about? It's about a farm labourer, surely, and the way agricultural work beats a man down. R. S. Thomas looks at the labourer, and sees him as a natural object, something that hardly emerges from the landscape, 'a vague movement among the roots of the young grass'. In the longest and most careful passage of the poem, he compares him with a tree, and it is a comparison which degrades. True, there are suggestions of timeless strength ('the slow heart beating to the hidden pulse') but dominating them is the feeling that this labourer is not even a man. This is clearest in the brilliant opening of the conceit:

> *Bend down and peer beneath the twigs of hair.* . . .

We are being shown a specimen. We feel awe, but an awe shot through with revulsion, with pity, almost with contempt: is man no more than this? If that were not the dominant note of the comparison, there would be little point in the last lines, the most direct, the most explicit in the poem. Man is more than this, they answer: even that creature has to be called a man. The lines are not very powerful in themselves, and perhaps they do not need to be. The power lay in the degrading conceit, and if they are not altogether convincing as a reply, perhaps that is as well, for the sake of honesty.

To say that this poem is 'about' the labourer is only half-true. There is a tremendous effort to decide just what the labourer is like, just how human he is: and that effort, that deciding, is the subject of the poem. Hence the importance of the 'you'. It does not matter whether 'you' means the reader, or whether the poet is addressing himself; though if we remember that Mr Thomas is a priest, and one who first came to his parish from outside, then there is a special poignancy in the latter. What is important is that there is a consciousness studying the labourer, trying to lay aside its illusions, trying to be sure.

A later poem by Thomas—called this time 'A Labourer'—looks at that same subject, and asks the same question:

> *Is there love there, or hope, or any thought*
> *For the frail form broken beneath his tread,*
> *And the sweet pregnancy that yields his bread?*

A very matter-of-fact poem, this other, ending on the lovely image —prominently lovely—of the sweet pregnancy of the earth in which the corn grows. It is obviously not the labourer's own image, but that of the consciousness which is watching him, and this sudden blurting in of someone else's style makes the question so agonised. Looking back, we can see that the same technique was used, less obviously, in the earlier poem. Not only the conceit of the tree, but all the images, came from the 'you', and we know that the labourer would not have used any of them, could not even have thought of them—not of 'tacking against the fields' uneasy tides', and certainly not of the pathetic fallacy of the 'spruce birds' in whose eyes he is shamed. It is not surprising, then, to turn to another poem, 'Iago Prytherch', and find an explicit admission that the concern here is overwhelmingly that of the observer. It is an apology to a peasant for writing about him: 'forgive my naming you'. The poet asks himself what in fact his attitude to Iago Prytherch has been:

> *Fun? Pity? No word can describe*
> *My true feelings.*

This could be mere introspection, idle self-curiosity, but it is com-bined (here lies the poem's power) with a deep respect: so that in the end he is smaller, in our eyes and his own, for not knowing what he is doing to the 'dark figure' of the peasant.

> *My poems were made in its long shadow*
> *Falling coldly across the page.*

Here are three poems, then, in something like a rising order of self-consciousness: we can see the poet himself drawing nearer to the centre of our attention. If now we ask, is Thomas, like Robert Frost, a poet who sees nature just as it is, stripped of illusions, of the sentimentalities of ignorance, or the mistakes and prejudices of the outsider?—our answer must be, yes and no. Yes, that is Thomas' purpose; but the purpose itself is the subject of the poems. He is trying to see his peasants without illusions, and the poems, often deeply moving, chronicle the difficulty of the attempt: the double difficulty of shedding illusions without falling into a cynical contempt.

What then would a poem be like which retained illusions? Which did not strive towards the matter-of-fact gaze of the expert, but deliberately saw nature in terms of an outsider's expectations? Which brought to the countryside emotions and expectations which were not rejected, but which determined the way the poem was written? Would it not be like this:

O sweet woods, the delight of solitariness!
O how much I do like your solitariness!
Here nor treason is hid, veiled in innocence,
Nor envy's snaky eye finds any harbour here,
Nor flatterer's venomous insinuations,
Nor cunning humourist's puddled opinions,
Nor courteous ruins of proferred usury,
Nor time prattled away, cradle of ignorance,
Nor causeless duty, nor cumber of arrogance,
Nor trifling title of vanity dazzleth us,
Nor golden manacles stand for a paradise.
Here wrong's name is unheard, slander a monster is.
Keep thy spright from abuse; here no abuse doth haunt:
What man grafts in a tree dissimulation?

No poem could have a simpler structure than this. It is a plain, insistent assertion that the country is free from certain evils. This negative point is the only one it makes. Almost every detail mentioned is a detail not about the country but about the court—it is a poem about what the country is *not* like. This gives it a curious kind of strength, a kind that is incompatible with subtlety: a growing passion of indignation and need mounts in its cumulative rhetoric, and its very formality adds to its power, in a way that is only possible in Elizabethan poetry, when men sometimes (especially for emotions like hate and indignation) seem to have thought, and felt, in rhetorical patterns.

Sidney shows us the poetic mechanism we are looking for so clearly that his poem consists entirely of an announcement of what kind of poem he is writing. Let us turn to someone who has the same point to make, but spent rather longer in the woods:

Now my co-mates, and brothers in exile
Hath not old custom made this life more sweet
Than that of painted pomp? Are not these woods
More free from peril than the envious court:
Here feel we but the penalty of Adam,
The seasons' difference, as the icy fang
And churlish chiding of the winter's wind,
Which when it bites, and blows upon my body
Even till I shrink with cold, I smile, and say
This is no flattery: these are counsellors
That feelingly persuade me what I am:
Sweet are the uses of adversity

16

Which like the toad, ugly and venomous,
Wears yet a precious jewel in his head:
And this our life exempt from public haunt,
Finds tongues in trees, books in the running brooks
Sermons in stones, and good in everything.

Nothing in this passage is an attempt to see the countryside as it is. One point runs through it all, that the country is not the court. The contrast with 'painted pomp', with 'flattery', with 'public haunt', determines everything. Real toads are not venomous, and carry no jewels. Frost would have known this, Thomas would have made it his business to find out, but to the Duke it does not matter, for the toads of Arden are not real. It is as if Thomas had not given his hard look at the labourer, but had continued to see him in terms of his own feelings.

The next example is also highly conventional: but it is non-dramatic, and of greater verbal complexity than the Duke's lines. It is by the most sophisticated and, probably, the most pastoral of seventeenth-century poets:

Ametas and Thestylis Making Hay-ropes

A. *Thinkst thou that this love can stand,*
  Whilst thou still dost say me nay?
  Love unpaid does soon disband:
  Love binds love as hay binds hay.

Th: *Thinkst thou that this rope would twine*
  If we both should turn one way?
  Where both parties so combine,
  Neither love will twist nor hay.

A: *Thus you vain excuses find,*
  Which yourselve and us delay:
  And love ties a woman's mind
  Looser than with ropes of hay.

Th: *What you cannot constant hope*
  Must be taken as you may.

A: *Then let's both lay by our rope,*
  And go kiss within the hay.

Marvell is a poet of paradox: not flagrantly, like Donne and Crashaw, but delicately and deeply. The deepest paradox in this poem is both hidden and obvious: it is the contrast between its rustic image and its verbal sophistication. The poem depends utterly on the figure of the hay-ropes, as if the two lovers had no other way of expressing themselves: their dialectic consists in modifying the analogies that can be drawn from this one vehicle. Yet it is not as if they think in images: for the comparison is regularly deployed as a formal simile, and at least in a technical sense the thought exists independently of it. It is a poem in which we can see the rhetorical art, and admire the poet's skill.

Yet as long as we admire the skill, the lovers stay apart: the better they express their feelings, the less they love. This is the paradox of 'The Definition of Love' too, that perfection and fulfilment are incompatible:

> *My love is of a birth as rare*
> *As 'tis for object strange and high;*
> *It was begotten by Despair*
> *Upon Impossibility.*

The perfect love, that poem says, does not exist: 'Ametas and Thestylis' moves in exactly the opposite direction. Here is a perfect image for love, it says, look how much can be expressed through it; but its lovers, rejecting despair and impossibility, must reject the attempt to express their love. They must lay aside the rope and go kiss within the hay. The poem is over, and the rest is silence.

Is this poem on the side of Robert Frost or the Duke in its view of nature? No simple answer is possible. For obviously it is on the Duke's side: its sophistication completely prevents us from seeing haymaking as it really is, and country life is shamelessly subordinated to the poet's wish to turn a polished analogy. And then, in the end, the poem gaily rejects everything it has done. That's how you *talk* about love, it says: now these country folk are, of course, going to stop talking and get on with it. They are going to show good sense—more sense than the poem.

Marvell always lets us down when we ask for a clear preference; but though his choice may evade us, he has, I hope, made the contrast itself plainer. It is the contrast to which all the foregoing discussion has been leading: that between seeing nature as it is, and seeing it mainly as the opposite to something else, between a direct and a mediated vision. When the priest or the courtier comes to the countryside, he brings with him a set of expectations—of wishes, fears and hopes—that shape what he sees. His view of nature will not necessarily be false (though his toads will tend to be

18

venomous and his birds spruce) but it will be illusory: for this is
exactly Freud's sense of the word 'illusion':

> An illusion is not the same as an error, it is indeed not neces-
> sarily an error. Aristotle's belief that vermin are evolved out
> of dung . . . was an error. . . . On the other hand, it was an
> illusion on the part of Columbus that he had discovered a new
> sea-route to India. The part played by his wish in this error
> is very clear.

An illusion, Freud concludes, is a belief in which 'wish-fulfilment
is a prominent factor in its motivation'. The wish to find in country
life a relief from the problems of a sophisticated society formed
itself, in Renaissance times, into a set of poetic conventions. These
are the conventions of pastoral.

The Renaissance poets were, of course, well aware that their
version of the countryside was an illusion. To show this, we can
turn to the first and most famous of them all, Jacopo Sannazaro,
whose *Arcadia*, published in 1502, began a vast literary fashion. In
the Epilogue to this work, Sannazaro defends himself for writing
pastoral. Addressing his pipe ('sampogna') he says 'Do not mind if
someone, accustomed perhaps to more exquisite sounds, rebukes
your baseness or considers you rude'; nor (the opposite criticism)
if they say that you have not followed the laws of shepherds
properly, and 'that it is not fitting for anyone to pass further than
what belongs to him' ('passar più avanti, che a lui si appartiene':
which seems to refer both to social and stylistic climbing). To this
latter criticism Sannazaro replies that he has been the first in this
age to

> awaken the sleeping woods, and teach shepherds to sing the
> songs they had forgotten. All the more since he who made you
> out of these reeds came to Arcadia not as a rustic shepherd
> but as a most cultured youth, although unknown and a pilgrim
> of love.

Pastoral poetry, in other words, is the work of courtiers: for that
reason, it would be inappropriate to censure it for baseness (it isn't
really) or for presumption (why shouldn't he 'passare più avanti',
considering who he really is?). Sannazaro is having his oatcake and
eating it. Not surprising then that when Selvaggio meets Montano
(*Prosa Secunda*) and asks him to sing, he addresses him 'con voco
assai umana'. This 'humanist voice' (a modern translation renders
it 'in a most courteous phrase') is no doubt a deliberate slip of the

tongue, a quiet reminder of how educated these shepherds actually are.

There is a formal device that corresponds to the fact that the version of the countryside is mediated. The song which Montano sings in reply to Selvaggio's request tells how he found Uranio stretched out sleeping, and woke him, and they then discussed whether to sing. In *Prosa Terzia* the shepherds go to the feast of Pales, and as they enter the holy temple they see various scenes painted on the gate—nymphs, Apollo guarding Admetus's cattle, Endymion, and so on. When we hear the priest's prayer in the temple, we realise that we are in the same world as these mythological paintings: he prays not to see Diana bathing, or the vengeful nymphs.

What we have in these two examples is the obliqueness of presentation so common in pastoral. The shepherd poet sings only after announcing he is going to sing, or discussing what, or taking part in a contest. Rural or mythological scenes are not described direct, but paintings of them are described. The method is old, and goes back to Virgil, even Theocritus; and some scholars tell us that it has its origin in the actual shepherd contests of rural Sicily. Whether that is true or not, its place in Renaissance pastoral is surely the opposite—not as a sign of realism, but as a sign of sophistication, a way of removing us from the immediacy of real rustics in real fields. Sannazaro knew that he was no Robert Frost, and had no wish to be taken for one.

II

Every culture has one or more centres of social, artistic and moral standards, a place where the educated people live, where the King's English is spoken, where the theatres perform and the political decisions are taken. In the sixteenth and seventeenth centuries this centre was the court; by the nineteenth it was the city; in modern America it is becoming the university. Most literature is written from and for this centre; but there are always corners of society, rural or provincial pockets, lower social levels, with their own less articulate, less sophisticated traditions, sometimes imprinted by old-fashioned court mores, sometimes seeming to live an older, more unchanging life of their own. It used to be true that the literature of the centre was written, that of the corners oral, but literacy and radio have changed that.

Let us now take two pairs of terms. To describe this contrast, we can speak of court, or metropolitan, or (more generally) centric literature, and set it against unsophisticated, rural, popular or (more generally) provincial literature. We have already developed the contrast between direct and mediated writing; and by using these pairs as two axes, we have a fourfold scheme of classification. The centric can be direct or mediated; so can the provincial.

The first class, centric and direct, will contain most of the great literature of Europe, which has naturally emerged from and deals with the court or the city. Tragedy belongs here (Hamlet's Denmark and Thésée's Athens are part of Renaissance court culture, wherever they are ostensibly situated), and so do most novels. It would be odd if this were not the area in which greatness harboured.

In the provincial-direct class we must put the ballads, which emerge from and belong to regional pockets of our culture; the narrative poems of Wordsworth, proudly proclaiming their setting in humble and rustic life; the regional novel; dialect poetry.

Centric-mediated can take two forms, positive and negative. If positive, then the view of court or city is mediated by longing and respect, it is seen from far as the desirable top where, if we're lucky, there may be room. The archetype of such writing is the Dick Whittington story. If it is negative, we get pastoral satire: denunciation of court by contrasting it with Arcadian simplicity.

Finally, there is provincial-mediated, which is (as we have seen) pastoral. This too can be positive or negative. If the poet's need is to escape from the sophisticated corruption of court life into the freshness, simplicity and honesty of an unspoiled countryside, the result is pastoral properly speaking. If, however, he looks at the country not through the eyes of his wishes but through those of fear or dislike, if he believes in courtly grace and subtlety and is simply pausing to laugh at rustic boors, we can call the result anti-pastoral.

III

Of course the same work may hover between positive and negative—as for instance *As You Like It* does. The Duke, we have seen, is a poet of simply pastoral enthusiasm; but the play as a whole sets pastoral and anti-pastoral constantly against each other, and does not encourage us to form a clear preference.

They are set against each other most directly in III.2, the

conversation between Corin and Touchstone on the shepherd's life. Each speaks unequivocally for one of the attitudes: courtly trickery against the good sense of Arden, or courtly polish against the slow-witted rustic chewing his straw. It is an old argument, going back at least to the twentieth idyll of Theocritus, in which Eunica despises the neatherd for his coarse smell, and he tells himself indignantly about the neatherds who have been loved by goddesses. Who wins that argument? And who wins this one?

> *Touchstone:* Hast any philosophy in thee, shepherd?
> *Corin:* No more, but that I know the more one sickens, the worse at ease he is; and that he that wants money, means and contentment is without three good friends. That the property of rain is to wet, and fire to burn. That a good pasture makes fat sheep; and that a great cause of the night is lack of the sun. That he that hath learned no wit by nature, nor art, may complain of good breeding, or comes of a very dull kindred.
> *Touchstone:* Such a one is a natural philosopher.

It is quite wrong to play this scene (as I have seen done) with a sly Corin winking at the audience, and smiling to see whether Touchstone will take him seriously. If Touchstone believes in courtly wit, as he clearly does, then Corin must be allowed to believe in rustic sense, and not turn into a secondary Touchstone. It is easy to say what each stands for; but it is not so easy to say who has the better of it.

A natural philosopher has no need of artificialities or rhetoric, for he goes directly to what is really important; a 'natural' who philosophises will produce nothing but empty platitudes like these. Touchstone is consciously punning, but which meaning of 'natural' more truly describes Corin? 'The property of rain is to wet', he says—just like the Bachelierus of Molière, who has been taught in medical school the reason why opium makes us sleep:

> *A quoi respondeo*
> *Quia est in eo*
> *Virtus dormitiva,*
> *Cuius est natura*
> *Sensus assoupire*
> Chorus: *Bene, bene, bene respondere. . . .*
> > *Le Malade Imaginaire,*
> > 3me Intermède

Isn't Corin, too, offering a tautology as if it were a substantive point: that's what rain *is*. Or is he? Shakespeare is at his most elusive here. These are the things that a countryman needs to know —not how to kiss hands, but how to look after his sheep, who have to be protected from the elements. In a world of servants, coaches and umbrellas, rain doesn't wet any more.

Of course it would be wrong for either of them to win clearly in the third act. The balance must continue to the end—a balance between the play's official self and its undercurrents, for of course it is officially pastoral, and on the deepest level, I believe, it stays so. Act I is certainly pastoral in its preference. The court is corrupt, as Le Beau admits with a sad gesture towards a happiness that he can locate only by saying it is not to be found here:

> *Sir, fare you well,*
> *Hereinafter in a better world than this,*
> *I shall desire more love and knowledge of you.*

We have already been told where this better world is. In (surely) one of the most haunting sentences in English—given, with an irony the play can easily handle, to Charles the thug—we have been told of the Duke's banishment:

> They say he is already in the Forest of Arden, and a many merry men with him; and there they live like the old Robin Hood of England: they say many young gentlemen flock to him every day, and fleet the time carelessly as they did in the golden world.

England and France are casually mixed up because we are in neither England nor France: this Arden is out of space and time. C. S. Lewis has described very well where it is, in his defence of Spenser's shepherds:

> Some readers cannot enjoy the shepherds because they know (or say they know) that real country people are not more happy or more virtuous than anyone else; but it would be tedious to explain to them the many causes (reasons too) that have led humanity to symbolise by rural scenes and occupations a region in the mind which does exist and which should be visited often.

Arden is the world that Le Beau was longing for (though he, alas, never gets there). The visitors to Arden sing its praises in much the same terms as the Duke's simple solemn eulogy:

> *Blow, blow, thou winter wind,*
> *Thou art not so unkind*
> *As man's ingratitude.*

What little action there is mostly confirms this idyllic view: Orlando 'thought that all things had been savage here', but he finds only hospitality and friendship. Above all, Arden is the place of happy lovers: there they find what they could not find at court—leaving, if necessary, their wickedness behind them. To dress Corin up as Hymen is an ingenious way of relating the happy love-stories to the pastoral element—though at a price, since it destroys the atmosphere of mystery, even magic, that seems to be growing at the end.

All this, then, makes *As You Like It* a pure pastoral—but: inevitably, there are buts. First, the action: however much the Duke may like Arden, the moment he is offered his kingdom back he forgets the sermons in stones and takes it. This point is more neatly made if we accept the common emendation of II.1.18. In the Folio text, the Duke's opening speech is followed by:

> Amiens: *I would not change it: happy is your Grace*
> *That can translate the stubborness of fortune*
> *Into so quiet and so sweet a style.*

Many editors give 'I would not change it' to the Duke. The change is plausible enough: Amiens is not likely to thrust such a naked expression of personal opinion on his duke, and 'Happy is your Grace . . .' makes a natural opening for his deferential response, like a round of polite applause. And, probable on local grounds, it is doubly attractive in the light of the later action, because it makes a quiet joke at the Duke's expense, i.e. at the expense of the pastoral preference naïvely expressed. The Duke, we realise, was speaking as exiled dukes no doubt should in Arden; but he did not actually *mean* it.

As we look carefully at them, all the pastoral points grow slightly dubious. Orlando finds kindness in the forest, but at the hands of courtiers, not countrymen. The lovers marry, but then they leave Arden: it is the place for love but not for marriage. And, most important of all, there are Touchstone and Jaques.

The task of these two choric characters is to comment and to mock: to remind us of what the others forget. Touchstone, as we have already seen, is explicitly anti-pastoral, mocking the Arcadian life as he mocks romantic love—and often both at once:

> I remember when I was in love I broke my sword upon a stone, and bid him take that for coming a-night to Jane Smile, and I remember the kissing of her batlet, and the cow's dugs that her pretty chopped hands had milked. . . .

Jaques is a more complicated character, and his relation to the pastoral theme is less obvious. Central to Jaques is his role as Malcontent, and the infinite subtlety, in Shakespeare's hands, of the point that denouncing vice may be self-indulgent but that the denunciations may none the less be valid. Here I simply want to point out that Jaques too (though it may not be so obvious) is anti-pastoral. Of course it is part of his general sourness: he mocks at romantic love more churlishly than Touchstone ('Rosalind is your love's name?': we can hear the sneer), at poetry ('call you 'em stanzos?'), and at the pastoral life—

> *If it do come to pass*
> *That any man turn ass,*
> *Leaving his wealth and ease*
> *A stubborn will to please . . .*

> I.5

He is anti-pastoral from the moment he appears—indeed, even before he appears, for the corollary of telling the Duke that he usurps more than his brother (Jaques' first, reported opinion) is that there should not be any people in Arden—or at any rate, no courtiers. Jaques welcomes Touchstone into the forest along with that un-Arcadian property, a watch; he thinks marriage should obey the proper rules and not be carried out under a bush, like a beggar—in this his morality is centric; and, most interesting of all, he refuses to go along with the others at the end of the play.

Most interesting: for what he is refusing is to go back to court, yet this does not make him a pastoral character. He is not staying in Arden either, not even for the rest of the dance. During the brief time remaining to the play, he would rather stay at the abandoned cave, a forest without pastoralists. After that, he will go where he really belongs: to a monastery, or hermitage. There, his sneers can be sublimated into *contemptus mundi*; in Arden, they are merely killjoy. Pastoral and monasticism are both retreats from the world, but quite different from each other. A monastery is an act of pure withdrawal, and because of this it can be accepted by the community it withdraws from. Retreat is a human need, and the occasional or partial retreats everyone needs are symbolised and reinforced by the existence of groups who have retreated totally. The countryside, however, is accepted by the court not psychologically but economically: it represents not withdrawal but simply farming. The pastoral poet is therefore exploiting his medium as the hermit is not, turning country life, which is community life, into an occasion for withdrawal from the community. Out of this exploitation can come a fruitful artistic tension, but this tension will be destroyed by anyone who has no interest whatever in the medium, only in withdrawal. That is why Jaques never felt at home in Arden. Touchstone disliked it because it was not the court. Jaques discovers only at the end that his true vocation is that of an old religious man.

Touchstone and Jaques were added by Shakespeare to Lodge's story. This makes it obvious that he has changed his source by complicating the simple pastoralism into something more ambivalent, where the choruses undermine the official message. It is not surprising that a few other changes mock the pastoral world—or stand tiptoe on the edge of mockery. Thus Shakespeare removed the violence. Lodge's wrestler kills the franklin's sons and is killed by Rosader; Charles breaks their ribs ('that there is little hope of life in them') and when he is thrown by Orlando, Le Beau reports 'He cannot speak, my lord' (the line usually gets a laugh), and Charles is then carried out. No actual deaths, but very nearly. Lodge's usurper is killed in battle, but Shakespeare's, though he raises an army, turns out at the last minute to be harmless:

> *And to the skirts of this wild wood he came;*
> *Where meeting with an old religious man,*
> *After some question with him, was converted*
> *Both from his enterprise and from the world,*
> *His crown bequeathing to his banished brother*
> *And all their lands restored to them again*
> *That were with him exiled. This to be true*
> *I do engage my life.*

V.4.165

He needs to engage it, the whole story is so gloriously improbable. The outcome reeks gaily of fairy-tale. Having removed the battle,

Shakespeare makes fun of what he has done, as if all you have to do, to get rid of the violence, is to wave a happy ending at your story.

The one touch of violence that remains is the wounding of Orlando, which is brought right on stage in the form of the bloody napkin—at whose sight Rosalind forgets her shepherd's role and almost puts an end to the game she has been playing. This is Shakespeare's comment on the tone of his play. 'Look,' he has already said, 'no blood.' Now he says 'See what blood would do to my pastoral, it would spoil everything'.

IV

I must now introduce one large distinction that will enable us to demarcate—and limit—the subject of this book. It can best be done, perhaps, by pointing out that there are two senses in which *As You Like It* is a pastoral play. The whole play is pastoral because it takes place in Arden, the heroine disguises as a shepherd, and the imagery is rustic. The scene between Touchstone and Corin, or the songs, or Duke Senior's speech, are pastoral in a further sense, because they are explicitly concerned with the nature of country life. This is the distinction between pastoral as convention and pastoral as theme. Much—perhaps most—pastoral is not about the court-country contrast at all, nor even about any similar sophisticated-simple contrast. It is about love and death. Sometimes it is even about the excellence of a patron or prince, who is referred to as Dameotas or Pan. As an example of poetry which is pastoral in convention only, we may take Marot's *Eglogue au roy soubs les noms de Pan et Robin* (1539). It is a short autobiography, which concludes by asking the king for protection and modest help: not for two thousand acres (*deux mille arpentz*), but simply for the safety of himself and his flock,

> *car l'yver que s'appreste*
> *A commencé à neiger sur ma teste.*

(for the coming winter has begun to snow on my head.)

Since the poem is an eclogue, the poet is a shepherd playing on rural instruments, and the king is called Pan: the whole world is reduced to a pastoral community. Yet 'Robin' says near the beginning:

> *Je te supply (si onc en ces bas estres*
> *Daignas ouyr chansonnettes champestres),*
> *Escoute un peu, de ton vert cabinet,*
> *Le chant rural du petit Robinet.*

(I beg you (if you ever deign to hear the rustic tunes of lowly creatures), listen for a while, in your green chamber, to the rural song of little Robin.)

There is a sense, we see, in which the poet does not trust the convention, for unless we step outside it this apology is nonsense: François I might notice that the poem is a *chansonnette champestre*, but Pan can't, since that must be the only kind of song he knows.

I don't know if there is a link between the fact that the poet occasionally mistrusts the convention, and the fact that it is no more than a convention. It would be possible to rewrite the whole poem in non-pastoral terms: for '*la musette entonner*' we would say 'publish a book of poems', for '*tyssir paniers d'osier*' we would say whatever is here allegorically described (the tasks suitable to youth, '*choses . . . à tel age sortables*', are perhaps only vaguely linked to literal equivalents). For the '*deux mille arpentz*' we would mention whatever he really wanted from the king, presumably a pension. And, of course, for Pan and Robin we'd say François and Marot.

If we did this, we'd have changed the literary form of the poem radically, but the content not at all. Perhaps this is even clearer in Marot's religious eclogue the *Complaincte d'un pastoureau chrestien*, where God is addressed as Pan.

> *Jusques à quand, ô Pan grand et sublime,*
> *Laisseras tu ceste gent tant infime,*
> *Et faulx pasteurs et meschans,*
> *Dessus troupeaux dominer en tes champs?*

(How much longer, O great and sublime Pan, will you allow this ignoble race, and these false shepherds, so perjured and evil, to lord it over the flocks in your fields?)

What would be changed if we said '*Jusques à quand, ô Dieu, grand et sublime?*' Nothing at all: for in his heart Marot never ceased to say 'Dieu'. Some details would be absurd if he had:

> *Car je suis tant, ô Pan, de dueil espris,*
> *Que presque suis hors de tous mes esprits,*
> *Si tout à coup ta clémence divine*
> *N'use envers moy d'une grace bénigne.*

(For I am so far in the grip of sorrow, O Pan, that I am almost completely out of my mind—unless your divine clemence show benignant grace towards me.)

Pan has neither *clémence* nor *grace*, but God has. The poem is simply written in code—a very transparent code, that deceives no one. Pastoralism in Marot is pure convention: that is, he is not interested in the idea of the countryside at all. The effect of wrapping up his characters in pastoral names is nil.

The same is largely true of most pastoral elegies: it is even true of *Lycidas*, and also of *Adonais* (though not of the third great pastoral elegy in English, *Thyrsis*). In *Lycidas* we find lines that are not only a pure example of pastoral as convention only, they are perhaps the purest examples imaginable:

> *Together both, ere the high lawns appeared*
> *Under the opening eyelids of the morn,*
> *We drove afield, and both together heard*
> *What time the gray-fly winds her sultry horn,*
> *Batt'ning our flocks with the fresh dews of night,*
> *Oft till the Star that rose, at evening, bright*
> *Towards Heaven's descent had slop'd his westering wheel.*
> *Meanwhile the rural ditties were not mute,*
> *Temper'd to th' Oaten flute;*
> *Rough satyrs danc'd, and fauns with cloven heel,*
> *From the glad sound would not be absent long.*
> *And old Damoetas lov'd to hear our song.*

Studying can be called 'driving afield', reading books 'battening our flocks', vacation exercises—i.e. poetry readings—'rough satyrs danced', and the college tutor can be called Damoetas. If we are meant to notice the effect of this terminology on the subject-matter, if we are meant to remember that reading is *not* driving sheep, and that to call it so is to see it differently, then we have pastoral as theme. But no such thought is meant to come to us here. Milton does not mean us to ask what a natural philosopher is, or whether it is better to be Damoetas among the fauns than Joseph Mead among the undergraduates.

Yet Milton has his reasons for writing *Lycidas* as a pastoral. The reasons are formal, and we may indicate them by saying that though he was not interested in the pastoral convention, he was interested in convention. He was concerned to write in a certain tradition, to invite comparison with Virgil, to show he knew the rules, to behave as a good Renaissance elegist. In a looser way, so much is true of Marot, but Milton makes serious poetic use of the fact. We can see *Lycidas* raising expectations as we read it, then fulfilling them triumphantly, or—sometimes—almost not fulfilling them. As an example, I take the device of the pathetic fallacy. This is an established technique of the pastoral elegy (and of the pastoral love-poem, too, in a different way). The elegist looks round the landscape, and sees that all nature is mourning with him: the flocks are unfed, the flowers are weeping,

> *The nightingales and the swallows to whom he taught their music*
> *They who had loved him well, wailed at the foot of the tree*
>
> (Moschus)

The *Lament for Bion* is virtually one long pathetic fallacy, and stylistically it must have been one of the most influential poems ever written (and so, inevitably, looks now like one of the most affected). Here is Milton's use of the figure:

> *Bid Amaranthus all his beauty shed,*
> *And daffadillies fill their cups with tears,*
> *To strew the laureate hearse where Lycid lies.*
> *For so to interpose a little ease,*
> *Let our frail thoughts dally with false surmise.*
> *Ay me! Whilst thee the shores and sounding seas*
> *Wash far away, where e're thy bones are hurled. . . .*

This marvellous passage turns round on itself in two steps. First there is a regretful shaking of the head at the admission that he has only given himself 'a little ease', then a horrified cry at the brutal truth of Lycidas' drowning. Now of course what the lines are saying is that the corpse can't be strewn with flowers because it is lost: the 'false surmise' concerns what happened to the body. But we have just had a dozen or more beautiful lines about nature's tribute to the dead poet:

> *And call the vales, and bid them hither cast*
> *Their bells, and flowerets of a thousand hues . . .*

(The appeal is a variation of the pathetic fallacy not differing much, in emotional effect, from the statement: the assertion that nature is mourning, and the instruction to nature to mourn, belong to the same stylistic genus, and both are found in the *Lament for Bion*). Now when these lines about the flowers, which suffuse an artificial device with such tender beauty, are swept aside by such a surge of feeling, it is difficult not to get the impression that the device itself is being swept aside, that a direct style is rushing in to state the grief that has so far been described in an artificial style.

If we turn back to the lines about 'battening our flocks', we shall see that they are followed by this:

> *But O the heavy change, now thou are gone,*
> *Now thou art gone, and never must return!* ...

Now these two lines are followed, not preceded, by the pathetic fallacy ('Thee shepherd . . .'); but all the same they have been preceded, as we have seen, by an extremely conventional use of stylistic tricks that belong to pastoral. Once again, a syntax of exclamation and a rhythm of release of feeling comes breaking in: and once again, though what is being said concerns Lycidas' death, i.e. subject-matter, I find it hard not to feel that what is being swept aside is the artificiality of the style itself. I think, though we do not pause to analyse it, this is how most of us read the lines—more, perhaps, than contemporary readers, less conscious of the 'artificiality' of the style, or less eager for the natural; yet I am sure the effect was, deliberately or half-deliberately, planted by Milton himself. With great poetic tact, he is allowing us something of the relief of hearing the true voice of feeling bursting in, without ever actually denying the convention. It is nice to imagine Milton hearing the tremor of Dr Johnson's pettish complaint against pastoral and appeasing it without, on the surface, taking any notice at all. This is what I mean by saying that *Lycidas* fulfils triumphantly the expectations of the genre, though at moments it almost refuses to do so.

What we have said about the pastoral addressed to a patron, and the pastoral elegy, can also be said about love-pastoral. If we glance through the best and most famous of Elizabethan anthologies, *England's Helicon*, published in 1600, we can see that it was intended as an anthology of pastoral poetry, from 'The Shepherd to his Chosen Nymph' at the beginning to 'The Shepherd's Consort' at the end. All the poems are about love and their use of the convention is usually automatic: the lovers are shepherds because the rules say so, that's all. Scholars have even noticed that some of the poems were not originally pastoral at all, but were touched up by the editor to make them fit his anthology. The result of all this is a hundred or so poems most of which are charming, and a handful something more, and no doubt they were meant to be taken one or two at a time; but if we are churlish enough to read them one after the other, the cumulative effect is one of tedium, because they are all so incurious about what they are doing.

This impression is confirmed if we ask what poems stand out. Well, none does quite that, since the uniformity of style is so marked, but one poet seems to me to emerge as clearly more interesting than the others. This is Nicholas Breton, who contributed eight poems, only one of which ('Sweet Phillis if a silly swain') is completely indistinguishable from the ruck of Bar Young, Shepherd Tony, and the rest. The most famous is very nearly the best:

> *In the merry month of May,*
> *In a morn by break of day,*
> *Forth I walked by the wood side,*
> *When as May was in his pride:*
> *There I spied all alone,*
> *Phillida and Coridon.*
> *Much ado there was, God wot,*
> *He would love and she would not.*
> *She said, never man was true,*
> *He said, none was false to you.*
> *He said, he had loved her long,*
> *She said, love should have no wrong.*
> *Coridon would kiss her then,*
> *She said, Maids must kiss no men,*
> *Till they did for good and all.*
> *Then she made the shepherd call*
> *All the Heavens to witness truth:*
> *Never loved a truer youth.*
> *Thus with many a pretty oath,*
> *Yea and nea, and faith and troth,*
> *Such as silly shepherds use,*
> *When they will not love abuse;*
> *Love, which had been long deluded,*
> *Was with kisses sweet concluded.*
> *And Phillida with garlands gay*
> *Was made the Lady of the May.*

What exactly is the delicate irony of this poem doing to it? How delightful love is, it tells us—and how easy for silly shepherds. We need the OED for 'silly' and not even that will find the exact tone for us: 'simple' is perhaps the best modern equivalent, and there is certainly condescension present, just as there is in 'pretty oath' ('*many a* pretty oath' makes it even more patronising—the silly shepherds can turn them out easily enough, and they're always charming). The narrator is half-amused (these youngsters take themselves so seriously) but half-envious too. We are meant to notice how cursory the last couplet is, yet to be swept on by it as well. The irony, clear but slight, is a matter of calling attention to the fact that the lovers are shepherds. Even the presence of the narrator who comes upon the lovers and tells us about them has the same effect. Admittedly it is a common device of pastoral—for it helps to make it a mediated rather than a direct view of the country-side—but it also prevents any direct outburst of emotion: we are all the time watching, not quite taking part. What Breton has done is to write a pastoral love-poem in which he withdraws, very gently, from the convention so that we shall notice what it means to see lovers as shepherds. That is, pastoral has become theme as well as convention.

'Shepherd and Shepherdess' is not, as it happens, in *England's Helicon*, but it will be convenient to look at it next. It seems, and on the whole is, a straightforward love-pastoral, with a pleasant breeziness and a rather different and fresher list of country delights than usual, culminating (of course) in fair Aglaia. One detail, however, must catch our eye. The poem begins with the usual assertion of the superiority of the shepherd's life to a king's. Then, as it gets swept away by its praises of Aglaia, it swears

> *Had I got a kingly grace,*
> *I would leave my kingly place*
> *And in heart be truly glad*
> *To become a country lad.*

What has happened now to the poem's earlier assurances? It began

> *Who can live in heart so glad*
> *As the merry country lad?*

Admittedly that was 60 lines back, and it is 30 lines since Aglaia appeared, but the reader who does remember it (and he is surely the best reader) must be tempted to read 'And in heart be *truly* glad': these later lines betray just how seriously we're meant to take the earlier ones, for they say 'I really mean it this time'.

'Shepherd and Shepherdess', then, calls attention to the form, but only once, briefly and mockingly. It is more clearly done in 'A

Report Song', the one poem that is perhaps even more delightful than 'The Ploughman's Song'—indeed, it is one of the gems of Elizabethan poetry, and deserves to be better known.

> *Shall we go dance the hay?*   The hay?
> *Never pipe could ever play*
>   *better Shepherd's Roundelay.*
>
> *Shall we go sing the Song?*   The Song?
> *Never Love did ever wrong:*
>   *fair Maids hold hands all a-long.*
>
> *Shall we go learn to woo?*   To woo?
> *Never thought came ever to,*
>   *better deed could better do.*
>
> *Shall we go learn to kiss?*   To Kiss?
> *Never heart could ever miss*
>   *comfort, where true meaning is.*
>
> *Thus at base they run,*   They run,
> *When the sport was scarce begun:*
>   *but I waked, and all was done.*

'Shall we go dance the hay?' This means of course 'fellow shepherds, shall we be gay?', but also 'Shall we use the pastoral manner?' The poem, that is, begins by drawing our attention to the convention it is using, and then moves towards love as subject. There is a double climax: it is more and more about love, and the love grows hotter and hotter, nearer *its* climax—and then the waking shatters both sexual and artistic tension, and the whole thing is left unreal because it was only, after all, pastoral.

It is sad to learn from the literary histories that Breton was a prolific and often a dull writer; one would prefer to think of him as contributing this lightness and grace to an otherwise too monotonous anthology, and then disappearing from view. That, however, is by the way, for my point here is not whether Breton or anyone else did it, or how, but what he did. What he did was give an extra dimension to pastoral love-poems by using the pastoral partly as theme.

v

And now, to limit the subject of this book: it is about pastoral as theme only. It does not discuss any poems simply because their characters are dressed up as shepherds and shepherdesses. It deals with poems that long to escape from the centre to the simpler world of Arcadia. And Arcadia, in this sense, need have neither sheep nor shepherds.

> They sailed to the Western sea, they did,
>   To a land all covered with trees,
> And they bought an Owl, and a useful Cart,
> And a pound of Rice, and a Cranberry tart,
>   And a hive of silvery bees . . .

Those trees are as unreal, in their way, as the trees of Arden on which Orlando hangs his verses. It is a sad comment—on the human condition, or on the nineteenth century, or perhaps on both (there are moments when one is tempted to equate them!)—that instead of the rich traditionalism of pastoral we have the eccentricities of the land where the Jumblies live, and that some of the happiest poetry of its age is the nonsense verse of Edward Lear—the happiness emerging from the obvious absurdity of his world, its gay rejection of the possible. That the poem knows what it is doing is clear from the delightful irony of 'useful': it has a child's solemnity, an attempt to convey importance by invoking a grown-up criterion, and so showing us more clearly than ever that we are not in the world of the adult and the sane. Much the same atmosphere is conveyed in 'The Quangle's Wangle's Hat':

> And the Quangle Wangle said
>   To himself on the Crumpety Tree—
> 'When all these creatures move
>   What a wonderful noise there'll be!'
> And at night by the light of the Mulberry moon
> They danced to the Flute of the Blue Baboon,
> On the broad green leaves of the Crumpety Tree,
> And all were happy as happy could be,
>   With the Quangle Wangle Quee.

This is all part of the Romantic movement—one step further in the Romantic fondness for the exotic. This is the mechanism of pastoral taken to the point of delightful absurdity; behind it lies all the seriousness of the poetry of escape.

As a typical Romantic poem of escape let us take Shelley's *Epipsychidion*. It contains the usual longing for a sheltered paradise, the usual links—sometimes embarrassing—with the poet's own life. An escapist poem spells out explicitly the feelings that

lie behind pastoral—and this is what we can see happening in
Epipsychidion. Its most overtly personal passage is the long appeal
to Emily to escape with him to the 'isle under Ionian skies':

> *Emily,*
> *A ship is floating in the harbour now,*
> *A wind is hovering o'er the mountain's brow;*
> *There is a path on the sea's azure floor—*
> *No keel has ever ploughed that path before. . . .*
> *The merry mariners are bold and free;*
> *Say, my heart's sister, wilt thou sail with me?*

And as he elaborates this longing, Shelley—as if to corroborate our
point—introduces a good deal of the material of pastoral. The
island he longs to escape to is 'a far Eden of the purple East'. Its
natives are called 'pastoral people', but this almost certainly means
'shepherd people' and no more. They do however breathe 'the
last spirit of the age of Gold', and later in the poem the lone dwelling standing on the island remains as a symbol of a distant past:

> *For delight*
> *Some wise and tender ocean-king, ere crime*
> *Had been invented, in the world's young prime,*
> *Reared it, a wonder of that simple time,*
> *And envy of the isles, a pleasure-house*
> *Made sacred to his sister and his spouse.*

(Were they the same person, one wonders? Was Golden Age sexuality so uninhibited?) The Golden Age is remote partly in space—on
the island—and partly in time—on the island long ago. The lone
dwelling house has now fallen into decay:

> *It scarce seems now a wreck of human art . . .*
> *For all the antique and learned imagery*
> *Has been erased, and in the place of it*
> *The ivy and the wild vine interknit*
> *The volumes of their many-twining stems;*
> *Parasite-flowers illume with dewy gems*
> *The lampless halls, and when they fade, the sky*
> *Peeps through their winter-woof of tracery*
> *With moonlight patches, or star atoms keen,*
> *Or fragments of the day's intense serene;—*
> *Working mosaic on their Parian floors.*
> *And, day and night, aloof, from the high towers*

And terraces, the Earth and Ocean seem
To sleep in one another's arms, and dream
Of waves, flowers, clouds, woods, rocks, and all that we
Read in their smiles, and call reality.

'I am seges est ubi Troia fuit': it is an old theme, that nature has regained what man had taken from her, and the town, or the dwelling, has fallen into decay. In Shelley, however, it is a cause for delight rather than for sad moralising. Nature has taken over, and all is purer than ever. The sky peeps through the broken roof, not to remind us that man's glory fades, but to give us glimpses of 'the day's intense serene'—an image for the sky, but with hints that we are glimpsing some higher realm of Forms. For the description is soaked in Platonism, as the last line shows. It is soaked, too, in the famous latent sexuality that gives Shelley's verse its individual flavour—and that gives *Epipsychidion* a very individual flavour indeed, for it is a love-poem, urging Emilia to run off with him. A sexual invitation is converted into a dream of ethereal escape— and that in turn is presented in almost-sexual terms!

What Shelley has done in this poem is to begin from the personal situation, and in developing it to rediscover fragments of poetic convention. By not writing a pastoral, he stumbles on a good deal of what pastoral uses. It is the reverse of the normal order. That reversal is part of what we call Romanticism.

VI

The Arcadian, then, need not be rural; and conversely, the rural need not be Arcadian. As an example of this, we may choose the most famous of all Renaissance pastoral dramas, Guarini's *Il Pastor Fido*. It may seem perverse, in view of its reputation and influence, to deny that this is really a pastoral play, but it is a perversity that follows from our conception of pastoral, and that is justified because it tells us something about what lies behind the form. Guarini's Arcadia is Arcadia in name only: it does not contrast with the court. Its shepherds are simply men and women, conscious of their social position and divine descent. Guarini gives the game away in his preface. *Il Pastor Fido* was widely discussed—and attacked—when it appeared, because there was no classical precedent or authority for its form. Guarini himself joined in the controversy in two anonymous pamphlets, in *Il Compendio della poesia tragicomica*, and in a brief preface to the 1602 edition of the play. The purpose of *Il Compendio* is to defend the writing of a pastoral tragicomedy, though Aristotle does not recognise such a genre as tragi-comedy, and though Guarini's opponent, de Nores, had claimed that sophisticated readers would not be interested in poems about rude shepherds.

Guarini's reply is that shepherd society, in early times, was as complex and hierarchical as that of the court or city today:

> All were shepherds, certainly, but with distinctions like those of the city, some great, some base, some poor, some rich. . . . Nor were they subject to the citizens, since in those days there were no cities, but they ruled themselves, and he who happened to excel was the commander—but that same commander was no less a shepherd than he who obeyed. So that it was not inappropriate to say 'the shepherd who is proprietor', 'the shepherd who rules the others'.

Though the 'shepherd who ruled' may not have looked after sheep, he was still a shepherd 'in his condition'. The great figures of the Old Testament—Moses, David, Joseph—were shepherds, and Guarini quotes a remark by Basil the Great that the shepherd's life is a fit training for kingship:

> David came to the throne from the shepherd's trade (ab arte pastorali). For the arts of keeping sheep and of ruling are sisters, in so far as the one has entrusted to it the care of animals, the other the care of those endowed with reason.

Pastoral society, then, is noble and capable of social distinction (capacissima d'ogni grado); and so it is proper that it should have produced its own drama. By a pastoral drama, Guarini explains, he does not mean a compound play with a pastoral element, but a single united 'favola' which is entirely set in a world of shepherds. All the qualities found in other plays are simply transposed into a pastoral setting, which is fit to receive them. What has Guarini done in this defence? He has rejected all that is specific to pastoral. Shepherd society does not contrast with that of court, it is a trans-posed version of it; the play contains exactly the kind of plotting and ingenuity that belongs to the 'fable' of a tragedy.

There is, in fact, only one explicitly pastoral passage in the play, Carino's denunciation of the lying, cheating and corruption of court:

That which elsewhere is virtue, is vice there:
Plain troth, square dealing, love unfeign'd, sincere
Compassion, faith inviolable, and
An innocence both of the heart and hand,
They count the folly of a soul that's vile
And poor. . . .

Carino is not really a character in the story, but an outsider who arrives in the last act only; and the subject of his denunciation is a very general picture of life at court, not related particularly to the main intrigue. The whole passage has the air of a set piece, dutifully added to a play in which it doesn't really belong.

VII

The essential pastoral contrast, then, is something which underlies that between courtier and shepherd: in a sense they are just trappings. We owe this point to William Empson, and it is widely accepted today. To see *The Beggar's Opera* or *Alice in Wonderland* as pastoral worlds is to perceive something important about their subject, the contrast with authority in the first, with grown-ups in the second. Each work has its own version of court, and is pleased not to be there.

In this book I accept Empson's extension of the term, but we have to realise what we are doing. The sixteenth century found no difficulty in knowing what a pastoral was: it was a poem about shepherds. For us to set what pastoral really is against what it was thought to be is to tamper with history; and since without literary history we would not have the concept of pastoral in the first place, we could be said to be knocking away the scaffold we are standing on.

The starting point of this book is that pastoral is a literary convention that conforms to a social contrast and a psychological attitude; that this attitude outlived the death of the form in the eighteenth century; and that there is therefore a good deal of the pastoral impulse in literature that is not pastoral in form—just as there were pastorals in the sixteenth century that observed no more than the mechanics of the tradition. Of course this is tampering with history: and this book is in no way a history of pastoral. What it has to say is in one, strictly literary, sense, peripheral to the form; in another sense it is central.

For if pastoral is an illusion there is a book to be written on it in a way that there is not, for instance, a book to be written on nature poetry. There are books to be written on Wordsworth and Frost, certainly; but to write on nature poetry, unless one is to stick to descriptive literary history, is to write on nature. This means to enter political economy (What was the social function of Wordsworth's beggars?) or biology (Why *do* birds sing?); and this seems too vast, and too far from poetry to be feasible or useful.

To write on pastoral, however, is to enter that region of the mind described by C. S. Lewis. It has several names. In terms of time it is the Golden Age. In terms of space it is Eden or Arcadia. Its goddess is Astraea, its worship is nostalgia. Its chronicle is pastoral.

In the next chapter I shall discuss nostalgia—its poetic possibilities, its connexion with pastoral, and the possibility of extending it to be the basis of other poetry too, even of all poetry. Then, for a few chapters, I shall discuss Arcadia—what the poets have told us it is like, and what its opposite is; its politics, its sex life, its satiric possibilities.

This first part of the book is arranged theoretically. The second part, though it still does not aspire to being a history of pastoral, does deal with individual poets in chronological order. They are all pastoralists, in a way, but they have not been chosen for their centrality in the tradition. They have been chosen for the very personal reason that they are the ones on whom I feel I have something to say, and the (perhaps almost as personal) reason that their relation to the pastoral impulse seems to tell us something central about their work.

II

ON NOSTALGIA

To establish that nostalgia is the basic emotion of pastoral, we can begin at the beginning—or almost at the beginning. Virgil's first Eclogue is a conversation between two shepherds, Tityrus and Meliboeus, about their home. Tityrus, now an old man, has been to Rome and received his 'freedom' from a god, or at any rate someone who *erit mihi semper deus*:

> *libertas quae sera tamen respexit inertem*
> *candidior postquam tondenti barba cadebat*
> *respexit tamen et longo post tempore venit.* . . .

Freedom, which, lazy as I was, eventually took notice of me, after my beard had begun to show white hairs as I clipped it— in the end it took notice of me, and after long delay it came.

'Libertas' turns out to mean keeping his land and not being dispossessed: the god said to him

> *Pascite ut ante boves, pueri; submittite tauros.*
> Feed your cattle as before, lads; and rear your bulls.

Meliboeus on the other hand is going to be driven away to the burning sands of Africa or to *toto divosos ab orbe Brittanos*. He is envious of Tityrus' good fortune: he does not know when he will return to see his humble cottage, and what *impius miles* will then have it. Such is the result of civil strife, and he is bitter: he can plant and prune, but he won't be there to see the fruit. Tityrus offers him hospitality, asking him to stay that night at any rate; and the poem ends.

Loss of home, and the sadness of Meliboeus at being driven out: this Eclogue is drenched in nostalgia. The beauty of home is seen through the eyes of loss:

> *Nos patriam fugimus; tu, Tityre, lentus in umbra*
> *formosam resonare doces Amaryllida silvas.*

We have to leave our home; while you, Tityrus, lying in the shade, teach the woods to resound with the beauty of Amaryllis.

Not only the woods but thousands of years of poetry have echoed the praise of Amaryllis. It is still echoing in Spenser:

> *Nathlesse doe ye still loud her prayses sing.*
> *That all the woods may answer and your echo ring.*

and the last strains are heard, graceful in their complete artificiality, in the literary exercises of the young Pope:

> *Where'er you walk, cool gales shall fan the glade,*
> *Trees, where you sit, shall crowd into a shade:*
> *Where'er you tread, the blushing flow'rs shall rise,*
> *And all things flourish, where you turn your eyes.*

The first listener to this long series was the dispossessed Meliboeus; the first ear to be ravished was that of one setting off for exile. The longest idyllic passage in the poem (46-58), lingering lovingly on each rural sight, each rural sound, is introduced by the same contrast: Meliboeus congratulates Tityrus, *fortunate senex*, that his flocks will not have to make trial of unfamiliar pasture, and only in the last three lines does the description break free of the shadow of Meliboeus' consciousness. And the most famous descriptive touch of all comes from him, not from Tityrus:

> *non ego vos posthac viridi projectus in antro*
> *dumosa pendere procul de rupe videbo.*

I shall no longer watch you (his goats), as I lie stretched out in a green cave, hanging in the distance on a bushy rock.

Wordsworth singled out *pendere* as a detail found by the imagination not the fancy, but his comment, true as it is ('the goats [do not] literally hang, as does the parrot or the monkey, but, presenting to the senses something of such an appearance, the mind in its activity, for its own gratification, contemplates them as hanging') does not fully account for the beauty of the lines. He has described the mind's activity, but not the emotion that links that activity to the scene, and infuses the passage. The shepherd lying in his green cave, watching his goats hanging from the bushy rock, is a figure of happy repose, and of sadness, as we have seen. Both these feelings are hinted at by the image: he is secure in possession (lying at ease, he notes that the goats are still there) but he is also deprived (they are so far he cannot reach them). With the ambivalence of the whole Eclogue, the glimpse of idyllic contentment hints at an undertone of loss.

The ninth Eclogue is a parallel to the first. Lycidas meets Moeris taking some kids to town, to the man who now owns his farm. Lycidas is surprised: he had heard that Menalcas had saved all the land from dispossession with his songs. No, says Moeris bitterly, he did no such thing: not only did they fail to save their farms, they nearly lost their lives in trying. Against this background they walk on together, recalling snatches of Menalcas' poetry. Moeris breaks off at one point to remark that he is no longer young, and has forgotten so many songs. *Omnia fert aetas.* The moment is slightly eerie: using a country superstition, he says he is losing his voice because the wolf saw him first. The beauty of the pastoral mood is sharpened by the bitterness of the situation.

Examples abound in the *Eclogues.* Daphnis' beauty is most eloquently asserted in death:

> *Daphnis ego in silvis, hinc usque ad sidera notus,*
> *formosi pecoris custos, formosior ipse.*   V.43-44

I was Daphnis in the woods, famous from here to the heavens, guardian of a lovely flock, lovelier myself.

Gallus in the tenth Eclogue thinks of how happy he would have been if he'd left war alone and stayed among his shepherd friends

> *serta mihi Phyllis legeret, cantaret Amyntas*

Phyllis would have picked out garlands for me, Amyntas would have sung—

(it does not matter in that carefree life who your sweetheart is, or even whether it is a girl or a boy). But all this is in the conditional: just as the picture of him hunting with his Parthian bow is broken off by

> *—tamquam haec sit nostri medicina furoris,*
> *aut deus ille malis hominum mitescere discat!*
>
>   X.60-1

As if all these things could be a medicine for my madness. As if that god could learn to grow mild at the sufferings of men.

Both the pastoral visions of Gallus are dreams, attempts to forget his sorrow.

Several of the *Eclogues* (1, 2, 6, 10) end at evening: they leave as their last impression the lengthening shadows and the need for shelter. And evening in the tenth sounds deeper reverberations:

surgamus. solet esse gravis cantantibus umbra,
iuniperis gravis umbra, nocent et frugibus umbrae.
ite domum saturae, venit Hesperus, ite capellae.

X.75-78

Let us go. Shade is usually bad for singers. The shade of the
junipers is bad. Shadows harm crops. Go home now, goats, now
that you have fed. Hesperus is coming. Home, goats.

Before the reposeful cadence of the last line comes the sophisticated playing with literal and figurative senses of *umbra*. What is
bad for crops is bad for poets: so the shadow is not that of night
alone.

There is a further point. Even Tityrus, who is keeping his farm,
has been to Rome, and it opened his eyes. He thought when he was
still a yokel that it must be just like the local market town, but it
towers above that:

quantum lenta solent inter viburna cupressi.

as cypresses tower above the supple undergrowth.

Tityrus is no longer the naïve countryman: he can now see his
simple love of home as part of something larger. There is no simple
love of home in the *Eclogues*: it is seen through eyes that have
changed, or eyes that are losing it. Country life does not lead
directly to country poetry: to express the sweetness of content,
you must have stepped out of the world of golden slumbers.

II

The nostalgia that impregnates the *Eclogues* never left pastoral;
and eventually it came to the surface, as the evident shaping
spirit of poems. It follows from the view of Romanticism sketched
in the last chapter, that in the nineteenth century, when the
pastoral convention is no longer used, poems will deal quite openly
with the emotion to which that convention corresponded; and if
they use the convention it will be by rediscovering its usefulness.

Any emotion can provide the impulse of a lyric poem; but
nostalgia can provide its structure as well. For nostalgia posits
two different times, a present and a longed-for past, and on this
contrast a poem can be built.

There is no lack of nostalgic poetry in the nineteenth century—
no lack of longing for a simpler, happier condition, for the freshness

44

of the early world, for escape from the great city, pent mid cloisters dim. Such escape is normally from town to country

—To one who has been long in city pent,
  'Tis very sweet to look into the fair
  And open face of heaven,—to breathe a prayer
Full in the smile of the blue firmament—

but the psychological mechanism is the same if the longing is not for the familiar and rural (Buttermere or Combray) but for the exotic isles under Ionian skies, perilous seas and faery lands forlorn. As the first example, then, I choose Baudelaire's fascination with tropical landscapes.

The voyage is one of Baudelaire's central symbols for escape from the mud and gaslight of Paris, the *noir océan*, to another ocean, blue, clear and profound. His poems vary from simple longing to the rich interwoven ironies of *Le Voyage*. Nowadays of course, corrupted by modern literature, sharpened by modern criticism, we tend to prefer the more ironic treatments of the theme, even to equate such a poem's excellence with its degree of detachment from the longing. I have to say at once that I do not accept this preference. A nostalgic poem must draw its power primarily from the expression of nostalgia, whatever is then done with this in the poem's total effect. It seems perverse to believe negative expression is preferable to positive, that what makes, say, the *Ode to a Nightingale* great is not the intensity of 'Away, away for I will fly to thee' but the fact that he returns to earth and ordinariness at the end, as if the undoing meant more than the doing. Even Baudelaire, master of irony, has to have something to be ironic about.

À Une Malabaraise is early and comparatively simple Baudelaire, and though it shows the nostalgic mechanism in reverse, it shows it in simple form.

Tes pieds sont aussi fins que tes mains, et ta hanche
Est large à faire envie à la plus belle blanche;
A l'artiste pensif ton corps est doux et cher;
Tes grands yeux de velours sont plus noir que ta chair.
Aux pays chauds et bleus où ton Dieu t'a fait naître,
Ta tâche est d'allumer la pipe de ton maître,
De pourvoir les flacons d'eaux fraiches et d'odeurs,
De chasser loin du lit les moustiques rodeurs,

Et, dès que le matin fait chanter les platanes,
D'acheter au bazar ananas et bananes.
Tout le jour, où tu veux, tu mènes tes pieds nus,
Et fredonnes tout bas de vieux airs inconnus;
Et quand descend le soir au manteau d'écarlate,
Tu poses doucement ton corps sur une natte,
Où tes rêves flottants sont pleins de colibris,
Et toujours, comme toi, gracieux et fleuris.
Pourquoi, l'heureuse enfant, veux-tu voir notre France,
Ce pays trop peuplé que fauche la souffrance,
Et, confiant ta vie aux bras forts des marins,
Faire de grands adieux à tes chers tamarins?
Toi, vêtue à moitié de mousselines frêles,
Frissonante là-bas sous la neige et les grêles,
Comme tu pleurerais tes loisirs doux et francs,
Si, le corset brutal imprisonnant tes flancs,
Il te fallait glaner ton souper dans nos fanges
Et vendre le parfum de tes charmes étranges,
L'œil pensif, et suivant, dans nos sales brouillards,
Des cocotiers absents les fantomes épars!

Your feet are quite as delicate as your hands, and your broad hips would arouse envy in the loveliest of white women; the thoughtful artist finds your body a delight; your big velvet eyes are blacker than your flesh. In the warm blue lands where your God granted your life, your task is to light your master's pipe, to provide flasks of cool water and perfume, to chase away the mosquitoes circling round his bed, and as soon as the plane-trees have started to sing with morning, to buy pineapples and bananas in the bazaar. All day your bare feet lead you wherever you wish, and you softly hum old and strange tunes; when evening with its scarlet coat descends, you lay your body gently down on a mat, where your wandering dreams are full of humming birds, and always (like yourself) gracious and blossoming. O happy child, why do you want to see our France, this overpeopled land cut down by suffering, and entrusting your life to the strong arms of the sailors, say a long goodbye to your dear tamarinds? Half-dressed in your frail muslin, shivering there in the snow and hail, how you would weep for your sweet and honest leisure, if, your sides imprisoned by the brutal corset, you had to glean your supper among our filth, and sell the perfume of your strange charms, your eye thoughtful and tracing, in the dirt of our fogs, the scattered phantoms of the absent coconut trees.

46

The beauty of this *heureuse enfant* is the beauty of the exotic. Her world fascinates the poet because it is so different from ours. Her God is not our God. Her country is *chaud et bleu*—or rather *chauds et bleus,* and the plural adds to the strange charm: she is not quite an individual, she comes from a bewildering richness of foreign lands. Sometimes the exotic is achieved by simple naming of objects: when she goes shopping it is for pineapples and bananas, when she dreams it is of humming birds. Her world is innocent, strange and distant.

And he tells her to stay there. The shepherd should not leave Arcadia and seek out the court, *ce pays trop peuplé que fauche la souffrance.* To be half-clad in Malabar is neither suggestive nor cold, but in France she will turn prostitute (*vendre le parfum de tes charmes étranges*), and she will shiver in the snow. And what will she do when she is there? She will weep for her *loisirs doux et francs*; she will make out the shapes of *cocotiers absents* in *nos sales brouillards.* She will write *Le Cygne,* in fact; or she will write this poem. *Le Cygne* is set entirely in the Paris of the *sales brouillards,* a Paris that changes and is rebuilt while the poet's melancholy stays the same, a Paris through which the poet walks and feels like an exile, recalling other exiles—Andromaque longing for the little river Simois, the swan he once saw, *près d'un ruisseau sans eau,* banished from its native element to the dreary filth of the city, and a negress who must surely be the same woman, poetically, as the Malabaraise:

> *Je pense à la Négresse, amaigrie et phtisique,*
> *Piétinant dans la boue, et cherchant, l'œil hagard,*
> *Les cocotiers absents de la superbe Afrique*
> *Derrière la muraille immense du brouillard.*

I think of the Negress, skinny and consumptive, tramping through the mud and searching with haggard eye for the absent coconut trees of her superb Africa through the immense wall of fog.

The similarity of phrasing is no accident. *Le Cygne* describes the future that awaits the Malabaraise—poverty, disease, ugliness, and the unbearable beauty of her nostalgic dream of home. To discover what the pastoral vision means to her, she must go to Paris and lose it. The same happened to poor Susan.

At the corner of Wood Street, when daylight appears,
Hangs a thrush that sings loud, it has sung for three years:
Poor Susan has passed by the spot, and has heard
In the silence of morning the song of the Bird.

'Tis a note of enchantment; what ails her? She sees
A mountain ascending, a vision of trees;
Bright volumes of vapour through Lothbury glide,
And a river flows on through the vale of Cheapside.

Green pastures she views in the midst of the dale,
Down which she so often has tripped with her pail;
And a single small cottage, a nest like a dove's,
The one only dwelling on earth that she loves.

She looks, and her heart is in heaven: but they fade,
The mist and the river, the hill and the shade:
The stream will not flow, and the hill will not rise,
And the colours have all passed away from her eyes!

This is surely inferior to Baudelaire's poem because of its naïvety.
It is as naïve as Susan, and simply relates her dream. Comparing
the two poems, we see that the modern fondness for irony which I
began by dismissing is based on real reasons, that merit restating.
The weakness of *Poor Susan* is a lack of complexity: so simply does
it surrender to the nostalgic dream, that only one half of its
contrast is present in the poem.

What is missing is the town. If we think of the richness of interest
in London that informs Book 7 of *The Prelude*, we can say that
Wordsworth did not write this poem with his whole being, because
he is not a pastoral poet. He does not believe, as Baudelaire does,
that the idyllic vision rests on a deep intimate loathing, a careful
complex love-hate for the town. Only in one stanza does the poem,
briefly, take on some of the poignancy that so wonderfully informs
Le Cygne: this is the second, in which we can for an instant feel the
very process of transformation. The first brilliant touch is 'ascending': the mountain grows before her eyes, and the purely physical
point made by the adjective converts the mountain into something
wholly visionary—and all the more real. Then for two magical lines,

Bright volumes of vapour through Lothbury glide,
And a river flows on through the vale of Cheapside.

the banality of rhythm that is so striking in the other stanzas is
suddenly, perfectly apt: not banality but simple intensity. This

48

rhythm holds the very movement of mountain mist and river, while the names keep us in London. But Wordsworth cannot keep it up. For the last two stanzas he retreats into a coy diction and a mere wish that he was back in the Lakes. The poem ends not with the stark reality of being back in London, but with a feebly explicit statement that the dream is over.

What Baudelaire's poem shows, and Wordsworth's doesn't, is the paradox of articulateness. Only by leaving Malabar can the woman become fully conscious of it. The poet has to urge her to stay there, but to know the beauty of his appeal she must disobey. It is a common enough paradox. Hardy's novels are a hurt cry of protest against the destruction of the rural economy of South-West England, and of the folk-lore and attitudes based thereon: but the novels could never have been written until that way of life had begun to crumble, and as the destruction grows more complete the books grow more moving. In *Far from the Madding Crowd* the forces of disintegration either belong entirely in the rural community (Bathsheba's letter to Boldwood) or are barely removed from it (Sergeant Troy was a local lad, originally). The result is a charming but limited book, with none of the harsher and profounder reach of *The Mayor of Casterbridge* and *Tess*. And the last novel of all, *Jude*, is also the harshest. It is a flawed and at times absurd book, but one that it is impossible to read unmoved. The disintegration is now so great that Hardy has not been able to make art out of it, yet the rough note of *Jude* has meant more to English fiction than the artistic success of *Far from the Madding Crowd*.

Somewhere on the scale between these two novels fell the point at which Hardy's art could touch greatness: at which the bitterness of his regret could impregnate his vision of Wessex without destroying his power to make art from it. If the Malabaraise had had Baudelaire's own gift of words, she too might have passed through such a cycle, from simple lyricism to something deeper, then to broken phrases and finally silence.

III

Meliboeus, la Malabaraise, Thomas Hardy: the list is varied of those who learnt to sing of what they loved by losing it. Is that what singing is? Is nostalgia the basis not only of pastoral but of other art too?

The greatest of modern novels contains a doctrine that almost says this. Its very title announces nostalgia, and with an interesting ambiguity. *À la recherche du temps perdu*: you can look for the past in two ways, with memory, and in some mysterious manner with your whole self, and to find it could be to remember your childhood or to return to it. The point of Proust's novel, though it does not become clear till the last volume, is that these can be combined, that the mental operation of remembering (provided it is done by the involuntary memory, not by the voluntary memory that produces only conventional and insignificant images) can so join two parts of our life that a new plane of being is created, a plane emancipated from the clutch of time:

> Une minute affranchie de l'ordre du temps a recréé en nous pour la sentir l'homme affranchi de l'ordre du temps.
>
> (Gallimard edition, XV.15)

> A minute emancipated from the temporal order has recreated in us for its apprehension the man emancipated from the temporal order.

This man is the artist and the subject of art: art too is *affranchi de l'ordre du temps*, and so the endlessly postponed attempt of the narrator to be an artist only becomes possible when a few trivial sense experiences reveal to him moments of his past, and transport him to the plane of being on which that man exists, and in which we attain to the only kind of immortality possible to us—transport him there because for an instant the physical sensations that brought stabs of memory from the past had offered to his imagination (which normally can only apprehend what is absent) the chance to grasp for a moment what it can never normally get hold of—a bit of time in its pure state (*un peu de temps à l'état pur*). The reason this state deserves to be called 'immortality' is not that it lasts for ever, but that it frees us from the fear of death. The being we then become is extra-temporal:

> Seul il avait le pouvoir de me faire retrouver les jours anciens, le Temps Perdu, devant quoi les efforts de ma mémoire et de mon intelligence échouaient toujours.   (ibid)

> It alone had the power to enable me to recapture the old days, Lost Time, before which the efforts of my memory and my intelligence always failed.

What are these *jours anciens*? The first and most famous case of the *mémoire involontaire* in the novel is the taste of the *petite madeleine* that reminds him of his aunt drinking her herb tea, and takes him back to his childhood, so leading in to the wonderful idyllic account of childhood in *Du Coté de chez Swann*—idyllic but also desperately unhappy. For us, who have grown up with psycho-analysis, a return to childhood seems a natural way to find the springs of one's being, and we nod in assent at Proust's dismissal of the conscious memory, knowing as we do that it is at the mercy of the defence mechanisms, and has no access to the important and therefore repressed material of infancy.

But there are other examples of involuntary memory in the novel, all of them occurring only in the very last of its fifteen volumes. There is the *sensation de pas inégaux*—the slight loss of balance as he stands on two paving stones that are not quite level, that takes him back to a similar sensation when he was in Venice. There is the *bruit métallique* of spoon on cup, that takes him back to a similar sound made by a hammer on the wheels of the little train he had travelled in, and recalls the experience of watching the wood, and realising that he took no pleasure in the thought of describing it. This had occurred only a short time earlier, and is narrated in the first volume of *Le Temps Retrouvé*. Finally there is the *raideur de la serviette*, the stiffness of the towel which reminds him of a similar stiffness in the towel he used the day of his arrival in Balbec, where as a young man he spent the summer.

Only the first of these reminders takes him back to childhood. The narrator's age at the end of the novel is left deliberately uncertain: his friends all have grey hair, and Swann's grand-daughter is now sixteen. This uncertainty is necessary in so realistic a novel, since if we do the arithmetic we'd notice that this last episode must be taking place later than the moment the book is being written—in fact, after the death of the author! Because of this, we cannot say just how far back each memory is taking him, but it is clear that the distance in time varies, and is not important. Watching the wood from the train is recent; the trip to Venice earlier; Balbec earlier still; and the *petite madeleine* takes him back virtually to the beginning of memory.

What was important for Proust was the joining of a sensation from the past with one from the present; where it came from in the past did not matter. And it follows from this that what is remembered will not matter either. Here is the central and profound difference between Proust and Freud. Childhood memories are, to Freud, the most important because they operate at the deepest level; the first five or six years of life provide, as he tells us, the content of the adult's unconscious. The breaking down of repressions and the release of forgotten material is important, for Freud, because the material itself is important. The very fact of its repression and return is evidence of its emotional importance. But for Proust the actual memories that return are arbitrary—others might have emerged, called up by other sense impressions, and they would have done as well. What matters is the fact that at the moment of recalling the past you are actually there—or rather that you and it have both taken on existence *affranchis de l'ordre du temps*. A new mode of being has been established.

Nothing about Proust seems more obvious than that he is a psychological novelist. His values are psychological: though he may use religious metaphors, it is to replace religion by human experience as the starting point for understanding the human condition. His explorations are psychological: the narrator's belated awareness of his grief for his grandmother is a discovery of his own emotions, even of his own consciousness. The drama is psychological: Morel and the Baron de Charlus, for instance, enact their Racinian battles through phrases and tone of voice: a misread telegram can lead to a new consciousness. All this is true; and yet, observing this difference between memory in Proust and memory in Freud, we can see that Proust's conception of happiness is not psychological at all, but ontological.

If this is true, it is important for our argument because of the great importance Proust gives to nostalgia. Longing is what makes art possible: for Proust, this is the same as saying that longing is what gives sense to living. This point is eloquently made in a short but crucial essay in *Contre Saint-Beuve*, called 'Journées' —a wonderfully moving piece, suffused with the emotion it describes.

'Journées' describes his extreme sensitivity to weather, so extreme that he did not need to go outside to know what sort of day it was:

À sentir le calme et la lenteur de communications et d'échanges que règnent dans la petite cité interieure de nerfs et de vais-

52

seaux que je porte en moi, je sais qu'il pleut, et je voudrais être à Bruges ou, près du four rouge comme un soleil d'hiver, les gélines, les poules d'eau, le cochon cuiraient pour mon déjeuner comme dans un tableau de Breughel.

From the quietness and slow pace of the communications and exchanges ruling in the small internal city of nerves and vessels that I carry within me, I know that it is raining, and I'd like to be at Bruges where, close to the red fire that is like the winter sun, the pullets, the moorhens and the pig would be cooking for my dinner as in a picture by Breughel.

This sensitivity is so great it is fearful, it is impossible to disentangle delight from pain when

j'entends tout au fond de moi une petite voix gaie qui dit: il fait beau—il fait beau—, des larmes de souffrance me tombent des yeux, je ne peux pas parler. . . .

I hear in the depths of myself a little gay voice saying, It's a fine day,—it's a fine day—, tears of suffering gush from my eyes, I am unable to speak. . . .

He does not even need to be awake to be aware of the weather. When he had developed the habit of staying up all night and in bed all day, he still knew with trembling exactitude what the day was doing. And this awareness of what he took no part in enriched his experience, gave him fresh reasons for living. A woman passes his window:

Ah! si j'étais levé. Mais, du moins, je sais que les jours sont riches de telles possibilités, mon appétit de la vie s'en accroit.

Ah! if I were up. But at least I know that the days are rich with such possibilities, and my appetite for life is increased by them.

Sometimes he found it necessary to peep through the curtains, just to reassure himself that his inner world did correspond to the other—like a musician composing on paper, who needs to play a note on the piano, to make sure that he is in tune with real sound. One note suffices, so intense is his awareness. The intensity and the withdrawal are obviously related. A new face, a new country rekindles our delight in living by what they offer:

Qu'importe si nous ne partons pas, nous savons qu'il existe, nous avons une raison de plus de vivre.

What does it matter if we don't set off, we know that it exists, we have one more reason for living.

Hopkin

It may lead to vision and with many reservation
vision may

The theory of this essay is that deprivation leads to creation.
When we are not part of the life we long for, the longing retains its
intensity, and can even offer the joy of attainment without the
fact. (It offers it to the imagination: and the importance of the
état affranchi de l'ordre du temps in *Le Temps Retrouvé* is that it
enables the imagination to have the illusion of dealing with what
is real, not just what is longed for.) The final example of 'Les
Journées' illustrates the point perfectly. What is the most intoxi-
cating of all the smells of the countryside? For Proust, it is the
smell of petrol: for that is the smell that offers. When it came
through the window, his joy was complete:

> Cette délicieuse odeur de pétrole, couleur du ciel et du soleil,
> s'était toute l'immensité de la campagne, la joie de partir,
> d'aller loin entre les bleuets, les coquelicots et les trèfles violets,
> et de savoir que l'on arrivera au lieu désiré, où notre amie
> nous attend.

> That delicious odour of petrol, the colour of the sky and the
> sun, it was the countryside in all its vastness, it was the joy of
> departure, of moving away through the cornflowers, the
> poppies, the purple clover, and of knowing that you will reach
> the longed-for spot where your girl is waiting for you.

To say that the smell of cars spoils the countryside is to make a
simple mistake: it is to believe that originality is a question of
facts, not impressions. In Proust's sensibility the effect of impressions is immediate and overwhelming: the smell of petrol
contains what it promises—provided, of course, that he doesn't
actually get to the countryside. Shelley's invitation to Arcadia,

> *A wind is hovering o'er the mountain's brow . . .*
> *The halcyon broods along the foamless sea . . .*

led, as we saw, to a long account of the 'isle under Ionian skies'.
Mallarmé expressed the same emotion in a sonnet, indeed in the
second half of a sonnet that begins with the boredom from which
he needs to escape. It ends where Shelley begins:

> *Je partirai! Steamer balançant ta mâture*
> *Lève l'ancre pour une exotique nature.*

I am off! Steamer balancing your masts, weigh anchor for an
exotic nature.

To say that Mallarmé's omission makes his poem superior to
Shelley's expansion would be absurd and puritanical: but in the

on a area where religious statements are valid but is a humanist.

light of Proust's theory we can say at least that there is a kind of wisdom in it. The sight of the steamer (and the song of the sailors a line or two later) is Mallarmé's smell of petrol. By stopping there, he assumes what Proust explains, that the invitation may contain a more intense experience than the fact.

This theory, that creation springs from longing and therefore depends on deprivation, is central to Proust: and it is not merely a theory of art. It is an obvious parallel to his belief that love depends on separation and is destroyed when the possibility of fulfilment is offered. It is a theory that covers all human experience.

IV *to be Freudian with all limitation that implies*

To find the theory outside literature, as part of a general theory of human development, I turn to Hanna Segal and Melanie Klein. In an essay called 'A Psychoanalytic Contribution to Aesthetics' (*New Directions in Psychoanalysis*, ed. Klein and others, Chapter 16), Hanna Segal claims that a feeling of loss is at the centre of artistic creation. Her starting point is Melanie Klein's theory of 'the depressive position'. The infant reacts to certain inevitable painful experiences by undergoing a neurosis: weaning, and the recognition of other human beings as real persons separate from himself, seem to be the crucial experiences, and to be related to each other. This neurosis must be worked through and overcome, first, through a series of defence mechanisms which offer partial adjustments and must themselves be outgrown, and ultimately by an acceptance of reality: the testing of reality is the main task of this phase of development. 'In my view', writes Melanie Klein,

> there is a close connection between the testing of reality in normal mourning, and early processes of the mind. . . . In mourning the (adult) subject goes through a modified and transitory manic-depressive state, and overcomes it, thus repeating, though in different circumstances . . . the processes which the child normally goes through in his early development.
> ('Mourning and its Relation to Manic-depressive States')

In this essay, Melanie Klein explores the tasks and difficulties of mourning, and relates them to this infantile neurosis which, with Freud, she considers rather the rule than the exception in human development.

From this, Hanna Segal develops a theory of art. 'All creation,' he claims,

> is really a recreation of a once loved and once whole, but now lost and ruined object, a ruined internal world and self. . . . The wish to create is rooted in the depressive position, and the capacity to create depends on a successful working through it.

Inability to work through one's depressive anxieties can thus lead to the inhibition of artistic activity. The successful artist is like the successful man: he can handle his situation. He is distinguished from the neurotic day-dreamer by the fact that in two fields he has a high reality-sense: in relation to his own internal life (he perceives the nature and implications of his longings), and in relation to the material of his art.

Seeing art as a form of sublimation, Hanna Segal accepts Freud's view that sublimation involves the successful renunciation of an instinctual aim. This can only happen through a process of mourning. 'The giving up of an instinctual aim or object is a repetition and at the same time a reliving of the giving up of the breast.'

The resemblance of this theory to Proust's is clear, and Hanna Segal admits the debt (though she does not mention 'Les Journées'). '*On ne peut recréer ce qu'on aime qu'en le renonçant*', says Elstir; and she adds, 'It is only when the loss has been acknowledged, and the mourning experienced that re-creation can take place. *Le Temps Retrouvé* corresponds to a situation of mourning: seeing his friends after so many years, the narrator finds that the beloved objects are dying or dead. This leads to his decision to write.'

Now Hanna Segal's theory is clearly a psychological one; Proust's, as I have admitted, is only partly so, and the boundary between what is and isn't psychological in it is not easy to draw. Deprivation is a state of the psyche, and the process by which it leads to substitute gratification of peculiar intensity, and so to art, is one that psychologists can explore and generalise from. But on the other hand, artistic experience is not, ultimately, nostalgic for Proust, since it culminates in the attaining of a state of aesthetic fulfilment. *Le Temps Retrouvé* crowns the novel, and fulfilment crowns fourteen volumes of frustration.

It is obvious in a formal sense that the last volume crowns and justifies Proust's great novel, but it is possible to respond very differently to this effect. The reader who accepts the symbolist aesthetic will feel that the climax justifies, that the *état affranchi de l'ordre du temps* is the experience to which everything, we now see, was pointing. But the reader who sees the narrator as constantly failing in insight or will, as a sensitive neurotic unable to cope with the demands of reality, must surely reflect that this state owes little to the reality-principle, and that aesthetic bliss is not human maturity. It is a happiness that contrasts with life, not the happiness of controlling it.

À la recherche du temp perdu is a long story of loss and gain; and I now suggest in conclusion, that the loss is psychological, the gain aesthetic. Its explanations of how deprivation leads to intensity are deeply true renderings of experience; what it offers as the overcoming of deprivation is (for the reader whose expectations are psychological) an evasion.

V

To set forth a theory is not enough; I must, however hesitantly, end by asking how true it is, or at least how we would set about asking if it is true.

First, we can observe that the theory is Freudian, but better than Freud's. For Freud, art was an expression of fantasy, parallel to day-dreaming. The artist achieves vicariously the mastery of reality that he is not able to achieve in fact; to this extent his work resembles the substitute gratification of neurotic fantasy. But the artist also has a power denied to the day-dreamer. He can 'soften the egotistical character of the day-dream by changes and disguises', and he also 'bribes' us 'by the offer of purely formal, that is aesthetic, pleasure'. Generations of critics have pointed out the weaknesses of this view—that it tells us much more about content than form, that it applies much better to bad literature than good. Freud himself comes close to admitting this, in the very hesitant language of his essay, 'The Relation of the Poet to Day-dreaming'. But too many of these critics have then concluded that psycho-analytic theories of art must necessarily be reductive. It is quite possible to accept Freud's view that art is built out of fantasy material without accepting his naïve claim that what the artist does with the fantasy is simply to submit to it. Hanna Segal's theory attempts to find in the handling of artistic material the same complicated reconciling of pleasure-principle

and reality-principle that Freud found in actual living. There are
other neo-Freudian theories—that of Kubie, for instance, or of
Simon O. Lesser—which attempt the same necessary task.

Hanna Segal's theory takes art seriously: a necessary but not
a sufficient condition for a good theory of art. When we now ask
what exactly she tells us, we seem to find a double claim. First,
she describes art. 'In a great work of art, the degree of the denial
of the death instinct is less than that in any other human activity.'
Like so many psycho-analysts, Hanna Segal chooses tragedy as
the central literary form, and she analyses the success of a great
tragedy into, first, an unshrinking expression of the full horror of
the depressive fantasy, and second, an impression of wholeness
and harmony. 'In tragedy, the content is ugly, the form is beautiful.' This is a particular example of her more general view that
both beauty and ugliness must be present for a full aesthetic
experience: the fear of the world must in one sense be faced, in
another sense transcended. When it comes to a more particular
description of art, the theory asserts that it resembles mourning.
Because art contains negative as well as positive elements and
seeks to organise them so that they illuminate each other, we
must seek its analogue and prototype in a similarly dialectical
experience. This is the experience of loss and acceptance of loss,
in which defence mechanisms (for instance, the wish to triumph
over the lost love-object) both uncover and distort elements in the
situation, help us to handle it but in a way that brings other
psychological difficulties. Our hatred of the dead person for dying,
for instance (which may conceal other hatreds), helps us to resist
our pining, but must in its turn be overcome as we slowly acquire
the strength to accept reality.

How useful is this as a description of the artistic experience?
It fits Proust very well, as we have seen; and it fits half of Proust
perfectly. I believe it fits pastoral poetry well too, and such neo-
pastoral lyrics as *Epipsychidion* or 'À Une Malabaraise'. But no
theory can be tested only on the kind of material that suggested
it. If it is a general theory of art, it must fit all kinds of art: an
honest methodology will try it on the least promising examples.

All we are offered for this is the discussion of tragedy, and
though Hanna Segal's account seems true in a general way, it does
not help us much on actual plays. The greatest tragedies certainly
do not control the terror of their material only by formal means:

that description fits Corneille much better than Euripides or Shakespeare. The form of *Lear* belongs, if anything, on the side of terror: the reconciliation of Lear and Cordelia is clearly 'content'. The form of *Hamlet* is notoriously untidy, and full of loose ends; its occasional profound effects of reassurance ('the readiness is all') are very moving but formally clumsy: we wonder, even, why they are there. As a description of tragedy, we have been given something very approximate.

No, this claim that art is like the experience of loss is really an account of those works of art that are based on loss. As a general theory it is useless, since Hanna Segal has not even begun the task of showing a wider validity. Having said this, we have not robbed it of its interest for us, since what drew us to it was the fact that it starts from the experience of nostalgia. Certainly the poetry of nostalgia is like mourning.

So much for the description of art. The second part of the theory is an account of what the experience of mourning is. Before examining it, I need to say that the first half of the theory does not need the second: the parallel between mourning and art (some art) may hold, whatever we say to the theory of the depressive position.

It is a Freudian theory, with heterodox elements. It claims to find many of the psychic processes of the adult in the very first year of life, and claims that the infant passes through a paranoid-schizoid position in the first few months, and then enters the depressive position, whose processes are no longer psychotic but neurotic. Both these 'positions' must be worked through, but can never totally be outgrown.

The main evidence for these steps and these processes is dreams. Both Klein and Segal interpret dreams by the basic Freudian methods of complicating the simple (since manifest elements are overdetermined) and they give us a monstrous deal of interpretation, sometimes, to a ha'porth of dream. Such interpretations, clearly, will be accepted by Freudians and by no one else, and for this the Freudians have their explanation—as have the others! Psycho-analysis has come to be marked out from the rest of psychology by its brilliant, lunatic sense of what constitutes evidence; but also by its concern with infancy. Klein and Segal move with abandon from child to adult, supporting a theory about the first by quoting (and interpreting) the dreams of the second. This is of course permissible if you grant the premiss that the deepest adult anxieties are a reactivating of infantile anxieties that have not been fully worked through—that there is 'a close connexion between the testing of reality in normal mourning and early processes of the mind'. This is too vast a subject for us here. Perhaps it is even too vast for psycho-analysis. But a few remarks are necessary.

It is especially hard to distinguish speculation from evidence in the accounts of what goes on in a child's experience. This is not altogether the fault of the psycho-analysts: the material here is speculative and untestable, yet crucially important, for obviously the shape of our psychic life *is* formed in infancy. Yet perhaps it is their fault that they don't notice the difficulty. And there is another difficulty they perhaps ought to notice. Even if we accept the parallel between adult anxieties and the infantile depressive position, it is hard to know if it is more than a resemblance. These two psycho-analysts (like all the others) slip in and out of causal terminology when speaking of the parallel. Melanie Klein claims that what Freud considered the *basic* infantile danger-situation in girls (dread of loss of love) is a *modification* of being robbed by the mother of the contents of her body; and I do not know if the words I have italicised are causal or chronological, or neither. It is not certain either if the *re-living* of early anxieties is different from their *repetition*: and if so, whether the difference is a matter of intensity or cause. And I cannot resist quoting a wonderful phrase from Melanie Klein's brief essay 'Infantile Anxiety-Situations reflected in a work of art and in the creative impulse': 'My work has *proved to me* that both these danger-situations are modifications of yet earlier ones.'

I have dwelt on this point for two reasons. First, because Hanna Segal's seems to me a prototype of psycho-analytic theories of art. At their rare best, these theories describe art sensitively, and sometimes (this is rarer still) illuminatingly; and they offer stimulating parallels with other human experiences. When it comes to describing these other experiences, they often combine a just sense of the whole with a lurid elaboration of hidden levels in the details; and when it comes to explaining them, they do what the behaviourists, alas, hardly ever do, they treat man as the product of his past, including his earliest past—and then, alas, they burrow into the untestable unfoldings of hidden motives in that now inaccessible past.

He is by no means a doctrinaire Freudian.

None of this has to do with the poetry of nostalgia. But there is another parallel to be drawn now (this time I am sure it is no more than a parallel) which will take us back to a question that arose in the first chapter, and will occur again in others. This is the question of childhood. What are we longing for, in our nostalgia? Is it for a host of lost objects and lost experiences, or for one in particular, that underlies them all? Are we longing as representatives of man, for the lost unity of primitive society (as a Marxist critic claims)? Or as individuals, for our own lost childhood? Let us take one last quotation from the *Eclogues* (we shall have occasion to take it again):

> saepibus in nostris parvam te roscida mala
> (dux ego vester eram) vidi cum matre legentem.
> alter ab undecimo tum me iam acceperat annus,
> iam fragiles poteram ab terra contingere ramos.
> ut vidi! ut perii! ut me malus abstulit error!
>
> VIII.37-41

When you were small I saw you (I was then your guide) with your mother, picking the dewy apples in our orchard. I had just entered the year after my eleventh year; already I could touch the delicate branches from the ground. I saw you and, ah, was lost: this wicked treachery of love caught me.

Macaulay found this the most moving passage in Latin poetry. Why? Because Virgil happened to write better about a longing that came to him from childhood than about the loss of a farm? Or because it was the link with childhood that enabled him to write better? I have saved this example till the end in order to ask if it has a special status among the others. Is it one more example, consummately expressed, or is it the emergence into explicitness of the one longing that underlies all longing—the longing for the time when you could not reach the branches?

Is Arcadia really childhood? Childhood reminiscences are frequent, and frequently moving, in nostalgic poetry; and as we'd expect, more frequent in romantic poetry than in traditional pastoral. Tasso wrote, in two famous lines:

> *il mondo invecchia*
> *et invecchiando intristice.*

the world grows old; and as it grows old it grows sad.

Does he simply mean 'the world'? Or do the lines draw their power from the hidden parallel, that *we* have grown older, and as we have done so, sadder? That we have 'entered the thorny wilderness, and the golden gates of (our) childhood for ever closed behind us'.

I do not know how to answer this question, because I don't know what sort of question it is. Is it a question about poetry or not? Does it concern the nature of nostalgia as it is found in pastoral poetry? Or have we finished talking about Virgil and Shelley when we have pointed out the presence of nostalgia and what the poet does with it? Is this further question simply that of a theory of nostalgia, on which psychologists could differ, though they read the poems alike?

The problem, alas, overspills the bounds of literary criticism. When Freud and Melanie Klein describe mourning, they are clearly writing psychology; at what point does their explanation of childhood origins turn into meta-psychology? Can one reject the latter and at the same time salute the shrewdness of the account of adult experiences? As long as psychologists and philosophers are defeated by this problem, the literary man may be forgiven for drawing back from his.

ARCADIA AND UTOPIA

'Ｆｉｒｓｔ of all,' Hesiod tells us, 'the deathless Gods who dwell on Olympus made a golden race of mortal men who lived in the time of Cronos when he was reigning in heaven. And they lived like Gods without sorrow of heart, remote and free from toil and grief; miserable age rested not on them; but with legs and arms never failing they made merry with feasting beyond the reach of all evils. When they died, it was as though they were overcome with sleep, and they had all good times; for the fruitful earth unforced bore them fruit abundantly and without stint.'

This Golden Age ended, and it was succeeded by a silver, then a bronze, then a fourth, and now at last a fifth age, when 'men never rest from labour and sorrow by day, and from perishing by night'. Every age runs its course, and perishes: 'Zeus will destroy this race of mortal men also', says Hesiod in a wonderful image, 'when they come to have grey hairs on the temples at their birth.'

Hesiod's account of the Golden Age is the first of a long series in ancient literature. Plato has various modified versions of it. The third-century poet Aratus has a version that introduces the virgin Astraea, who represents Justice, and thus gives a moral as well as a physical superiority to the first age:

> Not yet did men understand hateful war or vituperative disputes or din of battle, but they lived simply . . . and Justice herself, mistress of the people, giver of just things, furnished all things a thousandfold.

But the most familiar version of the Golden Age does not, of course, come from classical literature at all. 'Men never rest from labour,' says Hesiod: 'In the sweat of thy face thou shalt eat bread,' said the Lord God to Adam, 'till thou return into the ground.' The biblical story of the Garden of Eden is a version of the same myth, and phrases like these show how it must have originated—as an attempt to explain why life is so hard. In Eden, as in the Golden Age, the fruitful earth unforced bore fruit.

It is not simply a modern quirk to compare the Christian and pagan versions of this story. From patristic times to at least the seventeenth century there was a tradition that pagan mythology was really about the same thing as Christianity. It underlies the whole medieval tradition of 'moralising' or allegorising the classical authors; and it will engage us again in the chapters on Milton. For a sixteenth-century example here is part of the prefatory Epistle to Arthur Golding's translation of the Metamorphoses:

> *Moreover by the Golden Age what other thing is meant,*
> *Than Adam's time in Paradise, who being innocent*
> *Did lead a blest and happy life until that thorough sin*
> *He fell from God? From which time forth all sorrow did begin.*

In one respect, Golding is certainly wrong: he has compared not only Eden itself, but also its loss, to the classical story. Now Eden and the Golden Age are the same while we still have them; but they do not come to an end in the same way.

We all know how Eden was lost; but Hesiod's golden race perished through the whim of Zeus. There is nothing you can do about the arbitrariness of the gods except lament and submit; and the implications of the Golden Age story are therefore quietist. But Adam fell: there is a moral dimension in his story. And a moral decision can be discussed, defended, protested against, and perhaps, eventually, reversed. History now becomes a long effort to make ourselves worthy of Paradise again: the story that starts with Eden will culminate in the New Jerusalem.

> Behold, a king shall reign in righteousness, and princes shall rule in judgement . . .
> And the eyes of them that see shall not be dim, and the ears of them that hear shall hearken . . .
> Then judgement shall dwell in the wilderness, and righteousness remain in the fruitful field . . .
> They shall not build and another inhabit; they shall not plant and another eat: for as the days of a tree are the days of my people, and mine elect shall long enjoy the work of their hands . . .
>
> The wolf and the lamb shall feed together, and the lion shall eat straw like the bullock: and dust shall be the serpent's meat.
> They shall not hurt nor destroy in all my holy mountains, saith the Lord.

Isaiah's Paradise is different from Hesiod's. It belongs not at the beginning of time but at the end. It is ruled not by magic but by

justice. It is not amiable but fiercely moral. The good are to be
rewarded, and perhaps their reward is sharpened by the punish-
ment of the wicked: 'dust shall be the serpent's meat'. In the
Golden Age there was no agriculture; but in Isaiah's New Jerusalem everyone will work, and distribution will be just.

Lost Paradise is called Eden, if you are a Christian; or the
Golden Age, if you are thinking of the time; or Arcadia, if you are
thinking of the place. Paradise to come is called by Christians,
Heaven if it is in another world, New Jerusalem if in this. The
secular term is Utopia—or the withering away of the state.

The terms could be disputed, perhaps, but the dispute is not
important. It is true that Arcadia is an actual region of Greece,
but as the setting for pastoral poetry it is a land entirely of the
fancy. This transformation goes right back to the ancient world:
Bruno Snell claims it was due to Virgil. And it is true too that the
relation between Heaven and the New Jerusalem is sometimes
more complicated. In the Book of Revelation there is a period of a
thousand years when Satan will be bound and the martyrs will
reign with Christ; then the loosing of Satan and a final battle; then
the new heaven and the new earth and 'the holy city, new Jerusalem, coming down from God out of heaven, prepared as a bride
adorned for her husband'. All this can be variously interpreted,
according as the thousand-year binding of Satan is placed in the
past or the future. After the Reformation, when apocalyptic ideas
surged into European thought, it was often held that the thousand
years were just over. But if they were yet to come then there were
two millennia ahead, and the first or earthly one might well
(though this is not John's terminology) be called the New Jerusalem. Yet it does not really matter if the millennium is simple or
compound, for in both cases it offers an abolition of history by
violent divine intervention, and a kingdom of justice in the end.
All this is utterly different from Arcadia and the Golden Age. The
one structures our experience with sadness, the other with fierce
hope. One speaks an elegy, the other a call to action.

In Christian mouths this call has often had a note of sharp
paradox. Though the Fall introduces a moral dimension into
history, one prominent strand of Christianity (justification by
faith alone) contains a deep rejection of morality. To the Calvinist,
we do not make ourselves worthy of Heaven, we are permitted by
grace to enter into it. One might have expected this to lead to

quietism—the Calvinist, like Hesiod, sadly shrugging his shoulders and waiting for what God is pleased to give him. It has of course been one of the great paradoxes of Calvinism that this has not happened—a paradox it shares with Marxism, the great secularised belief in the New Jerusalem. In both cases we have an all-embracing theory that claims understanding of first causes; in both cases the first cause is beyond the control of the individual; and both systems therefore contain a strong potential quietism that has never emerged, for they are both deeply moral. With often astonishing subtlety, both systems tell you that the coming of Jerusalem does not depend on you, and urge you to strive for it.

The most brilliant description I know of the difference between Eden and Utopia is by W. H. Auden. 'Eden', he says,

> is a past world in which the contradictions of the present world have not yet arisen; New Jerusalem is a future world in which they have at last been resolved. Eden is a place where its inhabitants may do whatever they like to do; the motto over its gate is 'Do what thou wilt is here the Law'. New Jerusalem is a place where its inhabitants like to do whatever they ought to do, and its motto is 'In His Will is our peace . . .'

This is from Auden's essay on *Pickwick Papers* 'Dingley Dell and the Fleet'. He has also written a poem on the subject, 'Vespers', in which he describes an encounter between himself and his antitype: 'I am an Arcadian, he is a Utopian'. The Arcadian's reactions to the world are aesthetic, the Utopian's are political:

> Glancing at a lampshade in a store window, I observe it is too hideous for anyone in their senses to buy. He observes that it is too expensive for a peasant to buy.

Each has his own dishonesty:

> Passing a slum child with rickets, I look the other way: he looks the other way if he passes a chubby one.

And each has his own kind of religion, the Arcadian's ritualistic, the Utopian's reduced to mere morality:

> In my Eden each observes his compulsive rituals and superstitious taboos, but we have no morals; in his New Jerusalem the temples will be empty, but all will practise the rational virtues.

Eden is amiably inaccurate, New Jerusalem is planned:

> In my Eden our only source of political news is gossip; in his
> New Jerusalem there will be a special daily in simplified spell-
> ing for non-verbal types.

Auden's preference is clear—the resigned preference of a conservative. The Arcadian, having retreated into memory, will not
change the world; but at least this means that he will not hurt
anybody. People with superstitions instead of morals get nothing
done, but they are nice to know. Auden is afraid of zeal, because
it can be an outlet for aggression.

II

The Golden Age belongs to the past; and to put it in the future is
likely to change it into Utopia. The restoring of the Golden Age
was a commonplace of Renaissance panegyric; but if it is to be
restored by the prowess of a prince, it is difficult for it to keep its
primitive innocence. I take as an example an inoffensive work by
Ben Jonson, his masque on *The Golden Age Restored*. A masque
is not likely to explore concepts (the one great exception is, as it
happens, the subject of Chapter VIII), so that what Jonson does
to his terminology will be the more or less accidental result of his
subject. Jonson uses a good deal of traditional Golden Age imagery
and did not, I am sure, intend to write an unconventional work.
But simply because the Iron Age, as anti-masque, appears at the
beginning, it must in some way be defeated. This means that there
must be a struggle, and a victory: Pallas shows her shield, and the
evils are turned to statues.

> *So change and perish scarcely knowing how*
> *That 'gainst the gods do take so vain a vow . . .*
> *Twas time t'appear, and let their folly see*
> *'Gainst whom they fought, and with what destiny*
> *Die all that can remain of you but stone.*

The return of Astraea is meant to restore harmony, but it is
accompanied with fierceness:

> *Let narrow natures how they will mistake*
> *The great should still be good for their own sake.*

67

'Narrow natures': the intensity of this moral vocabulary destroys the Arcadian spirit. Flattery and politics have no place in the true primitive ideal.

Yet the most famous of all versions of the Golden Age, and the one that introduced it into the pastoral tradition, is set in the future; somehow carefully preserving its true nature. This is the fourth of Virgil's *Eclogues*, probably the most famous short poem ever written. From the first, it stood out among the *Eclogues*: it is the only one which is neither in dialogue nor about named pastoral figures, and it announces in its opening lines that it is to be read with special awe:

> *Sicelides Musae, paulo maiora canamus*

(Sicilian Muses, let us sing of something rather greater)

What made the poem so celebrated in the Middle Ages was of course its announcement of the birth of a child who would rejuvenate the world; and to the natural interpretations (that the child is the son of Pollio or the son of Octavianus—neither quite fits) was added a supernatural one, that Virgil the magus was foretelling the birth of Christ forty years later. This goes of course with the *sortes virgilianae* and with his selection as Dante's guide through Hell and Purgatory.

So far we seem to be dealing with New Jerusalem; and it has even been suggested that Virgil knew a Greek version of Isaiah. But when we look at what this promised new age is going to be like, we can see that it is purely Arcadian. The earth will yield gifts without cultivation. Goats will run around oozing milk. The sheep will grow coloured wool, so that we shan't need dyes. No one will sail on the sea; or rather, they will at first, because of *vestigia priscae fraudis*, but once the child has grown up

> *cedet et ipse mari vector, nec nautica pinus*
> *mutabit merces.*

(the voyager will abandon the sea, and no tall-masted ship will carry goods from one place to another.)

It is a bad mistake to render *priscae fraudis* (as one translator does) by 'primal error', or indeed by any phrase that suggests sin or the Fall. It simply means 'the way we live now'. What will impede our regeneration is not human wickedness, but the slow revolving of the spindles of Fate. The Parcae have already given the command:

'talia saecla' suis dixerunt 'currite' fusis
*concordes stabili fatorum numine **Parcae***

(The Fates, in accordance with the unalterable will of destiny,
said to their spindles: 'Run through these new ages'.)

The whole thing is to happen without human action: there is no
Day of Judgement. For though a day of Judgement is God's work,
not man's, its purpose is to *judge*, to separate sheep from goats,
and what happens will therefore in some degree depend on man.
Even the fierce arbitrariness of the Calvinist God is presented as if
it was moral, not as the waywardness of a world of natural magic,
whereas Virgil's new age is quite unselective: it is simply what's
going to happen to the world, and is for the just and unjust alike.

The stages of the new Golden Age are marked in the poem by the
growth of the child. At first he is an infant, then he has learned to
read, then full-grown age has made him a man. But these steps in
his growth simply accompany the unfolding of the new age, they
do not cause it. 'When he can read'—what follows is not what he
will now be able to do for mankind, but simply what the spindles
of the Parcae bring next:

molli paulatim flavescet campus arista,
incultisque rubens pendebit sentibus uva,
et durae quercus sudabunt roscida mella.

(Gradually the plain will grow yellow with supple corn, without cultivation the grape will hang ruddy on the brambles,
and tough oaks will ooze honey-dew.)

I can find only one truly Utopian touch in this Arcadian idyll:
that is line 17:

pacatumque reget patriis virtutibus orbem.

The child will rule over a world pacified by *patriis virtutibus*. Now
here is an ambiguity. If it means 'by the prowess of his father' then
there is going to be some political cleaning up by the child's father
—Octavianus, or Pollio, or whoever it is—to make things ready.
Such cleaning up, as Auden brilliantly reminds us, is Utopian, not
Arcadian:

When lights burn late in the citadel, I (who have never seen
the inside of a police-station) am shocked . . . He (who has
been beaten up several times) is not shocked at all, but thinks:
'One fine night our boys will be working up there'.

But if *patriis virtutibus* means 'by our ancestral virtues', then Octavianus' boys are not going to be working late in the citadel, for the line is about the past only.

Certainly this is the only political line in the poem, the only line that looks forward to the fearful virtue of the *Aeneid*. It is a line which Pope leaned on very heavily for his free rendering of the Eclogue:

> *No more shall nation against nation rise,*
> *Nor ardent warriors meet with hateful eyes,*
> *Nor fields with gleaming steel be covered o'er;*
> *The brazen trumpets kindle rage no more.*

All that is squeezed out of 'pacatum'. Pope set out to rewrite Virgil in the light of Isaiah, and to show 'how far the images and descriptions of the Prophet are superior to those of the Poet'. This meant turning Arcadia into Utopia, and he even called his version 'Messiah'.

Virgil however, has not left the Arcadian world: his first line was at least partly misleading. If he is writing prophecy, it is not Messianic prophecy: looking into the future he sees the original Golden Age. The Virgil of the *Aeneid* is a long way off: even the Virgil of the *Georgics* is not yet present.

The *Georgics* are nature poems. They tell of crops and weather, of the planting of trees and vines, of the raising of cattle and bees. They are almost a practical handbook, by a poet who prided himself on his knowledge of the countryside. They also contain (Book II.1.458-end) a long praise of rural content, contrasted with the restless life of soldier or merchant, and seen as a thing of the past

> *hanc olim veteres vitam coluere sabini,*
> *hanc Remus et frater*

(this was the life which the ancient Sabines once led, or Remus and his brother)

So the Golden Age is naturally mentioned; but when Virgil speaks of it at length, he speaks of its end:

> *ille malum virus serpentibus addidit atris*
> *praedarique lupos iussit pontumque moveri*

(he—Jupiter—gave deadly poison to the black snakes, and ordered wolves to pillage and the sea to rage in storms)

Not the Golden Age itself but the evils that have followed it is the theme of the *Georgics*; not Saturn's earth that yielded crops *nullo culto*, but the details of husbandry rendered necessary by the reign of Jove; not pastoral but nature.

Each of Virgil's three poems has its version of the Golden Age; and that in the *Aeneid* is different again. They had no agriculture, not because their life was easy but because it was hard; they weren't able to lay up stores,

> *sed rami atque asper victu venatus alebat*

(but lived off the hard fare of hunting and fruit from the bough . . .)

This stern existence no doubt fits the epic spirit; and it puts Virgil (for the moment) among the hard primitivists. I take the term from Lovejoy and Boas's useful contrast between soft primitivism, which delights in the freedom of primitive man to do as he pleases, in the dream 'of a life with little or no toil or strain of body or mind' (*Primitivism and Related Ideas in Antiquity*, p. 9); and hard primitivism, which praises the austerity and stern character training of primitive society. The finest example of hard primitivism in English poetry is the eighth book of *The Prelude*, in which Wordsworth contrasts the life of classical or Mediterranean shepherds with those of Cumberland:

> *Smooth life had flock and shepherd in old time,*
> *Long springs and tepid winters, on the banks*
> *Of delicate Galesus.*

But the bleak life of the Lake District produces 'a free man, wedded to his life of hope And hazard'—austere, difficult and imaginatively far richer:

> *The lingering dews of night*
> *Smoke round him, as from hill to hill he hies,*
> *His staff protending like a hunter's spear.*

Hard primitivism is unpastoral: goes, even, with its explicit rejection. The shepherds of the Golden Age leapt from no rocks, battled through no mists, but spent their hours

> *In unlaborious pleasure, with no task*
> *More toilsome than to carve a beechen bowl.*

71

Wordsworth is the great unpastoral poet in English—not anti-pastoral in the sense of Touchstone and Sidney, rejecting country for court, but unpastoral in his concern with incidents and situations from common life: a poet of the direct, not the mediated provincial. So it is appropriate that he finds soft primitivism slightly unreal and not altogether admirable.

III

Both Eden and the New Jerusalem—the myth of the Golden Age and the myth of the millennium—are ways of refusing history. If the ideal version of man's life is placed outside ordinary time, then we have a way of protecting ourselves against the incessant suffering that human history offers. This is the theme of Mircea Eliades' fascinating book, *The Myth of the Eternal Return*: mankind has been able to tolerate suffering because it was given a meta-historical significance. True meaning for the primitive mind lies out of time.

But neither of these myths, after all, seems very effective in providing reassurance. What comfort is it that there was a Golden Age if it is now lost? And even the millennium is only a comfort if you have learned to accept one-way time—a sophisticated concept that presupposes a certain acceptance of history. The true defence against history is neither the Golden Age nor New Jerusalem, but the Great Year.

Cyclic views of history are very old: they underly New Year regeneration ceremonies, the expulsion of demons and diseases, and the belief that the settlement of a new land is a re-enacting of the Creation. Such views embody the natural attitudes of primitive man who—according to Eliade—lives in the paradise of archetypes. His truest experiences are the least individual: 'his life is the ceaseless repetition of gestures initiated by others'. And the Golden Age is obviously a reassurance if it is going to recur.

Both the myth of decline and the myth of the millennium have been confounded with—perhaps originally emerged from—cyclic theories. There were cyclic touches in the fourth Eclogue:

> *iam redit et Virgo, redeunt Saturnia regna;*
> *iam nova progenies caelo demittitur alto*

72

(Now the Virgin returns, and the kingdom of Saturn is again instituted. A new race (? child) is now being sent to us from Heaven)

It sounds as if it has all happened before. The prophet of such cyclic change is the Sybil:

> *ultima Cumaei venit iam carminis aetas.*

I take this to mean 'now the last age which the Sybil prophesied has arrived'; the other interpretation, 'now the age of Sybilline prophecy is over', which I must confess to finding more moving, is far more Utopian, as if a series of historical cycles is now at last ended. And even if we accept this meaning we are leaving the heart of the poem Arcadian still. It is moving, surely, because it announces the end of the magic world that produced the rest of the poem, whose beauty is that of mysterious innocence, not of prophecy.

Later in the poem, the cyclic theory grows more specific still: all the famous events will be re-enacted:

> *alter erit tum Typhis, et altera quae vehet Argo*
> *delectos heroas*

(then there will be another Typhis, and another Argo which will set off with its chosen heroes)

This has found its way into English poetry:

> *I saw a staring virgin stand*
> *Where holy Dionysus died,*
> *And tear the heart out of his side,*
> *And lay the heart upon her hand,*
> *And bear that beating heart away.*
> *And then did all the Muses sing*
> *Of Magnus Annus at the spring,*
> *As though God's death were but a play.*
>
> *Another Troy must rise and set,*
> *Another lineage feed the crow,*
> *Another Argo's painted prow*
> *Drive to a flashier bauble yet.*
> *The Roman Empire stood appalled:*
> *It dropped the reins of peace and war*
> *When that fierce virgin and her star*
> *Out of the fabulous darkness called.*

Yeats held a cyclical theory of history, and regarded the moment of the birth of Christ as pivotal, when one Great Year ended and a new one began, which is now ending. A Great Year is instituted in a time of violence, with all the apparatus of prophecy and salvation, and therefore what the virgin is bringing in is an utterly Utopian version of history; the poet, however, sees it against a larger background, and does not believe the prophecy is absolute. Hence the strange mood of the songs in *The Resurrection*; they present the fierce moral enthusiasm of the new, but by putting it in a cyclical setting, they do not believe it. The muses may at first seem to offer comfort: God is not really dead. But below this they are depriving us of the fierce comfort of prophecy: the ultimate age is not coming, it's just a turn in the wheel of the recurring drama. 'God's death is but a play' may be good news for your grief, but it's bad news for your millennarianism.

Behind this poem of Yeats' lies Shelley's famous chorus from Hellas, which also mingles the Utopian and the cyclic—but more drastically, since the Utopian is presented in the poet's own person.

> *The world's great age begins anew,*
>   *The golden years return,*
> *The earth doth like a snake renew*
>   *Her winter weeds outworn:*
> *Heaven smiles, and faiths and empires gleam*
> *Like wrecks of a dissolving dream.*
>
> *A brighter Hellas rears its mountains*
>   *From waves serener far;*
> *A new Peneus rolls his fountains*
>   *Against the morning star;*
> *Where fairer Tempes bloom, there sleep*
> *Young Cyclads on a sunnier deep . . .*

This poem is about the future, but calls on the past for its images. To say that a new and brighter Hellas is coming could be Utopian or cyclic. New Jerusalem means *new* Jerusalem (Utopia will be so much finer than the world we know) but 'another Troy' means another *Troy*—the cycle is beginning again, and could begin again indefinitely. It is not at first clear which of these Shelley has in mind. The tone of the poem seems, at first, one of radiant optimism: yet the word 'anew', and the image of the snake renewing its weeds suggest the cyclic; and the most enthusiastic stanza of all seems to suggest it too:

> *Another Athens shall arise,*
>   *And to remoter time*
> *Bequeath, like sunset to the skies,*
>   *The splendour of its prime;*
> *And leave, if naught so bright may live,*
> *All earth can take or Heaven can give.*

In the very flush of excitement, these lines predict the death of the new Athens: it will arise, and since 'naught so bright can live', it will die too. The 'remoter time' will be the time after it has passed away—and that time too is suffused with splendour because of what will be bequeathed to it. Shelley cannot bear to assert the limitations of a cyclical view, and tone outdoes content.

Until the last stanza. The change of tone in this stanza is so violent and unexpected that its relation to the rest is very hard to make out.

> *O cease: must hate and death return?*
>   *Cease! must men kill and die?*
> *Cease! drain not to its dregs the urn*
>   *Of bitter prophecy!*
> *The world is weary of the past—*
> *O might it die or rest at last!*

Who is telling whom to cease? Is it part of the splendid prophecy of the future that the violent present will be displaced: another Athens is coming, cease all this warfare? This reading fits the poem into its context: Athens has been saluted as the future, and then at the end we turn to Xerxes, the main character of the play, and he is told that all he stands for is now to cease. I suspect this is how the poem is usually understood, but to read it this way is to ignore something of the stanza itself. For the stanza is protesting against the *prophecy*; it does not lament that hate and death are around us now, but that they will return. Yet at the same time it says 'the world is weary of the past': why the past, if we are dealing with prophecy?

It seems that the cry of distress in this stanza is directed at elements of the past which lie in the future. 'Cease!' can only be addressed to the prophet, telling him to stop his prophecy at the moment of triumph, telling him to let the new Athens come, and

then let it endure. This makes sense of 'drain not to its dregs'—
though perhaps it does not make the best sense of the last line,
which seems close to despair, and to a refusal of the whole of the
future. But that would be to make nonsense of the optimism that
so thoroughly pervades the rest of the poem, and to impose on it a
reversal at the end both more violent and more unexpected than it
could sustain.

I cannot find Shelley wholly consistent in this poem, but it takes
us very near to consistency to say that it is an assertion of Utopian-
ism against a cyclical theory. Utopian tone strives with cyclic
content for six stanzas, and then the Utopian breaks out into
explicitness: the cyclical vision is not what he wants to believe in,
even though he hailed it with such joy.

The impulse to believe that history is cyclic is clearly very old
and deep-seated; but the actual belief, held in cold prose, must be
almost obsolete today. This is one reason why Yeats' poems
(which contain the feel of such a theory) are so much finer than his
prose theorising in *A Vision*, which works it all out in figures and
phrases. For us, there can be no more cyclic theories. They may
have been primitive man's protection against the terror of history,
but we are ineluctably civilised. We lead our own lives, not an
archetypal life through which we re-enact primordial situations.
Time for us is one-way time.

IV

And linear history, once it has disengaged itself from recurrence,
has these two possible myths, the New Jerusalem and the Golden
Age. The one sees it as going upward, the other downward, to
or from the paradise that transcends history. These two mythic
patterns have always contended for man's imagination, and
determined his view of history—sometimes in complicated ways.
A very common belief in the sixteenth century, for instance, was
that the Second Coming must be nigh because the world was
growing worse and worse. Thus John Donne, in a sermon of 1594,
asserts that the world

> is not only in the staggering and declining age, but, which
> exceedeth dotage, at the very upshot, and like a sick man which
> lyeth at death's door, ready to breath out the last gasp;

and Henry Bullinger (1573) actually makes this point in terms of the successive ages. In the past thousand years the Devil's actions have been bad enough.

> But if ye consider what hath been done since those thousand years, and what is done at this day: you will say those ages of the thousand years were golden, and silver worlds; and ours now for these five hundred years are of brass, iron, lead and clay.

Here we find another paradox of Christian historiography. All this sounds like a myth of decline, but in a wider view it is optimistic. Since the Apocalypse prophesied a final struggle between Satan and the Saints just before the Last Judgement, the sickness of the world may be a good sign: the thousand-year binding having ended, the present troubles must surely prove that heaven and earth are soon to pass away, and the new heaven and new earth are imminent. Once again, there is a parallel with Marxism. The proletarian revolution is to be heralded by an increasing disintegration of capitalism; and some have claimed that for the early Marx the revolution itself—the dictatorship of the proletariat—was to be bloody, protracted and tyrannical. A secular Apocalypse has the disadvantage that you cannot rely on God's power to see that the damage is checked.

Both these theories then are ultimately optimistic, though immediately pessimistic; and perhaps we can press the parallel further. Just as one line of Marxist thought has led to reformation —apocalypse replaced by steady improvement—so the chiliasm of the Reformation, as Ernest Tuveson has shown in *Millennium and Utopia*, grew more comfortably optimistic in the course of the seventeenth century, turning slowly into an unalarming doctrine of progress. As the millennium was absorbed into history, it ceased to be a sudden reversal, or an intervention from outside, and became a pattern that acted itself gradually out. Thus John Edwards (1699):

> I confidently aver Christ's Kingdom, whereof I am speaking, shall be set up and maintained by the Kings and Rulers of the Earth; Christianity shall arrive to that excellent pitch, by the Assistance of the Civil magistrate, by the Incouragement which shall be given to it by the secular powers . . .

Here is the nineteenth-century belief in progress, almost secularised by now. Has Edwards (who is typical of many) still got a historical myth? Perhaps the best way to answer this is to say, Yes, he has, but it is now immanent, not transcendent. Now it informs history, instead of destroying it from outside. Either myth can be treated in this way: the New Jerusalem will become a general belief in progress, the Golden Age a general belief in decline.

This still leaves history with a pattern; but another step is possible. You may claim that no general direction is perceptible, that historical change is a complicated succession of movements and problems—not Improvement but improvements, not Decline but setbacks. The historian who holds this view will follow Ranke, and set himself the modest task of finding 'wie es eigentlich geschehen ist'. It is quite common among historians nowadays to be sceptical about this programme, but the scepticism seems only to attack the feasibility of finding out, not the desirability of trying.

And the man of action who holds this view will believe that controlling our lives is not a matter of choosing the winning side or the right direction, but of mastering specific situations. With science and politics, with technology and patience, man can learn not to abolish suffering, not to bear it, but to try and cure it. That takes a long time, and myths are for the impatient and the desperate.

v

Here are four views of history, three of them myth-shaped. To each corresponds an attitude and a form of art, and to conclude I shall try and suggest what these are. I begin with the last: the sober theory that accepts history and refuses its myths, that tells us that Utopia is nowhere and nowhen. It offers us a tempered hope in the possibility of action and improvement. Its literary mode, aware of possibilities and limitations, is realism—the replacement of dream by reality-principle.

The New Jerusalem, in contrast, offers a different kind of hope: a sacred not a profane hope, transfiguring not patient, a hope that needs faith—a burning faith in the possibility of breaking out of the frustrations of this actual life on to another plane where spiritual freedom will at last be possible—or even compulsory.

It is hard to say what its literary form is. The Book of Revelation and the Prophetic Books of Blake are literary sports, and there is a sense in which such determined and single-minded zeal is actually inimical to literature. Yet in another sense it leads to the greatest literature. When such zeal fails, we see that it has to, and we regard it with fear and pride. We see that it was exhilarating and dangerous, like a hero so obsessed that he cannot compromise or accept the limitations of mere living. It is out of such passions that tragedy is made.

What cyclic theories offer is reassurance, a way of not regarding personal loss as final—irrevocable for us, it can be redeemed in the cycle of time. The literary form of this is comedy. Prospero and Leontes have made a shabby mess of things, but Miranda and Perdita will have another chance. Comedy ends in marriage because that leads to birth, the greatest of all reassurances, and offers the joy of recurrence.

And finally the Golden Age. Well, we know where it belongs and the point was a commonplace of literary theory. 'Pastoral' said Pope, 'is an image of what they call the golden age ... We are not to describe our shepherds as shepherds at this day really are, but as they may be conceived then to have been; when' (a lingering trace of Guarini's snobbery) 'the best of men followed the employment.' Dr Johnson could not understand this habit:

> 'I cannot indeed easily discover why it is thought necessary
> to refer descriptions of a rural state to remote times ...'

Nor does he make much effort to discover it, for with his usual sturdy empiricism Johnson deduces the qualities of pastoral not from a conception of the genre but from what he finds in pastoral poems—i.e. (since he is an equally sturdy defender of the Ancients) in Theocritus and Virgil. Surprisingly, he does not notice the Golden Age in the fourth Eclogue in which, he tells us, 'all the images are either taken from the country or from the religion of the age common to all parts of the Empire'. This is certainly untrue: neither the Italian countryside nor the religion of the age produces rams which

> *iam suave rubenti*
> *Murice, iam croceo mutabit vellera luto*

(will change their fleece, now to a pleasant purple colour, now to the yellow of the crocus)

There are two answers to Dr Johnson. The first (from literary history) is that Renaissance pastoral is not really the work of Theocritus and Virgil but of Sannazaro, Tasso and Marot. The second (more important for us) is that we should wonder why a court poet would want to write about the country; and if I am right in suggesting that his interest is mediated not direct, then it is not enough to describe his concern as 'effects upon a country life'.

'We must . . . use some illusion,' said Pope, 'to render a pastoral delightful, . . . in exposing the best side only of a shepherd's life, and in concealing its miseries.'

Pastoral, in other words, is part of the poetry of illusion. Just as the Golden Age is part of its historiography.

IV

SEX IN ARCADIA

A FAMOUS controversy in sixteenth-century poetry set two ideals of Arcadian love against each other. In Tasso's *Aminta*, the most celebrated of all pastoral dramas, there is a chorus that celebrates the sexual freedom of the Golden Age; it was much quoted and much translated, among others by Samuel Daniel.

> *O happy, golden age!*
> *Not for that rivers ran*
> *With streams of milk, and honey dropped from trees;*
> *Not that the earth did gage*
> *Unto the husbandman*
> *Her voluntary fruits, free without fees;*
> *Not for no cold did freeze,*
> *Nor any cloud beguile*
> *Th' eternal flowering spring,*
> *Wherein lived every thing,*
> *And whereon th' heavens perpetually did smile;*
> *Not for no ship had brought*
> *From foreign shores or wars or wares ill sought.*

All these details are, as we have seen, part of the traditional picture of the Golden Age—food freely provided by the earth without tilling, no commerce, no needless travel, no uncomfortable weather. But it was not these, Tasso tells us, that really made the age golden, but sexual freedom: the fact that Honour, 'that empty sound',

> *Was not yet vainly found;*
> *Nor yet sad griefs imparts*
> *Amidst the sweet delights*
> *Of joyful, amorous wights;*
> *Nor were his hard laws known to free-born hearts;*
> *But golden laws like these*
> *Which Nature wrote: 'That's lawful, which doth please.'*

This Golden Age is based on the pastoral contrast between sophistication and nature: on the one hand, Honour, a sophisticated

F

concept, which first encased the golden hairs of maidens, and on the other the freedom and simplicity of

> *Whisperings with songs, then kisses with the same,*
> *Which from affection came.*

To round off this pagan paradise, this happy land with no super-ego, Tasso concludes with the most famous of all pagan common-places, loved and quoted by scores of Renaissance poets—Catullus'

> *soles occidere et redire possunt:*
> *nobis cum semel occidit brevis lux,*
> *nox est perpetua una dormienda.*

Daniel renders it thus:

> *Let's love; the sun doth set, and rise again;*
> *But when as our short light*
> *Comes once to set, it makes eternal night.*

The *Aminta* was produced in 1573; seventeen years later Guarini published *Il Pastor Fido*, which was partly intended as a reply. Guarini's play is also set in Arcadia, and he too has a chorus on sexual morality, which contrasts with Tasso's.

> *Fair golden Age! when milk was th' only food,*
> *And cradle of the infant-world the wood*
> *(Rocked by the winds); and th' untouched flocks did bear*
> *Their deer young for themselves! None yet did fear*
> *The sword or poison: no black thoughts begun*
> *T'eclipse the light of the eternal sun:*
> *Nor wandering pines unto a foreign shore*
> *Or war, or riches (a worse mischief) bore.*
>
> Fanshawe's translation (1647), II.4179-4186

The traditional details of the Golden Age are here invoked not to be dismissed, but to be praised and lingered on. As for love,

> *Then sports and carols amongst brooks and plains*
> *Kindled a lawful flame in nymphs and swains.*
> *Their hearts and tongues concurred, the kiss and joy*
> *Which were most sweet, and yet which least did cloy*
> *Hymen bestowed on them. To one alone*
> *The lively roses of delight were blown;*
> *The thievish lover found them shut on trial,*
> *And fenced with prickles of a sharp denial.*
> *Were it in cave or wood, or purling spring,*
> *Husband and lover signified one thing.*　　　II.4195-4204

The chorus then lashes the 'base present age', which 'givst desire the reins', and appeals to the King of Kings to 'create In us true honour'; and to support this virtuous aspiration it rejects the pagan basis of Tasso's *carpe diem*, turning the image from Catullus into a Christian assertion

> *Let's hope: our ills have truce till we are hurled*
> *From that: Let's hope; the sun that's set may rise,*
> *And with new light salute our longing eyes.* II.4222-4224

Here then is a clear contrast offered to the reader (and writer) of pastoral. Against Tasso's *'s'ei piace, ei lice'* (if it pleases it's lawful), Guarini writes sententiously, *'piaccia se lice'* (if it's lawful, it pleases). Arcadian sex can be free or chaste, rejecting honour or following 'true honour'. It is a choice that Renaissance poets were conscious of, and whichever way they inclined, there was a tradition to support them.

Yet, in the terms in which Tasso and Guarini pose it, we may feel that for the pastoral poet there was no choice at all. Why do poets write pastoral, and why has mankind for so long been haunted by the dream of a Golden Age? I have claimed that the underlying psychological mechanism is the desire to escape from the complex to the simple, from court to an idealised country, from the problems of maturity to an earlier stage when there were no problems. Honour, virtue, marriage customs, moral decisions —these are what pastoral wants us to get away from, but Guarini's stern exhortations thrust them all too freely upon us.

And if we look at *Il Pastor Fido* as a whole, we can see that it is not, anyway, a pastoral play. I have already claimed this in Chapter I, talking of the view of society advanced in the Preface; and the same is true of the handling of the love intrigue. True, it looks at first as if we are being offered a chaste pastoral, contrasting the honest love of the principals with the corruption of Corisca who has had a courtly upbringing, who has 'in cities oft been courted by Gallants and wits'. She likes to have 'many servants' (i.e., suitors): 'courtly Dames' know this is a sign of honour, and think it 'clownishness' to reject any. This is a clear foil to the simplicity of the pastoral world.

But on inspection, that world is not so simple. Corisca's corruption is a foil both to the Hippolytus-like chastity of Silvio, and to the faithful love of Mirtillo and Amaryllis. Mirtillo and Amaryllis

are chaste, yet in an oddly prurient fashion. Mirtillo tells in **II.i**
how he disguised as a woman and joined in a kissing-contest. The
act ends with a chorus on the delights of kissing

> *the sweet echoing and the dove-like billing*
> *of two encountering mouths, when both are willing*

and in **III.iii** there is a game of blind man's buff, in which Amaryllis
catches Mirtillo, thinking he is one of the girls:

> *Twas thee I wished to catch; that I might use thee*
> *Just as I list, and thus, and thus abuse thee;*
> *And thus, and thus.*

No doubt Guarini would have said that kissing was innocent and
permitted to virgins; and that since Amaryllis didn't know she
was holding a man, there was nothing prurient in the language. It
is a nice question whether, if he'd said this, he'd have believed it
himself; but it is quite certain that we can't believe it today. The
state of knowing-and-not-knowing that these lines capture is
exactly what we mean by prurience, and no bandage is strong
enough to keep the overtones of such language out of awareness.
As for the kissing, I know no poet who reminds me so strongly as
Guarini does that the kiss, in Freud's view, is really a sexual per-
version which happens to be licensed by custom.

This is a negative reason for deciding that the loves of *Il Pastor
Fido* have nothing of pastoral simplicity in them. There is also a
positive and explicit reason. It is Corisca, of whom we are meant to
disapprove, who defends her sexual freedom in terms of nature;
the play's official morality is delivered by Nicandro. When
Amaryllis protests that she has not transgressed the law, he
answers sternly

> *Not Nature's law perchance,* Love where thou wilt,
> *But that of Men and Heav'n,* Love without guilt.

As it happens, Nicandro is wrong on the fact, but he is meant to be
right in his principles; and they are the same as the principles of
the chorus:

> *But thou that art the King of Kings, create*
> *In us true honour.*

Guarini's play, then, lives up to the views of his Golden Age
chorus; as it happens, Tasso's does not. There is plenty of resistance
in *Aminta* to the doctrine of unstinted enjoyment, mainly from

the heroine, Sylvia, who for most of the play resists the advances of
Aminta; he in his turn loves Sylvia and wants only her, so the
question of free love really does not arise, and the plot differs little
from that of other love stories, except in its simplicity and naïvety.

As a play, *Aminta* has little to do with free love: the theme
appears in more or less detachable fragments of poetry. There is a
prologue spoken by Amore, which establishes immediately the
pastoral contrast: he tells how his mother thrust him into the
court, but he prefers to take refuge in woods and humble homes.
There is an 'aria' by Daphne on how all nature is in love:

> *Come tutte le cose*
> *Or sono innamorate*
> *D'un amor pien di joia et di salute.*

And there is the *Bell'età d'oro* chorus, and that is really all.

The Tasso–Guarini contrast then, is a genuine one, but it is a
contrast between the two choruses: it blurs when we look at the
two plays as a whole. And in the terms in which they pose it, it is
not really a contrast between two versions of pastoral. Yet such a
contrast is possible: the pastoral love poet *has* a choice between
chaste and free. To see it clearly, we must push aside the senten-
tious Guarini, and imagine our own anti-Tasso.

The civilised adult finds that love entails stress because of the
conflict between law and desire. There are two ways of escaping
this: to have no law, or to have no desire. If there is no law, all
desires are declared innocent and granted fulfilment: sex is for
everyone, and costs nothing. This is the Golden Age of Tasso's
chorus, though not of his whole play. If on the other hand there is
no desire, we are spared the problems of sex by being spared sex.
There may be a wild wood filled with satyrs, but they are not the
inhabitants of Arcadia. They may threaten it, and even make
raids (Arcadia is always frail), but they do not belong in a paradise
of chaste love.

For the true opposite of Tasso's chorus, we can look back at
lines already quoted in Chapter I:

> *saepibus in nostris parvam te roscida mala—*
> *dux ego vester eram—vidi cum matre legentem.*
> *alter ab undecimo tum me iam acceperat annus;*
> *iam fragiles poteram ab terra contingere ramos.*
> *ut vidi, ut perii, ut me malus abstulit error!*
>
> Virgil: *Eclogue* VIII.38-42

85

(When you were small I saw you (I was then your guide) with your mother, picking the dewy apples in our orchard. I had just entered the year after my eleventh year; already I could touch the delicate branches from the ground. I saw you and, ah, was lost: this wicked treachery of love caught me.)

This is an exact parallel to the contrast between court and country, but it is presented as a contrast between adult and child. The adult is a victim of love's complexities ('*malus error*'), and here he is recalling the moment before it all began, the moment when he was just beginning to develop the reach of an adult. The passage is no doubt playful—childhood simplicity is described in deliberately intricate, formalised language, and the histrionic exclamations are carefully inappropriate to the '*alter ab undecimo annus*'—but the emotion behind it is a serious one: nostalgia for the loss of innocence, for a pre-sexual paradise.

Both versions of Arcadian sex—freedom from law and freedom from desire—are very old. The former can certainly be found in Latin poetry, for instance in Tibullus'

> *tunc quibus aspirabat Amor praebebat aperte*
> *mitis in umbrosa gaudia valle Venus.*
> *nullus erat custos, nulla exclusura dolentes*
> *ianua: si fas est, mos precor ille redi.*
> Elegies II.iii.70-74

(In those days, gentle Venus openly offered her joys in a shady valley to those whom Love had breathed on. There was no guard, there was no gate to shut out sorrowful lovers. If it is right, I pray that such a custom may come back.)

Despite the brief Guarini-touch of respectability ('si fas est'), this is a longing for the time when 's'ei piace, ei lice'. It is not so easy to find an ancient specimen of chaste Arcadia to set against it. The reason is that praise of chastity is more likely in antiquity to belong to the counter-tradition of hard primitivism, and not to pastoral. Lovejoy and Boas (to whom I owe the Tibullus quotation) assemble a number of interesting passages from the Cynics and the Stoics in which the simple life is praised for relieving us of our civilised burdens, and it is here that we should expect the praise of chastity—though even here we find in the dialogue *Cynicus* (attributed to Lucian) that the Cynic defends the hardness

of his deliberately chosen austerity without finding it necessary
to include chastity:

> No need, either, to mention all the things that men do and
> suffer for the sake of sexual gratification—though that desire
> is easy enough to satisfy, if one is not too fastidious about it.

No doubt this could, at a push, be called pastoral: it is certainly a
way of making things uncomplicated. But it would take us into
quite a different tradition from the one this book is concerned with.
Arcadian primitivism is soft, not hard.

II

It is certainly an interesting, though not perhaps an answerable
question, to wonder which is the true version of Arcadian sex.
Wayland Young, for instance, in *Eros Denied*, claims vehemently
that the Golden Age was a time 'when all lovers loved reciprocally
and calmly, when there was no frustration in desire and no dis-
appointment in love'. He regards it as an example of projection
('the system of feeling which says: "We don't do this, but other
people do lots of it" '), and therefore as expressing one of mankind's deepest dreams of happiness, the dream of unstinted sexual
fulfilment. The fact that we attribute to the Golden Age a material
and sexual communism shows that in our civilisation we have a
great deal of (Mr Young explicitly hesitates to say 'too much')
property and chastity. So we dream of their opposites.

This is a plausible argument: though if this is the Freudian
concept of projection that is being used, by which what is projected
is a wish, then we *do* have to say that we have too much chastity,
i.e. more than we (unconsciously) want. And no doubt the same
explanation could be applied to the other attributes of the Golden
Age. In the Hesiod tradition it was usually vegetarian and peaceful; there was no commerce, no seafaring, no agriculture. Those
who wrote of it had no doubt done (or seen) a lot of fighting, eating
and travelling—though one might doubt whether it was the same
people who had too much agricultural work and too much meat-
eating!

Projection seems a good explanation for the Golden Age; but
before we explain we must describe. There is a preliminary, altogether less complicated way of deciding what 'true' Arcadian sex

was like, and that is to see what the poets claimed it was like. And this, of course, depends where we look. Mr Young looks at the visual arts, and finds several sensuous and direct sixteenth-century versions of sexual paradise, in particular four pictures by Agostino Carracci depicting four aspects of Eros. And there are others he could have cited, by Vasari, or Cranach, or Giorgione. He looks at Tasso's chorus, and he could perhaps have added Sannazaro: there is disagreement among scholars on how erotic his Eclogues are. But though there may be traces of free Arcadia in Italian pastoral, if we turn to English poetry it begins to look as if Mr Young's account is simply wrong. The Elizabethans clearly loved the *Aminta*-chorus, but they didn't much attend to what it says.

The English equivalent of Tasso and Guarini is Fletcher's *Faithful Shepherdess*, which opens, like *A Midsummer Night's Dream*, with the lovers all agreeing to meet in the woods that night, thus taking us into a pastoral world clearly contrasted with the everyday. But it is not a world of free love; rather one in which lasciviousness is a crime and the innocent are blest. The Priest of Pan performs ceremonies against lust:

> *Shepherds, thus I purge away*
> *Whatsoever this great day*
> *Or the past hours gave not good,*
> *To corrupt your maiden blood.*
> *From the high rebellious heat*
> *Of the grapes, and strength of meat,*
> *From the wanton quick desires*
> *They do kindle by their fires,*
> *I do wash you with this water;*
> *Be you pure and fair hereafter!*

I.ii

All sorts of lovers meet in the woods that night, and it soon grows clear that they form a sort of scale, from the completely pure to the completely corrupt. At the one extreme is Clorin, who has dedicated herself to a life of holy chastity because of the death of her lover, and who is presented as a kind of priestess, with magic powers and an attendant satyr, who—despite his name—reveres her innocence and helps the good. Then comes Clorin's wooer Thenot, whose only fault is that he sees Clorin as a woman and would like to marry her; but with a simple (if tasteless) trick she cures him, and he renounces. In the middle come Perigot and Amoret, two

normal healthy lovers, whose plot complications are caused by
mistaken identities and the machinations of others; who neither
renounce nor anticipate marriage. Next comes the wanton Cloe
('It is impossible to ravish me, I am so willing'), with her bashful
lover Daphnis and her insistent lover Alexis; and finally comes the
Sullen Shepherd, who represents naked desire, and who is allowed
one vicious and telling thrust at the play's morality:

> *Hath not our mother Nature, for her store*
> *And great increase, said it is good and just*
> *And willed that every living creature must*
> *Beget his like?*

Priest.   *You're better read than I*
> *I must confess, in blood and lechery.*

V.iii

Here is the germ of *Comus:* the eloquence is on one side, the
primness on the other, and we are simply told that the former is all
wrong.

The very existence of this scale of innocence among the characters makes it difficult to sustain the atmosphere of pastoral
chastity. For the mingling of such varied attitudes must produce
contrasts, and the complications of the plot must produce clashes,
so that we find ourselves with just that interaction of law and
desire from which pastoral should provide an escape. In fleeing to
the woods, Fletcher's lovers have not left enough behind. They are
still in a world of moral issues, a world in which the virtuous are
all too easily shocked. Perigot's indignation at the advances of his
beloved Amoret (as he thinks; it is actually Cloe in disguise) introduces the language of high respectability:

> *Forbear, dear soul, to try*
> *Whether my heart be pure; I'll rather die*
> *Than nourish one thought to dishonour thee.*

III.i

Moralising like this has no place in Arcadia; and if it remained as
mere morality it would surely destroy all the poetry. Fletcher is
sometimes able to acclimatise it by turning it into magic. Clorin,
the guardian of chastity, is also its priestess; she does not preach,
she performs holy rites and invokes the spirit of the woods, and
there is poetry in this.

In this flame his finger thrust,
Which will burn him if he lust;
But if not, away will turn,
As loath unspotted flesh to burn.—
See, it gives back; let him go.

V.iii

The Elizabethans (as we can see from *The Changeling*) obviously enjoyed the idea of chastity tests: and such tests surely belong in the forest at night, accompanied by a simple incantatory poetry like this. These parts of the play were clearly influenced by *A Midsummer Night's Dream* and passed on that influence to *Comus*, and naturally the double comparison is hard on Fletcher. But though he has neither Shakespeare's wit and charm, nor Milton's strange power, he is writing in their tradition.

Yet the very tradition that saves the play brings its own problems. Here for instance are a few lines from each of its two river spells:

Take this maid, thou holy pit
To thy bottom; nearer yet;
In thy water pure and sweet
By thy leave I dip her feet;
Thus I let her lower yet;
That her ankles may be wet;
Yet down lower, let her knee
In thy waters washéd be;
There stop.—Fly away,
Everything that loves the day!

III.i

Do not fear to put thy feet
Naked in the river sweet;
Think not leech, or newt, or toad,
Will bite thy foot, when thou hast trod;
Nor let the water rising high
As thou wad'st in, make thee cry
And sob; but ever live with me,
And not a wave shall trouble thee.

III.i

Reading these, we can nod and say, Yes, charming, though not great poetry; and, Yes, the play is better for striking this note. We are likely to say it equally about both, yet they are not alike. The first, spoken by the Sullen Shepherd as he changes Amaryllis to Amoret, is an evil spell; the second, spoken by the River God as he cures Amoret of her wound, is a good one; but who would know? Because Fletcher achieves poetry by turning morality into magic, it is the very presence of a spell that brings the poetry, and good spells will not be distinguishable, poetically, from bad.

There is a similar problem over the treatment of Pan. To make Pan the God of chastity is to fight against the tradition, but Fletcher has to do it if he is to create a chaste Arcadia. What gives Pan his numinousness—and what can therefore give the play its poetry—is too closely bound up with his nature as a sensual god to break free of it; so that when he lets himself go in praise of Pan, Fletcher is—not surprisingly—swept away to inconsistency:

> *Now, whilst the moon doth rule the sky,*
> *And the stars, whose feeble light*
> *Gives a pale shadow to the night,*
> *Are up, great Pan commanded me*
> *To walk this grove about, while he*
> *In a corner of the wood,*
> *Where never mortal foot hath stood,*
> *Keeps dancing, music, and a feast,*
> *To entertain a lovely guest . . .*

> III.i

Pan emerges from all this as a god who gets his priests to do what he isn't willing to do himself! It is an inconsistency that results from Fletcher's task and his medium: writing a chaste pastoral play does not go easily with writing poetry.

The same problem arises in the lyric. If we look through the pages of *England's Helicon*, we find a good deal of chastity and, sometimes, an uneasy confusion of purpose. I take as example 'Montanus his Madrigal' by Robert Greene. This is the story of how Cupid shot Diana and her maids, and is full of references to chastity—such as this stanza, describing Diana bathing:

> *Her taffeta cassock you might see,*
> *Tucked up above her knee,*
> *Which did show*
> *There below*
> *Legs as white as whales bone,*
> *So white and chaste was never none.*

This is either very confused or very knowing. 'So white and chaste': is that just prurience? To claim that the more suggestive the sight the better it can represent chastity has perhaps a kind of mad logic: but it is either a humourless logic that makes the poem simple-minded to the point of absurdity, or else a wink to the reader that Diana's chastity won't last the poem.

Another kind of muddle, or at any rate a revealing picture of the author's uneasiness, is found in William Browne of Tavistock. Somewhere in his vast *Britannia's Pastorals* he had to bring in the Golden Age: and so he simply stops the story in II.3 to insert an account of it. After some of the usual commonplaces about contentment and water drinking, he turns to sex:

> *None had a body then so weak and thin,*
> *Bankrupt of nature's store, to feed the sin*
> *Of an insatiate female, in whose womb*
> *Could nature all hers past, and all to come*
> *Infuse, with virtue of all drugs beside,*
> *She might be tir'd, but never satisfied.*
> *To please which ork her husband's weakened piece*
> *Must have his cullis mixed with ambergris:*
> *Pheasant and partridge into jelly turned,*
> *Grated with gold, seven times refined and burn'd*
> *With dust of Orient pearl, richer the East*
> *Yet ne'er beheld: (O Epicurean feast!)*
> *This is his breakfast; and his meal at night*
> *Possets no less provoking appetite,*
> *Whose dear ingredients valu'd are at more*
> *Than all his ancestors were worth before.*
> *When such as we by poor and simple fare*
> *More able liv'd, and died not without heir,*
> *Sprung from our own loins, and a spotless bed*
> *Of any other power unseconded. . . .*
>
> II.iii.242

The Golden Age was the time when we were free of our present constant need of aphrodisiacs in order to satisfy our insatiable wives! The time when our children were our own, not simply fathered on the last comer. If this was Browne's sexual fantasy, it is certainly, to us, unusual: a time when women's sexual prowess was less and men's more. The belief that women have stronger sexual appetites than men was well over a thousand years old when Browne wrote: it goes back to Juvenal and to Bernard of Cluny's *De Contemptu Mundi,* and had become a well-established literary convention. It can hardly, one feels, have been based on observation; and to say that it was based on literary habit does not explain anything. We seem to have another case of projection. All the poems on women's lustfulness were written by men, and may be seen as an attempt to attribute to women those pressures that men did not like to admit to. Browne's passage suggests a more complicated projective mechanism: that the original cause is fear of inadequacy. Anxiety about their own sexual performance could have led men to project not only their unconfined desires, but also their fears, and to attribute to women the kind of demands they were afraid of not being able to meet. This explanation seems particularly obvious here, because of the negative nature of Browne's description. The Golden Age is obviously, for him, a release from anxiety; for he describes it by describing the anxiety and attaching negatives—and even they are half-hidden by the syntax. Perhaps the anxiety was very strong; for the ideal that is greeted with such relief is in fact an ideal of ordinariness. Browne seems able to present with Arcadian intensity a Golden Age that consists of normal marital relationships: was he so frustrated as to long intensely for that?

Does all this suggest that chaste pastoral is impossible? Perhaps it is. How can an erotic element be kept out of love-poetry? And if it appears, either as plot complication or as sexual elements in the beauty of a chaste heroine, there can be no poetry of total innocence —certainly no sophisticated poetry, and pastoral is always sophisticated.

Perhaps however there is one way we can have it: by claiming that innocence is not weakened but strengthened by the presence of the feelings it rejects.

> No white nor red was ever seen
> So am'rous as this lovely green.
> Fond lovers, cruel as their Flame,
> Cut in these trees their Mistress name.
> Little, Alas, they know or heed,
> How far these Beauties Hers exceed!
> Fair Trees! wheres'eer your barkes I wound,
> No name shall but your own be found.

When we have run our Passions heat,
Love hither makes his best retreat.
The Gods, that mortal beauty chase,
Still in a Tree did end their race.
Apollo hunted Daphne so,
Only that she might Laurel grow.
And Pan did after Syrinx speed,
Not as a Nymph, but for a Reed.

Here we have a witty reconciliation of the two versions of Arcadian sex. Given the opportunity to withdraw from the world, says Marvell, I elect chastity because it has all the advantages of passion. Is it woman's complexion you admire?

> *No white nor red was ever seen*
> *So am'rous as this lovely green*

—green, the colour of natural growth, natural innocence: innocence is being substituted for sex. But green, too, the colour of lechery (Spenser's Lechery dressed in green; 'Green is the colour of lovers', said Armado; and there is 'giving a green gown'): so innocence contains sex. Marvell's wit has it both ways: the joke is that the associations of green make his comic point a true one.

Or is it the eccentric habits of lovers you are thinking of? The pastoralist can do the same, but in parody. Trees are so much nicer than women that he will enjoy carving 'Oak' or 'Elm' instead of Phyllis or Julia.

The second stanza also makes a comic point, and also backs it up with an ingenuity that makes us blink, and even believe ourselves convinced. Why are there all these stories about fleeing nymphs turning to plants? They show us that nature is against sex, and willing to protect Daphne and Syrinx from it; and since the Gods must surely know this, we can deduce their intentions from their actions, and conclude that what happened was what they wished to happen:

> *Apollo hunted Daphne so,*
> *Only that she might Laurel grow.*

What Marvell is asserting is something like the modern concept of sublimation: that by renouncing sex and then satisfying its

demands indirectly, we channel and use the energy that would be
used up if we looked for direct satisfaction. Marvell tells us that
his ascetic delights contain a finer version of what you get in sex.
How we take this depends on whether he is offering a bold parallel
or an unexpected explanation. If he believes his rural retreat is
genuinely ascetic, then he is showing the reach of his wit by
comparing it with what he knows to be its opposite: the brilliance
lies in the apt analogy found in a preposterous parallel. But if he
believes he has a point to make about the cause of his solitary
delights; if there is a sexual element in such ascetic intensity—
then the parallel is not preposterous, but simply paradoxical: he
is asserting a doctrine of sublimation, and telling of the origin of
his poem.

III

Is there any free pastoral in English? It depends how far we are
willing to stretch our definition. There are no descriptions of free
love among shepherds (though such a run-of-the-mill romance as
Greene's *Menaphon* hints at it in the comic underplot); but there
are works based on a contrast between the ordinary world of
repression and complications, and an uninhibited Arcadian
alternative. I end by discussing two of these—one lyrical and one
more or less dramatic; one Renaissance and one modern; both
outspoken and both superbly written. The first is Thomas Carew's
poem *A Rapture.*

Why is this poem so little known? It seems such a natural
candidate for the twentieth century to have rescued. Written with
all Carew's poise and verbal delicacy, it is outspokenly erotic in
a way that is rare, even unknown, in English poetry. Though it
never mentions the countryside, or calls Celia a shepherdess, it is
pastoral in conception:

> *I will enjoy thee now, my Celia, come*
> *And fly with me to Love's Elysium.*

Its erotic world is special and distinct—Elysium, because it is
an escape from the world of normal complications. Later he calls
it 'paradise'.

> *Come then, and mounted on the wings of Love*
> *We'll cut the flitting air, and soar above*

The monster's head, and in the noblest seats
Of those blest shades quench and renew our heats.
There shall the Queens of Love and Innocence,
Beauty and nature, banish all offence
From our close ivy-twines; there I'll behold
Thy bared snow and thy unbraided gold;
There my enfranchised hand on every side
Shall o'er thy naked polished ivory glide.

'Enfranchised' is a typical piece of metaphysical wit: this use of a technical term in a transferred sense is common in Donne. It has a further ambiguity here, which subtly reinforces the pastoral mechanism: he is enfranchised by her, and also by his situation—the fact that he is in Love's Elysium, where erotic gestures are given political rights. The 'noblest seats' are the Arcadia of this poem: they are the home of 'Love and Innocence, Beauty and Nature', the pastoral ideals. 'Innocence', of course, does not mean 'chastity' here: this is free Arcadia, where desire is released from law, and enjoyment is therefore innocent. 'Prisons are made with stones of law.'

We saw the pastoral mechanism at its simplest in Sidney's chronicle of what doesn't happen in the woods:

> *Here nor treason is hid, veiled in innocence,*
> *Nor envy's snaky eye finds any harbour here,*
> *Nor flatterer's venomous insinuations,*
> *Nor cunning humourist's puddled opinions . . .*

Carew uses the same rhetorical device.

> *There no rude sounds shake us with sudden starts;*
> *No jealous ears, when we unrip our hearts,*
> *Suck our discourse in; no observing spies*
> *This blush, that glance, traduce; no envious eyes*
> *Watch our close meetings; nor are we betray'd*
> *To rivals by the bribed chambermaid.*

This then is the poem's structure: an equivalent to pastoral. Its content is, quite simply, a celebration of sex. No one could call it a love-poem: the girl not only has no individuality (that is common enough in the seventeenth century), she has no conventional attributes except sexual ones. The poem presents the anonymity of desire. We can see, in fact, that the free tradition can do one thing which the chaste cannot—it can present the sexual act itself as an entry to Arcadia, an activity so intense and self-regarding that the pastoral flight from Court to Country could be seen as a metaphor for it.

Here is the poem's climax:

> Now in more subtle wreaths I will entwine
> My sinewy thighs, my legs and arms with thine;
> Thou like a sea of milk shalt lie display'd,
> Whilst I the smooth calm ocean invade
> With such a tempest, as when Jove of old
> Fell down on Danaë in a storm of gold;
> Yet my tall pine shall in the Cyprian strait
> Ride safe at anchor, and unlade her freight:
> My rudder with thy bold hand, like a tried
> And skilful pilot, thou shalt steer, and guide
> My bark into love's channel, where it shall
> Dance, as the bounding waves do rise or fall.
> Then shall thy circling arms embrace and clip
> My willing body, and thy balmly lip
> Bathe me in juice of kisses, whose perfume
> Like a religious incense shall consume,
> And send up holy vapours to those pow'rs
> That bless our loves and crown our sportful hours,
> That with such halcyon calmness fix our souls
> In steadfast peace, as no affright controls.

Direct description of sexual experience is a problem for any poet —before 1960, at least. The use of metaphor can be either evasive or enriching. If the metaphor is conventional and the tone of the poem suggests any embarrassment, the effect will be furtive or coy; and it is because of this that blunt description, even in four-letter words, can be so exhilarating. It is an exhilaration that soon wears off: you can only let fresh air in once, and after a while it grows tedious or raucous. I doubt if there is any form of sexual description that does not lead to some kind of problem (even, perhaps, since 1960). This poem is a model in the solving of the problem. Carew has used metaphor, but triumphantly. The whole atmosphere of his poem is so contemptuous of prudery that there is no danger at all of coyness: the metaphors are celebratory, not evasive, and the poem arouses no giggles.

That was the climax; but the poem does not end there. The

passage that follows is certainly brilliant, but in a tone very
different from what went before.

> The Roman Lucrece there reads the divine
> Lectures of love's great master, Aretine,
> And knows as well as Lais how to move
> Her pliant body in the act of love.
> To quench the burning ravisher, she hurls
> Her limbs into a thousand winding curls,
> And studies artful postures, such as be
> Carv'd on the bark of every neighbouring tree
> By learned hands, that so adorn'd the rind
> Of those fair plants, which, as they lay entwined,
> Have fanned their glowing fires. The Grecian dame
> That in her endless web toil'd for a name
> As fruitless as her work, doth there display
> Herself before the youth of Ithaca,
> And th' amorous sports of gamesome nights prefer
> Before dull dreams of the lost traveller.

There is a poem in this, certainly, and a highly entertaining one;
but its ingenuity does not belong with the Arcadian passion of the
rest. Where is the 'there' of the first line? Grammatically, it refers
to the 'Elysian ground' of I.110, and is therefore part of the
pastoral structure. But the Elysium of these lines is not the same
as the paradise of direct sexual fulfilment celebrated in the
previous passage. In that paradise all identity was forgotten:
Elysium contained nothing but a beautiful body, sexual desire, and
the exhilaration of being alive. In these lines, Lucrece and Penelope
retain their identity: they live both in the ordinary world, in which
they represent chastity, and in the new Elysian world, in which
they seem consciously to enjoy the reversal of roles. The resulting
impression is titillation rather than fulfilment; and it is notable
that Lucrece reads lewd books and practises 'artful postures',
while Penelope has become an exhibitionist. The spontaneity of
the rest of the poem has disappeared; we are in Court now, not
Arcadia.

IV

And finally, a modern pastoral that celebrates Arcadia as a land
of sexual freedom. By the stretched definitions of this book it
should not seem strange to call *Under Milk Wood* a pastoral: for

Llareggyb is a simple, happy place, sealed off from the world's complications. In Dylan Thomas' original design, the sealing-off was to have been quite explicit. The work was to be called *The Village of the Mad*, and was to have a crazy plot, in which an inspector would come down from London to declare the village insane. In the course of the trial, the villagers would decide that they preferred their madness to the world's sanity, and voluntarily declared themselves guilty. There are a few other variations that have been described by those to whom Thomas spoke, and all have in common a cutting-off of the village, as an oasis of madness in a world whose sanity is frightening.

Thomas seems to have been inhibited by this ingenious plot, and in the end dropped it. But he did not drop the underlying assumption that Llareggyb was Arcadia, that it led an idyllic life, freed from cunning humorists' puddled opinions, where the only poets are amiable, local and not too talented, and even the poisoner will never carry out his dreadful designs. We need not worry about the fact that Llareggyb is a town, since the only really urban thing about it is the closeness and curiosity of neighbours. Not much work is done there: Willy Nilly's occasional letter is simply an excuse for chatter, and Mfanwy Price sells a pound of sweets about as often as Damon's flocks stray off and have to be looked for.

The special madness of Llaregybb was to be that everyone is in love. This is more or less true of the final version, though it is pushing things a bit to say it of Mr and Mrs Pugh:

> Alone in the hissing laboratory of his wishes, Mr Pugh minces among bad vats and jeroboams, tiptoes through spinneys of murdering herbs, agony dancing in his crucibles, and mixes especially for Mrs Pugh a venomous porridge unknown to toxicologists which will scald and viper through her until her ears fall off like figs, her toes grow big and black as balloons, and steam comes screaming out of her navel.

Yet Thomas did claim something like love even for them. 'She likes nagging,' he wrote; 'he likes plotting, in supposed secrecy, against her. . . . How lucky they are to be married.'

This remark is from a letter to *Botteghe Oscure*, where about half the text was published (for the first time) in 1952. It is a most interesting account of how Thomas saw his own work. What emerges most vividly is his own enormous delight in his characters. After describing them he writes:

> And so with all of them, all the eccentrics whose eccentricities, in these first pages, are but briefly and impressionistically noted: all, by their own rights, are ordinary and good: and the First Voice, and the poet preacher, never judge nor condemn but explain and make strangely simple and simply strange.

We are in a never-never land of complete innocence, where all behaviour is different from our own. Often the comic point consists simply of an assertion of innocence in an outrageous situation, as with Mr and Mrs Cherry Owen. Cherry Owen staggers home drunk every night, dances on the table, and throws his supper across the room. This should be an occasion for indignation or compassion; but as it happens, Mrs Cherry Owen loves it, and she tells him next morning all that he did and has now forgotten —tells him not as a scold or a martyr but with enjoyment as great as his. Certainly Thomas is right in claiming that his voices (that is, himself) do not judge or condemn—though they surely don't explain either. This world is too far-fetched for explanations; the play simply narrates and describes.

It is obvious that love in Llaregybb is free not chaste, and Silenus keeps appearing. He appears in the thoughts of Gossamer Beynon, the dainty schoolmistress:

> Gossamer Beynon high-heels out of school. The sun hums down through the cotton flowers of her dress into the bell of her heart, and buzzes in the honey there and couches and kisses, lazy-loving and boozed, in her red-berried breast. . . . She blazes naked past the Sailors Arms, the only woman on the Dai-Adamed earth. Sinbad Sailors places on her thighs still dew-damp from the first mangrowing cockcrow garden his reverent goatbearded hands.
>
> *Gossamer Beynon:* I don't care if he *is* common. . . .

What reconciliation of Eden and Arcadia could be wittier than this? Sinbad is Silenus, yet as he touches her imagination she is Eve, 'still dewdamp' from her creation. Eden itself, then, was a free not a chaste paradise—a view for which there is the authority of Milton (the question of promiscuity does not, of course, arise). 'Reverent' is not simply a joke here, but as assertion of the poem's paganism.

This paradise of free sexuality is constantly presented as unreal —as 'strangely simple and simply strange' (a nice formula for pastoral). The clearest example of this is the love of Mfanwy Price and Mog Edwards, sweetshop-keeper and draper, who exchange touching simple-minded erotic letters every day:

> Throw away your little bedsocks and your Welsh wool knitted jacket, I will warm the sheets like an electric toaster, I will lie by your side like the Sunday roast.

Only at the end does Thomas tell us what, in a way, we knew all along, that they never meet: 'she looks around with pleasure at her own neat never dull room which Mr Mog Edwards will never enter'. Their love is perfect because unattainable, like that of Marvell's lovers:

> *It was begotten by Despair*
> *Upon Impossibility.*

Or they are like two Proustian lovers who have agreed to keep away from each other in order to achieve the perfect love that only frustration brings. In the same letter to *Botteghe Oscure*, Thomas has a comment on them that is both illuminating and misleading:

> . . . all their lives they have known of each other's existence, and of their mutual love: they have seen each other a thousand times, and never spoken: easily they could have been together, married, had children: but that is not the life for them: their passionate love, at just this distance, is all they need.

The misleading detail here is 'all'. To say that love at a distance is all they need suggests that if they had married and had children, they would have had something better. In an obvious sense they would have, but *Under Milk Wood* could never have been written if this obvious level were the only true one. The 'distance' that converts their love to a dream gives them more as well as less, for vision needs feeding as well as appetite.

Less obviously, we can make a similar comment on Captain Cat. Old and blind, he remembers the girls of his youth—all prostitutes but all, in memory, invested with a strange innocence. His memories of Rosie Probart are unutterably sad, and the sadness makes them pure. Time does for Captain Cat what distance does for Miss Price and Mog Edwards.

The clearest manifestation of free sexuality in the poem is, of course, the story of Polly Garter. She is the common woman of the town, to be found every night in the wood with a different man: enormously fond both of her men and her brood of illegitimate children. She enjoys her promiscuity, yet for her too there is sadness mingled with love. Her song is perhaps the most enchanting thing in *Under Milk Wood*:

> *I loved a man whose name was Tom*
> *He was strong as a bear and two yards long*
> *I loved a man whose name was Dick*
> *He was big as a barrel and three feet thick*
> *And I loved a man whose name was Harry*
> *Six feet tall and sweet as a cherry*
> *But the one I loved best awake or asleep*
> *Was little Willie Wee and he's six feet deep.*
>
> *O Tom, Dick and Harry were three fine men*
> *And I'll never have such loving again*
> *But little Willy Wee who took me on his knee*
> *Little Willy Wee was the man for me. . . .*

Her paradise of unrestricted sexuality is not presented as unreal: but it is tinged with the sad thought that the best of all exists only in memory.

What has she lost? She has lost Willy Wee, but to say that does not say all. Why is he given such a name? Why is her poem given the form it has? Thomas' most brilliant invention was getting her to sing a nursery rhyme. This says to us what he nowhere says explicitly, that what she has lost is childhood. If only Tasso, or Daniel translating him, had found a form like this, there would have been a new layer of magic on the 'bel etá d'oro' chorus, which looks almost strident compared with Polly Garter's song.

Under Milk Wood is full of children. The scene in which they play their kissing game has an effect all its own, less extravagant, less verbally eccentric, than the rest, more delicate in tone:

> *Gwennie Gwennie*
> *I kiss you in Goosegog Lane.*
> *Now I haven't got to give you a penny.*

The sexual symbolism (kiss me in Goosegog Lane, on Llareggyb Hill, Under Milk Wood) is clear but not obtrusive: the effect is still innocent. The third boy, who won't kiss 'because my mother says

102

I mustn't' reminds us that sooner or later the childhood world will submit to the reign of law.

The children are linked with Captain Cat, and at one point they are linked not only with Polly Garter but with her song:

> Children's Voices
> *When birds do sing hey ding a ding a ding*
> *Sweet lovers love the Spring . . .*
>
> Second Voice
> *Polly Garter sings, still on her knees,*
>
> Polly Garter
> *Tom, Dick and Harry were three fine men*
> *And I'll never have such*
>
> Children
> > *ding a ding*
>
> Polly Garter
> > > *again.*

What could say more clearly that the loving which Polly remembers with such joy is her childhood?

Free Arcadia and chaste Arcadia both bring us back to childhood as (surely) they both should. We do not need to choose which is the 'true' Arcadia, for the ambivalence itself is significant. Sexless or free of sexual restraints: are not these our two views of infancy? Childhood is the time when we have not yet been troubled by sex; but it is also the time when (like the nymphs in Tasso's chorus) we didn't have to wear clothes, and didn't have a super-ego. The paradox of childhood sexuality may be the paradox of Arcadia.

v

And finally, a brief moral epilogue. There are always Puritan voices raised against the paganism of Arcadia. Spencer's Piers objected to the merry-making of the 'love-lads masken in fresh array' with a stern exhortation to maturity:

> *For Younkers, Palinode, such follies fitte,*
> *But we tway bene men of elder witt.*
> > *The Shepherd's Calendar*, V

The Piers of *Under Milk Wood* is Mr David Holbrook, who in his book on modern poetry, *Llareggub Revisited*, finds the setting of the work unreal ('Llareggyb bears no relation to modern Wales'), and the whole as irresponsible as Tasso, since it offers 'the satisfaction of sexual needs without the acceptance of responsibility'. He also finds it implausible. Polly Garter, he points out, would hardly have loved Mr Waldo back, but would have found him disgusting. Mr and Mrs Cherry Owen's exchange is 'hopelessly unconvincing (under the circumstances)'.

Now who expects plausibility in Arcadia? Why, Celia and Oliver didn't even *know* each other. And Lycius—wouldn't he have found Lamia ('under the circumstances') just a little bit slimy? It is easy to make fun of inappropriate demands for realism; it is only unfair if the work itself seems to raise them. Now I have to confess that I find Mr Cherry Owen, sometimes, a little too real for comfort. He sounds so like a drunken husband, that I find myself sighing with relief that Mrs Owen doesn't, after all, mind. The next step after relief is to admire her: and once we do anything so moral as admiring, Llareggyb has ceased to be Arcadia.

The beauty of pastoral depends on freedom from plausibility. Once it drops into a realistic mode—once it actually seems to be about fat men and their lusts, or drunkenness as a homebreaker, rather than a projection of nostalgia—we must start to question it severely, and in a different voice.

Perhaps the poetry of Arcadia is above all a poetry of moments. A poignant phrase touches a nerve, and a stab of nostalgia shoots to the surface, leaving its glow suffusing the surrounding work. Yet it's a poetry of sustained works too, and if we ask what, on the scale of being, the poetry of nostalgia is worth, the answer is not easy. To assert with Piers and Mr Holbrook that immature dreams should not be expressed is to replace art by morality. But to say that all dreams are worth the same is to live in a universe without values. *Ceteribus paribus*, our profoundest impulses, springing from our fullest selves, lead to the greatest art.

If we are to stay inside the bounds of literary criticism, we must end on a tautology, and say that the poetry of Arcadia is worth as much in the scale of art as nostalgia is worth as an emotion to live by. It is not, among the range of our feelings, that which most richly nourishes the whole of our being. But if we allowed ourselves only those bracing joys that have no need of nostalgia, we'd live as grey and stern a life as those shepherds who are never allowed to fleet the time carelessly, as they did in the golden world.

V

GOLDEN SLUMBERS:
THE POLITICS OF PASTORAL

THE hierarchical structure of sixteenth-century society, and the political power of the Tudor monarchy, were, as everyone now knows, reinforced by powerful sanctions. A universe of correspondences was one in which the fitness of order and design in one area was strengthened by its fitness in another. If the glorious planet Sol is enthroned among the others, that is one reason more for keeping the king on his throne: if the bees are happy to contribute to the welfare of the hive, that is one reason more why the peasant should be glad to feed the layers of society above him.

The great chain of being (it is time our democratic century removed its capital letters) belongs to centric literature: from epics, from learned tragedies, from orthodox political treatises, from sermons that impose the official world picture on their hearers, we can illustrate it endlessly—as the literary historians have done. The aim of this chapter is to ask what centrifugal literature contributed to the case. When a poet wrote not about court but about country, did this alter the political implications of his work? Did *any* Renaissance poets, for that matter, write with different political implications?

I

But first, to illustrate the orthodox doctrine at greater length. I shall spin out the political implications of a thoroughly centric book. The example I have chosen is Sidney's *Arcadia*—chosen not without malice, since the literary histories like to refer to this book as a pastoral. In fact, the most pastoral thing about it is its title. Sidney's Arcadia is not a rural paradise where life is simpler and more idyllic than at court; it is a kingdom like any other, with a hierarchical social structure. Eclogues are introduced simply as light relief; the values are the central values of a Renaissance court —Platonic, absolutist, sophisticated. When the wicked Cecropia tries to seduce her virtuous niece Pamela, urging that virtue is little more than 'the staff of vulgar opinions', Pamela answers in a long eloquent assertion of the great chain of being and the argument from design. The best defence of virtue, we are to realise, is not simple innocence, but learning.

The politics of the book, too, are staunchly monarchic. The praise of the good King Eunarchus (II. ch. vi) describes how he found his kingdom torn by strife and ruled by 'the worst kind of oligarchy', 'the names of a king . . . grown even odious to the people', and how by strong centralised government in the best Tudor style, including 'some even extreme severity', he imposed peace and order and 'won a singular love in his people'. As for its taste, that is clearly anti-pastoral. True, the most famous passage in the book, the description of the Arcadian landscape in I. ch. ii, could be a description of Arden:

> . . . Here a shepherd's boy piping as if he should never be old: there a young shepherdess knitting and withal singing, and it seemed that her voice comforted her hands to work, and her hands kept time to her voice's music . . .

But this idyllic note does not last: not only has Arcadia a court, it has comic relief in the shape of the boor Damoetas, who is mocked for his rustic clumsiness and lack of good breeding:

> He began with a wild method to run over all the art of husbandry: especially employing his tongue about well dunging of a field: while poor Zelmane yielded her ears to those tedious strokes . . .   Book II. ch. iv

Very little of the apparently pastoral element survives scrutiny. Musidorus disguises himself as a shepherd in order to woo Pamela but there is no suggestion that the disguise has anything to teach him. When Calidore led a shepherd's life to woo Pastorella in *The Faerie Queene* he found that it taught him new values; not only does no such thought occur to Musidorus, he exploits his disguise to assert all the more strongly the courtly values he has never doubted. In order to woo the princess Pamela, he pretends to make love to Damoetas' daughter Mopsa; in the presence of both ladies he makes elaborate speeches, all addressed to Pamela, and then pleads with her to intercede with Mopsa for him; he tells the story of his own life, Mopsa thinking it is just a tale for her entertainment, Pamela realising the truth. It is hard to think of a grosser example of treating a human being as a means and not an end. The unfortunate Mopsa is in love with Musidorus, but it never occurs to him to take her love-sick glances seriously:

> . . . ever and anon turning her muzzle towards me, she threw such a prospect upon me, as might well have given a surfeit to any weak lover's stomach. But Lord, what a fool am I, to mingle that drivel's speeches among my noble thoughts?
>
> II.iii

We can hope, for the sake of his modesty, that the thoughts are noble because they are about Pamela, though it is possible he is simply reminding himself that he is above Mopsa in station. Of the fact of this Sidney has no doubt, and he draws some heartless consequences: Mopsa, though in love, is unable to keep awake through Musidorus' story—and when she drops asleep, she snores. Shepherdesses, if they are so bold as to invade the main plot, must snore, and the prince who disguises as a shepherd must remain patently a prince.

The *Arcadia* then is firmly anti-pastoral in its preferences; and its political attitudes are impeccably orthodox. By far the most interesting political episode, to the modern reader, is the rebellion in Book II. It is, of course, easily suppressed, by the valour of Zelmana; and once it is suppressed it has to be explained. Sidney's 'explanation' consists essentially of the belief that the multitude don't know what they want. When they are asked what their grievances are, everyone wants something different:

> . . . never bees made such a confused humming: the town dwellers demanding putting down of imposts: the country fellows laying out of commons: some would have the Prince keep his court in one place, some in another . . .   II.xxvi

It is not surprising that in the next chapter they fight among themselves. In the meantime, however, they have been pacified by a speech of Zelmana's showing the need for government and the advantages of monarchy.

Was Sidney interested in the causes of rebellion? In one sense, yes, for this rebellion later turns out to have had a very specific cause: the scheming of Clinius the agitator, who was employed by the wicked Cecropia to stir up trouble. This leads into a rather interesting account of Cecropia's son Amphialus, who decides to launch a milder and more constitutional revolution, accusing Basilius of neglecting his kingdom, threatening to call the general assembly of the states to settle the matter. He claims that since ends justify means, his mother was right to seize Basilius' daughters and hold them prisoner—and we begin to see that what Sidney most fears in politics is the reckless disregard of traditional sanctions, the assertion that, in the name of the weal-public, 'long-held opinions (rather builded upon a secret of government, than any ground of truth) are to be forsaken'. (The Hobbesian scepticism of the parenthesis belongs of course to Amphialus, not to Sidney.)

To the question whether he was interested in the cause of rebellion, we have therefore to say that he was interested in the clash between the traditional order and the reckless invoking of weal-public: that is, in what the mob-rising of Book II, ch. 25, and the seizure of the princesses in Book III, ch. 2, have in common. For Sidney, Cesare Borgia and Jack Cade are part of the same danger, the arrogant overthrow of traditional order. Now to the monarchist who hears the rattle of the great chain of being every time the king lifts his arm, they may well seem part of the same phenomenon, but to the historian who is interested in social movements they are quite different. How and whether a Clinius can manage to foment disorder (the question of Rudé, Talmon, Thompson and—ultimately—Marx) interests Sidney no more than it interested Coriolanus. Sidney looks at popular rebellion, and he simply sees rebellion.

Did any Elizabethan look at it and see that it was popular? See, that is, that a discontented populace has its own political language, which is not the same as that of the over-mighty subject—and then ask why they are moved to use it? Well Shakespeare, who did everything, did this too.

II

The issue which best illustrates the difference between official and popular views of politics is war; for in war it is clearest that the people pay the price and their rulers take the benefits. As an example of the orthodox, heroic attitude to war, we can take *Henry V*. This is the fourth play of a tetralogy, and ideologically it is much simpler than the other three. The structure of *1 Henry*

IV demonstrates a multiple view of military honour. On the one hand there is Hotspur—simple, impulsive, enormously likeable—whose acceptance of military ideals is single-minded even to the point of fanaticism. On the other hand there is Falstaff—corrupt, cowardly, cynical and enormously likeable—who rejects them with equal completeness. Between the two is Hal, not at all likeable when we pause to stare at him, who has to choose, and whose choice involved the rejection of Falstaff; whether it involves the complete acceptance of Hotspur's ideals is something we are never explicitly told, and the structure of the play leaves us to understand that his final political attitude will be richer and fuller than either.

Henry V, in contrast, is clear in its assertions. Falstaff has gone; and Hal has been simplified into Hotspur—his one sin is that he 'covets honour'. Well, perhaps not quite Hotspur, who is one of Shakespeare's most individualised characters, and whose impulsiveness continues to contrast with Henry's consciousness of responsibility; but certainly the social range of Hal's experience has not been incorporated into his personality as king. Walking through the English camp the night before Agincourt he recalls the age-old stories of the kings who mingle disguised with their people, but he does not mingle with them as the once-madcap Prince Hal. He

> *Bids them good-morrow with a modest smile,*
> *And calls them brothers, friends and countrymen*
>> Act IV, Chorus

exactly as his father had done before going into exile:

> *A brace of draymen bid God speed him well,*
> *And had the tribute of his supple knee,*
> *With 'Thanks, my countrymen, my loving friends'.*
>> *Richard II*, I.iv.32

When Hal's nobles urge him to war, they appeal to the Hotspur in him:

> *never king of England*
> *Had nobles richer and more loyal subjects*
> *Whose hearts have left their bodies here in England*
> *And lie pavilioned in the fields of France*
>> I.ii.126

There is no Falstaff standing by to paraphrase this, capturing the mixture of exhilaration and fear that accompanies the outbreak of war: 'thy father's beard is turned white with the news. You may buy land now as cheap as stinking mackerel.' Even the horrors of war are now made acceptable to us:

> And tell the pleasant prince this mock of his
> Hath turn'd his balls to gun-stones . . .
> . . . for many a thousand widows
> Shall this mock out of their dear husbands;
> Mock mothers from their sons, mock castles down;
> And some are yet ungotten and unborn
> That shall have cause to curse the Dauphin's scorn.
>
> I.ii.281

The destruction that is coming is here presented as a consequence of the splendid anger of Henry, an aspect of his refusal to let a Frenchman make fun of him.

That comes from the first part of the play, before hostilities begin. Once France has been invaded, we see what war is like:

> look to see
> The blind and bloody soldier with foul hand
> Defile the locks of your shrill-shrieking daughters;
> Your fathers taken by the silver beards,
> And their most reverend heads dash'd to the walls; . . .
>
> III.iii.33

None of the truth is baulked or avoided in Henry's threat to the governor of Harfleur, yet in an interesting way the king himself is protected from the taint of what he threatens. He very carefully disclaims responsibility for what will happen:

> What is't to me, when you yourselves are cause,
> If your pure maidens fall into the hand
> Of hot and forcing violation?
>
> III.iii.19

A thousand politicians, a thousand letters to *The Times*, have responded to stories of atrocities by saying, Yes it's unfortunate, but then war is a horrible thing. Hal is here describing what will happen if Harfleur does not surrender, and his description is almost dispassionate: it was misleading even to call it a threat. What he is threatening is to attack the town: the details of that attack will follow of themselves, and are not part of his personal design. The effect of the whole is that the horrors are a comment not on Hal but on war: this is how you have to behave when you're in a corner, and when you're not, then you can afford to be generous:

> we give express charge that in our marches through the country there be nothing compelled from the villages, nothing taken but paid for . . .   V.iii

Up to this point, nothing has questioned our simple admiration for the patriotism of Hal; and his walk through his camp dispensing 'a little touch of Harry in the night' seems the climax of his heroic royalty—until, wrapping a cloak round him for disguise, he stops to talk to his common soldiers. And then, for one short marvellous scene, we are in another world.

The difference is announced—as so often in Shakespeare—by a new kind of language. Against the public morality, the carefully balanced sentences of Henry

> —methinks I could not die anywhere so contented as in the king's company, his cause being just and his quarrel honourable—

comes the unanswerable bluntness of Williams: 'that's more than we know'. Williams is the irreducible element of popular cynicism, and he too describes the horrors of war—and without exempting the king from responsibility for them:

> But if the cause be not good, the king himself hath a heavy reckoning to make: when all those legs and arms and heads, chopped off in a battle shall join together at the latter day, and cry all: 'We died at such a place'; some swearing, some crying for a surgeon, some upon their wives left behind them, some upon the debts they owe, some upon their children rawly left. I am afeard there are few die well that die in battle; for how can they charitably dispose of any thing when blood is their argument? . . .
>
> IV.i

Heroism is for the nobs; in a war like this, the natural attitude of the people is pacifism. For Williams, who has not only a different conception of responsibility from Henry, but a different way of talking about realities, the deaths of soldiers are seen as deaths, not as the consequences of the regrettable fact that war is like that. Henry, of course, answers him:

111

So, if a son that is by his father sent about merchandise do sinfully miscarry upon the sea, the imputation of his wicked-ness, by your rule, should be imposed upon his father that sent him . . .

Henry asserts that every man is responsible for his own death, that if soldiers go into battle with the guilt of past sins on them, 'they have no wings to fly from God': their deaths will find them out, for 'war is His beadle'. To this Williams answers:

Tis certain, every man that dies ill, the ill upon his own head; the king is not to answer it.

How easy things are for a king, even when Shakespeare is his dramatist! Henry's reply is totally unconvincing, but he wins the argument. The very first words of his reply take us back from one world to another. 'So, if . . .': the tone has changed to one of discussion. 'We are going to die tomorrow' has given place to 'I can't quite accept that point'. And Henry has not only removed the immediacy, he has used false analogies. The sending of the son about merchandise was the accidental occasion of his death, not its cause. Henry is denying that war *matters*: he is treating a battle as the occasion when soldiers happen to die—and die in a way determined by their past lives only. This is to knock the basis from under Williams' case, without answering any of his points —and Williams accepts it all meekly, for he, after all, is only Williams, and we know who Henry is.

And as a matter of fact Williams' position has already been accepted by Henry. When he urges the Archbishop to weigh his words carefully before advising him, he accepts that he will himself be responsible for the consequences of war:

> For God doth know how many now in health
> Shall drop their blood in approbation
> Of what your reverence shall incite us to!
> Therefore take heed how you impawn our person,
> How you awake our sleeping sword of war . . .
>
> I.ii.18

—and as soon as he has parted from the soldiers, Henry, in his famous soliloquy ('Upon the King! . . .) accepts the burden of kingship in a way that it would not be difficult to turn into Williams' case. I think there is no doubt that Williams gets the better of his argument with Henry. It is bad enough that he gives way so easily, but worse is to follow. When Henry plays his elaborate trick with the gloves and exposes Williams as a man who answered back to the king, then fills the glove with crowns, audiences always enjoy the scene: they laugh, they feel nice and comfortable. Williams, whose bluntness they have warmed to, gets rewarded; Henry, by rewarding him, turns out to be a good fellow after all; everyone is happy. Of course Williams can't be mollified too easily, but Henry has seen to that too, by inserting Fluellen into the trick, so that he can offer Williams twelvepence and Williams can answer back to *him*—'I will none of your money' —while of course gratefully accepting the gloveful of crowns from the king.

There is only one way to describe all this: Williams has been bought off. The genuine radicalism of his attitude has been brushed aside, and the blunt honesty of his manner, by being rewarded, has been rendered harmless. He's a fine chap, he thinks for himself, says what he believes: *this* is what we are told, and it prevents us from listening to what he said, and wondering if it's true.

The conversation before the battle is immediately followed by the most chauvinistic and heroic touch in the play, the Crispin's Day speech, and by the splendid romp of the battle, in which the sombre notes are contributed by the defeated, while the victors end with the glorification of sword and altar:

> *O God! thy arm was here;*
> *And not to us but to thy arm alone*
> *Ascribe we all.*

IV.viii.102

For Williams, religion was a radical force: 'the latter day' is when the king will be shown the results of his war, and made to answer for them. For Henry's military regime, religion is a sanction for his policies, *Non nobis* and *Te Deum* will be sung in gratitude for victory, and Christian humility will be offered to God as a reward for letting them beat the French:

> *And be it death proclaimed through our host*
> *To boast of this, or take that praise from God*
> *Which is his only.*

IV.viii.110

Henry V is a simple, patriotic, militaristic play, with one or two subversive and pacifist streaks that are never integrated into the whole, and never convincingly answered. By far the most important of these is the sudden irruption of Williams into the middle of the play. He comes from nowhere and he is soon disposed of, but we cannot fail to hear his voice long after the rest of the play is silent.

Voices like that are rare in Renaissance literature. Even if we do not insist that the people speak in their own voice, but look for such bluntness, such potential subversion, in the comments of the leisured and the literate, we shall not often find it. Yet, sometimes, we may:

> L'on voit certains animaux farouches, des mâles et des femelles, répandus par la campagne, noirs, livides and tout brûlés du soleil, attachés à la terre qu'ils fouillent et qu'ils remuent avec une opiniâtreté invincible; ils ont comme une voix articulée, et, quand ils se lèvent sur leurs pieds, ils montrent une face humaine, et en effet ils sont des hommes; ils se retirent la nuit dans des tanières où ils vivent de pain noir, d'eau et de racines; ils épargnent aux autres hommes la peine de semer, de labourer et de recueillir pour vivre, et méritent ainsi de ne pas manquer de ce pain qu'ils ont semé.
>
> La Bruyère, *Les Caractères*, XI.128
>
> Certain wild animals, both male and female, can be seen all over the countryside, black, livid, and quite sunburnt, attached to the land which they dig and stir about with unconquerable obstinacy. It's as though they make articulate sounds, and when they stand up they show a human face—and they are, in fact, men. At night they retire to their hovels, where they live on black bread, water and roots. They release other men from the task of sowing, ploughing and reaping in order to live, and so they deserve to have some of the bread they sow.

This extraordinary passage is unique in La Bruyère, perhaps unique in the seventeenth century. In a way, it is more shocking than Williams, for by speaking in his own person La Bruyère can be blunter than ever. We have here shifted, of course, from war to the economy, but there is quite as much to say, and quite as violent a point to be made by a sudden shift in assumptions—or rather by the mere abandoning of certain previous assumptions. La Bruyère renders this shift by the brilliant devices of treating

the *animaux farouches* as animals, before slowly revealing that he
is talking about peasants. It is worthy of Swift, though it is turned
to different purpose: Swift's subject, when he wrote like this, was
always man's nature in general: La Bruyère's is social—not man
as he really is, but one class of men as social organisation has made
them. No doubt he thought such social organisation was inevitable,
and perhaps in the seventeenth century it was. It is not easy to
say whether the passage is socially radical. It may well be that
La Bruyère intended a cool, detached tone, a shrug at the inevitable: if that is so, the brilliant bluntness transcends the intended
tone. It may be too that the only radicalism it could inspire in
the seventeenth century was that of mere destruction: for the
peasant revolts of the time, as Roland Mousnier has shown in his
Fureurs paysannes, were almost completely lacking in alternative,
democratic ideologies. Perhaps only now, when technology has
opened up the possibility of an alternative social structure, can we
see in the passage a positive, even a revolutionary critique of
seventeenth-century society.

III

These then are the extremes. Sidney—and a thousand others
—shows the conservative tradition, asserting the political ortho-
doxies of the need for order and the religious sanctions that
underly social and political hierarchy: Williams, and (for an
instant) La Bruyère, refusing to believe a word of it, tell us to
look at what it all means for the people.

By juxtaposing these extremes, we are in a sense removing
ourselves from the real issues of sixteenth-century politics. The
threats to social order which the Tudor and Valois monarchs
feared did not come from peasants, shepherds or artisans, let
alone labourers; they came from overweening nobles, religious
fanatics and entrepreneurial courtiers. The threat from the common
people must have seemed to the sixteenth century more remote,
more merely destructive—and yet, in a sense, more fundamental.
If not so actual as a political threat, it would involve a completer
rejection of ideology, and the ideology shows signs of worry about
it.

And it is this fundamental, ideological threat that must concern
us if we ask what the politics of pastoral were. For pastoral is

about the lower orders. It is not the place to show struggles between courtier and monarch, between Erastian and theocrat; but it is the place to ask how peasant and shepherd regard their lot. And however peripheral the question may have been politically, it was certainly asked.

Further, the implications of pastoral are at least potentially democratic. It continually asserts that the peasant is a better man than the courtier. The pastoral Perdita is not afraid of King Polixenes:

> *for once or twice*
> *I was about to speak, and tell him plainly,*
> *The selfsame sun that shines upon his court*
> *Hides not his visage from our cottage, but*
> *Looks on alike.*
>
> The Winter's Tale, IV.iv.439

What in fact did pastoral have to say about the hierarchical society?

I begin with a work of no literary eminence, but of revealing ordinariness, Nicholas Breton's *The Court and the Country* ('A Brief Discourse between the Courtier and the Countryman; of the manner, nature and condition of their lives'). Though arranged as a dialogue, this work is completely one-sided. The countryman does more than three-quarters of the talking, and wins every point. Some of the courtier's arguments descend to sneers, others seem half-heartedly advanced. The pamphlet is a conventional eulogy of rural quiet and contentment.

What is praised about country life is simplicity, which is contrasted with affectation ('for kissing of the hand, as if he were licking of his fingers, bending down the head, as if his neck were out of joint . . . we allow none of that learning'); the 'true mirth' of country festivals, the good sense of farmers, and above all contentment:

> We are content with what we have, and keep somewhat for a rainy day: love neither to borrow nor lend . . .
> Then for a good rule of life, Fear God and obey the king, which perhaps some do not so well in the court as in the country . . .
> If we live within the compass of the law, serve God and obey our king, and as good subjects ought to do, in our duties and our prayers daily remember him, What need we more learning? . . .

There is an intimate link, we see, between the theme of rural content and a meek submissiveness to authority. The last thing Breton's countryman wants to do is to question a social order that keeps him in Arcadia.

It often happens in Elizabethan romances that the prince or courtier comes down in the world, through shipwreck or rebellion, and finding himself in the happy position of Breton's countryman, sings the praise of rural content and its golden slumbers. When this happens we can usually be sure of two things—first that he did not seek it voluntarily, but so far as the plot is concerned is making a virtue of necessity; and second that he will be restored to prosperity in the end. The reward for accepting the joys of poverty is to be deprived of them.

If you tell a man that his life is better than that of kings, that court brings corruption, and power brings care, that the recipe for happiness is

> To rise with the day rays, and go to bed without a candle, to eat when we are hungry, drink when we are thirsty, travel when we are lusty, and rest when we are weary: fear God, be true to the Crown, keep the laws, pay scot and lot, breed no quarrels, do no wrong . . .

—if you tell him all this, do you stir him up or calm him down? It depends just what you say and how you say it; and Renaissance pastoral managed, almost invariably, to say it in a conservative voice. The verse equivalent of Breton's dialogue is a poem like Southwell's 'Content and Rich':

> *In lowly vales I mount*
> *To pleasure's highest pitch;*
> *My silly shroud true honour brings;*
> *My poor estate is rich. . . .*
>
> *My wishes are but few,*
> *All easy to fulfil;*
> *I make the limits of my power*
> *The bonds unto my will*
>
> *Silk sails of largest size*
> *The storm doth soonest tear,*
> *I bear so low and small a sail*
> *As freeth me from fear . . .*

I envy not their hap,
Whom favour doth advance;
I take no pleasure in their pain,
That have less happy chance . . .

There is no need to multiply examples. This is the conservatism of 'Art thou poor yet hast thou golden slumbers?' It is conservative because the superiority of the shepherd depends on his staying where he is. It may not always be as explicit as Southwell, whose countryman actually tells us he is going to stick to a small sail; but that simply brings to the surface the constant implication of rural content.

To see how blind a sixteenth-century poet could be to radical implications, we can look at Philip Sidney's remarks on pastoral in the *Apology for Poetry*. Sidney defends pastoral in the simplest imaginable terms: that however humble the medium, it is possible to say something worth while.

> Is the poor pype disdained, which sometimes out of Meliboeus' mouth can show the misery of people under hard Lords or ravening soldiers, and again, by Tityrus, what blessedness is derived to them that lie lowest from the goodness of them that sit highest.

This is a reference to Virgil's first Eclogue, which as we have seen shows the brutality of Augustus' policy of rural eviction to make room for his veterans; and then praises Augustus for his clemency in granting Tityrus an exemption. It is a nice question whether that is radical or not; and it is certainly tempting to give more weight to the criticism on which the poem is built than to the flattery which overlays it. But whether or not Virgil is radical, Sidney certainly isn't; for Sidney's account clearly supposes a courtly audience, the natural audience of pastoral. It is to the courtiers that you need to defend the 'poor pype' in these terms; and whereas to 'show the misery of people under hard Lords' may be subversive if it is shown to the people, it is merely moral if shown to the Lords. The second half of Sidney's statement comes in so automatically to balance the first, that it really does not seem to have occurred to him that he was dealing with politics. If misery is alleviated, it will of course be through benevolence from above.

IV

Now to examine the political implications of the pastoral lyric. I want to treat one poet at greater length, and have chosen Ronsard. Ronsard is a pastoral poet quite literally because of his *Eclogues*, which rehearse most of the pastoral commonplaces (singing contests, Golden Age, cups carved with rural scenes) and are quite shameless in allowing the true material to peep through the convention: it is actually great princes who are speaking, we are reminded, and not shepherds. But he is also (and more interestingly) a pastoral poet because of the occurrence of pastoral themes and attitudes in some of his less formal poems, and it is these I want to discuss.

Indeed (before we turn to the politics) we can actually see the two elements of the pastoral coming together (or being dismantled) in *La Salade*. On the one hand, this poem is filled with a matter-of-fact love of the countryside. It names flowers—not richly symbolic flowers, rose, violet, and daffodil, but particular and obscure ones, to show the eye of the botanising country dweller:

> la boursette touffue,
> La pâquerette à la feuille menue,
> La pimprenelle heureuse pur le sang . . .
>
> the tufted lamb's lettuce,
> The daisy with its tiny leaves,
> The pimpernel that is good for the blood . . .

Ronsard is never afraid to go into detail. In his *Epitre à Ambroise de la Porte, parisien* he sings the praises of a very real countryside, where real work, such as pressing grapes, is done—and described at length, with an abundance of technical terms. Ronsard has several ways of making us feel we are in a real place: another is his note of judicious fussing, as of someone who is drawing up a menu:

> L'engraisserons de l'huile de Provence:
> L'huile qui vient aux oliviers de France
> Rompt l'estomac et ne vaut du tout rien.
>
> We will mix it with oil from Provence:
> The oil that comes from French olive-trees
> Ruins the digestion and is worthless.

On the other hand, *La Salade* presents the author as not a simple countryman. He likes the company of peasants, but is not one of

119

them. He is a scholar, who can't take his nose out of his books even in the open air.

> *Puis, en lisant l'ingénieux Ovide*
> *En ces beaux vers ou d'amour il est guide,*
> *Reguagnerons le logis pas à pas . . .*
>
> *Then, reading the ingenious Ovid,*
> *Those lovely verses in which he explains all about love,*
> *We will stroll back to the house . . .*

The violently playful reversal at the end of the *Epitre à Ambroise de la Porte* achieves the same effect in a very different way. After his eloquent praises of rural life, contrasted with the '*ville périlleuse*', Ronsard concludes by assuring Ambroise that nothing can make him forget Paris, and that as soon as winter comes he'll rush back to the city, his companions and his books

> *que j'aime*
> *Plus que ces champs, que toi, ni que moi-même.*
>
> *which I love*
> *More than these fields, or you, or even myself.*

The poet emerges as someone who was just playing at country pleasure.

Love of the country as it actually is: love of the country by a townsman. Put these together, and you get love of an idealised version of the country, you get mediated not direct rural poetry—that is, pastoral. Ronsard by separating them shows us what the mechanism is—and anticipates the nineteenth century.

La Salade has political implications almost as simple as Breton's *Dialogue*. Life in the country is contrasted with life at court, where lying and flattery are the rule: this is the usual praise of golden slumbers, with its implied exhortation to stay contentedly where you are. There is only one couplet whose effect is different:

> *Dedans le sac on met tout à fois*
> *Rocs, Chevaliers, Pions, Reines et Rois . . .*
>
> *Into the sack everything goes*
> *Rooks, Knights, Pawns, Kings and Queens . . .*

There is a curtness about this that might sound like a snarl, a willingness to insult the mighty; but it is tamed again by the whole thing being turned into an image from chess, and so kept at one remove.

120

There is the same conventional conservatism in the poem *Au cardinal Odet de Châtillon*. It, too, satirises the court, warning against flatterers, and then turns to praise of rural content, where there is no mob of followers, and where the earth, our common mother, feeds all alike. Like Breton's countryman, Ronsard expresses pity for those who have sold themselves to the king, and lost this happiness:

> *Misérables valets, vendant leur liberté*
> *Pour un petit d'honneur servement acheté.*
>
> *Wretched valets, selling their liberty*
> *For a scrap of honour servilely purchased.*

The most interesting word here is 'liberté'. It is a political term, and the lines appear to be making a political point about the advantages of the country. But the 'liberté' is freedom to *keep out of* politics, to eat bread and drink water: not freedom to do anything, to change, to criticise, to revel, but non-political freedom that no tyrant need begrudge.

Things are a little more complicated in the sonnet *A Monseigneur le Duc de Touraine*, in which the speaker is a garden nymph:

> *Ces grands, ces triomphants, ces superbes Romains,*
> *Qui avaient eu du ciel un si riche avantage,*
> *N'avaient que cinq arpents de terre en labourage,*
> *Et si tenaient pourtant l'Empire entre leurs mains.*
>
> *Ces grandeurs, ces honneurs, dont les hommes sont pleins,*
> *Ne sont pas les vrais biens qui font l'homme plus sage:*
> *Un petit clos de terre, un petit héritage*
> *Les rend plus vertueux, plus gaillards et plus sains.*
>
> *Ces arbres, qui pour vous leurs robes renouvellent,*
> *Ces fleurs et ces jardins et ces fruits vous appellent,*
> *Célébrants jusqu'au ciel vos faits et vos valeurs,*
>
> *Dignes d'avoir autels, temples et sacrifice;*
> *Et que votre beau nom écrit entre les fleurs,*
> *Se fasse compagnon d'Ajax et de Narcisse.*

Those great, those triumphant and proud Romans, so greatly favoured by Heaven, had no more than five acres of land to plough, and yet held the Empire in their hands. The distinctions and the honours with which men are overwhelmed, these are not the true goods that render a man wise; a little plot of land, a small inheritance, is what brings virtue, happiness and health. These trees, renewing their garments for you, these flowers, these gardens, and these fruits call you, celebrating your deeds and your courage as far as the heavens—deeds deserving altars, temples and sacrifice, and that your splendid name, written among the flowers, should be the companion of Ajax and Narcissus.

This praise of 'un petit de terre' has, apparently, the same quietist moral that is now familiar to us; and the quietism determines the structure of the last tercet. It begins as a courtier's dutiful praise of a great man and his deeds; then it turns from official eulogy into golden slumbers. 'Jusqu'au ciel' might suggest that his name will be written 'entre les astres', but it is only going to be 'entre les fleurs'; it might suggest that he will be inscribed as companion 'd'Alexandre et de César', but it is only 'd'Ajax' (for his death not his deeds) 'et de Narcisse'. And when we add (what was clearly known to all contemporary readers of the poem) that François d'Alençon was a political malcontent, 'rongé d'ambition' according to Larousse, that he plotted against his brother Charles IX, then the exhortation to seek only for a 'petit héritage' is even more clearly anti-political, and so conservative.

But there is another way of seeing the poem. Though malcontent, François, Duc de Touraine, was politically important. This means that the act of writing a poem to him is itself a political act: Ronsard is advancing himself, and the existence of the poem runs counter to its message. This is certainly the case in the next poem, in which a nymph of the woods speaks (as in the further poem where *la nymphe de la Fontaine de Baune* is the speaker). The whole forest, declares the *nymphe bocagère*, is ready to sing your praises to the skies; and in fact the poem is not really any different from the run of the mill sonnets of political flattery that Ronsard wrote to the king (whoever the king happened to be), declaring that Europe, Asia and Africa were too small for his greatness. We have here one of those delicate borderlines between the meaning of a poem and its social situation—considering how circumstantial the title is (it runs, in full, 'A Monseigneur le Duc de Touraine, François de Valois, entrant en le jardin de l'auteur'), it does not seem far-fetched to say that the circumstances are part of what it means; and as it happens there is one detail in which even the strictest refuser of social context would have to admit that we were talking about the poem. This is the fact that in the first quatrain, the 'cinq arpents de terre' are attributed to 'ces superbes Romains', and are even suggested as the cause of their political success. We have the Cincinnatus-legend, in fact, which is not at all anti-political. The sonnet, I conclude, is only partly a pastoral rejection of court; it also contains an acceptance of the world it is claiming to despise. And both these contradictory elements are conservative.

Where do we look for subversiveness in Ronsard? Perhaps in the Ode 'Au Laboureur':

> *Pourquoi, chétif laboureur,*
> *Trembles-tu d'un Empéreur?*

Wretched ploughman, why do you tremble at an Emperor?

The contempt for princes in this apparently aggressive poem is quite direct:

> *Courage, coupeur de terre!*
> *Ces grands foudres de la guerre*
> *Non plus de toi n'iront pas*
> *Armés d'un plastron là-bas*
> *Comme ils allaient aux batailles:*
> *Autant leur vaudront leurs mailles,*
> *Leurs lances et leur estoc*
> *Comme à toi vaudra ton soc.*

Courage, tillers of the soil. Those great thunderbolts of war will not, any more than you, go yonder wearing a breastplate, as they do going into battle. Their armour, their lances and their long swords will be worth just as much to them as your ploughshare to you.

The contempt appears in the glee at the uselessness of all those splendid weapons; and what can sound more inflammatory than *Courage, coupeur de terre!*, especially followed by *ces grands foudres*, which can be spat out like an insult. If we attend only to the tone of this ode, we might imagine we are hearing Shelley:

> *Men of England wherefore plow*
> *For the lords that lay ye low?*

Ronsard is writing an accepted kind of Renaissance poem, not pastoral but interestingly parallel to it. The most famous example in English is Shirley's moralising lyric, 'The glories of our blood and State'.

The glories of our blood and state,
  Are shadows, not substantial things,
There is no armour against fate,
  Death lays his icy hand on Kings,
    Sceptre and Crown,
    Must tumble down,
And in the dust be equal made
With the poor crooked scythe and spade.

Some men with swords may reap the field,
  And plant fresh laurels where they kill,
But their strong nerves at last must yield,
  They tame but one another still;
    Early or late,
    They stoop to fate,
And must give up the murmuring breath,
When they pale Captives creep to death.

The Garlands wither on your brow,
  Then boast no more your mighty deeds,
Upon Death's purple Altar now,
  See where the Victor-victim bleeds,
    Your heeds must come,
    To the cold Tomb;
Only the actions of the just
Smell sweet, and blossom in their dust.

The second stanza of this is strong meat. Disrespect appears in the very first words: 'some men' is no way for a seventeenth-century subject to speak of his prince. The irony of 'reap', too, is a social reversal. Kings are mocked because that is the only kind of reaping they can do: this establishes the 'poor crooked scythe and spade' as the poem's norm, and underlines the irony of 'poor': the speaker can use such a term of denigration because he is having the better of the contrast. The punch-line is the last line of the stanza: the pride of the mighty is humbled, and the long-drawn monosyllables speak the gloating of the moraliser. The last stanza follows effortlessly from this line. Its rhythm is smoother now, as befits these calmer corollaries: after such humbling of the great, we can naturally tell them not to boast, or mock at them in a sprightly pun.

Yet for all its fierceness, the poem is firmly protected from real subversiveness: for this humbling is removed to another world. The pastoral is not subversive, because the countryman is only better than the king if he keeps in his place; and death, similarly, is a parallel to rural content. Equality is asserted, but in a way that leaves politics alone. However revolutionary in tone, the poem is conservative, after all, in content.

The same is true of 'Au Laboureur'. To put it all in the next world is to render the appeal harmless. There is no real radicalism until someone says 'Why wait for death?', and Ronsard has not said this. Yet calling the next world *là-bas* has given it an air of familiarity, as if the ploughman were at home there, and the king ill at ease—and so has made it more like this world, this world as the poor know it. The hint of doggerel in the versification too, and even the string of technical terms, gives the poem a reality that threatens the easy formulas of pastoral convention; and all in all this is not a poem that the authorities should have felt too happy about.

v

Now if both the centrifugal and the centric, both pastoral and *The Arcadia*, both ways of reading the sonnet to the Duc de Touraine, are socially conservative, if even the poems which begin as a clarion call to the ploughman turn out to be conservative when we look at their content, is anything radical? Not very much Renaissance literature; but Ronsard's *Hymne de l'Or* is interesting. It begins like a conventional golden slumbers poem, despising riches, and pointing out that the Muses never managed to earn dowries by their writing, and that Homer died poor. But after about 40 lines it changes. Ronsard announces that he would rather imitate the *beaux vers* than the poverty of Homer, and the bulk of the poem is then devoted to a witty and cynical praise of money. It narrates fables to show the power of gold over the gods, quotes ancient poets complaining of poverty, and is full of illustrations of the usefulness, indeed necessity of money: Greek and Latin don't fill an empty belly. The argument that poverty, being the gift of God, must be beneficial, is soon disposed of:

> Celuy qui la loura pour estre un don celeste,
> Il faudra que de mesme il loue aussi la peste,
> La famine, la mort, qui sont presens des Dieux . . .

Whoever praises poverty as a celestial gift ought in the same way to praise plague, famine and death too, which are gifts of the Gods . . .

As for the argument that riches brings with it *ennuie, haine, querelles, procez, noises, debats, affaires et soucy*, it is simply untrue. It would mean that princes and emperors were more wicked the richer they were. And the argument that riches bring fear is equally stupid: it would mean that kings were always frightened, whereas they are much tougher (and better guarded!) than anyone else. All these conventional attacks on riches are dismissed as rubbish; and in fact it is not the rich but the poor who lead a life of care—and who become criminals: poverty leads men to rob and kill, and sharpens their ingenuity in breaking the law. In conclusion, the poem moves to a denunciation of the selfish and spendthrift rich, and of the miser, neither of whom put their money to socially beneficial uses.

This poem is in several ways the exact opposite of pastoral. Opposite in imagery: the gold it praises is not the mythic gold of the Golden Age, but the 'corrupting' gold of today. Opposite in tone: there is a no-nonsense realism about it that is impossible in pastoral. It constantly appeals from what is conventionally believed to what a sensible man can see if he opens his eyes. And there are touches too of a deeper and strangely bracing cynicism:

> *Et vien-çà, mon amy, puisqu'il nous faut joüer*
> *La farce des humains, vaut-il pas mieux loüer,*
> *Qui peut, l'habit d'un Roy, d'un grand Prince, ou d'un comte,*
> *Que l'habit d'un coquin duquel on ne fait compte.*

And come here, my friend. Since we have to take part in this human farce, is it not better to hire, if you can, the costume of a king, a great prince, or a count, than the costume of a rascal of no account?

The fable of gold and gods is neatly ironical. The account of how earth opened her bosom and showed her gleaming gold mines and so won the acclaim of all the gods, could well belong to a poem in praise of the Golden Age, the generosity of earth in pouring out gold for her sons, and gilding the heavens, could be a parallel to bearing fruits without tillage. But in the context, it has the effect of making fun of such primitivism, since by gold it simply means money.

How this poem, anti-pastoral in tone, in imagery, in its view of the simple life, is on the edge of being radical. Its message is not that poverty is to be pitied, but that poverty is a crime.

The universal regard for money is the one hopeful fact in our civilisation, the one sound spot in our social conscience. Money is the most important thing in the world. . . . The crying need of the nation is not for better morals, cheaper bread, temperance, liberty, culture, redemption of fallen sisters and erring brothers, nor the grace, love and fellowship of the Trinity, but simply for enough money.

Preface to *Major Barbara*

It is hard to imagine two writers more different than Ronsard and Shaw; yet when we make all allowance for the differences, we have to say that they are making the same point. And a belief in the universal excellence of money, a belief that poverty is 'the vilest sin of man and society'—*that*, if it falls into the hnds of the poor, is the really radical doctrine. The *Hymne de l'Or* is the exact opposite to 'The Glories of our blood and state', or the ode *Au Laboureur*. Not at all explosive in tone, it is really subversive in content.

VI

I have had a good deal to say on the ingenuity of Renaissance literature in avoiding radical implications; but there is one final ingenuity I have not yet mentioned and on which I will conclude. Essentially, the strategy for avoiding subversion was simple: to keep court and country separate, so that all the splendid promises only applied to the countryman if he stayed put. But there is one form of romanticism which mingles them as no other pastoral elements do: what if the prince falls in love with a peasant girl? Either he betrays the very purity that attracted him, or he comes down in the world.

The Winter's Tale is a tragedy for the first three acts, then turns into a pastoral. There were pastoral hints in the first part, above all Polixenes' marvellous account of childhood innocence, 'we were as twinned lambs that did frisk i' th' sun'; but it is only when we move to Bohemia that the court-country contrast becomes explicit. Act IV is of course profounder than most pastoral poetry, for under its rural charm is a sense of organic life permeating all nature. And in Act V this source of life is brought to court, where it rejuvenates and cleanses.

This sounds, at least potentially, good democratic stuff; and if we look at the changes Shakespeare made in his source it appears that he has pushed his pastoral towards radicalism. In *Pandosto* the young lovers both rebuke themselves for loving across such a social gap. Dorastus (Florizel) tells himself 'Shamest not thou, Dorastus, to name one unfit for thy birth, thy dignities, thy kingdoms?', and Fawnia (Perdita) has a long soliloquy on the wickedness of trying to rise above your station:

> No bastard hawk must soar so high as the hobby, no fowl gaze against the sun but the Eagle: actions wrought against nature reap despite, and thoughts above fortune disdain.

Of course these scruples are overcome in Greene, but Shakespeare removes them altogether. He removes too the pastourelle-type dialogue between the lovers, in which they rehearse some of the court-country commonplaces, almost in the language of Touchstone ('maids must love because they are young: for Cupid is a child, and Venus, though old, is painted with fresh colours'), and all hint of immodesty in Florizel ('Why, Fawnia, perhaps I love thee, and then thou must needs yield, for thou knowest I can command and constrain').

The love in Shakespeare is pure, lyrical and without social complications: as if he really believed that in the pure air of Bohemia a shepherdess was worth a prince, and difficulties vanished. The only trace of hierarchy left comes in Perdita's first speech:

> *Your high self*
> *The gracious mark o' th' land, you have obscured*
> *With a swain's wearing, and me, poor lowly maid,*
> *Most goddess-like pranked up . . .*
> *To me the difference forges dread; your greatness*
> *Hath not been used to fear. Even now I tremble*
> *To think your father by some accident*
> *Should pass this way, as you did.*

IV.iv.8

This is doubly different from Fawnia. Because Perdita is dressed as a Queen for the sheep-shearing feast she is 'pranked up' theatrically as well as socially. This enriches the idea: not, I think, because the theatrical situation enacts the social but for a reason nearer the opposite: Perdita is dressed up in play, and this is almost enough to account for our sense of reversal, thus distracting our attention from the real social upheaval. And secondly, Perdita expresses fear but no guilt: she is troubled only by the thought that Polixenes will prevent their marriage, not by the thought that she isn't a fit mate for Florizel. The democratic point comes to the surface in the lines already quoted earlier, on the sun that shines on all alike. All this seems democratic: where is the catch? It is so obvious that we can easily miss it: Perdita is not a shepherdess after all, but a king's daughter, as we have known all the time. This fact gives quite a different slant to the famous dispute with Polixenes on art and nature. Perdita rejects indignantly Polixenes' defence of grafting and interbreeding as unnatural and brushes aside his view that 'the art itself is nature'. But whatever we think of Perdita's opinions, the fact of her existence fits his theory rather than hers. As for her marriage, it is made doubly ironic. Polixenes is defending in general the very process he is about to attack in particular—marrying a 'gentler scion to the wilder stock'—until we remember the birth of Perdita; and then we realise that the whole debate was unnecessary, since there is no question of wilder stock. Instead of an enriching irony, we have a reassurance that they are only talking about flowers.

As for Perdita's 'democratic' speech on the sun that 'looks on alike'—why doesn't she make it to Polixenes? Then the Jack Cades at the Globe might have given it an ovation. As it is, it is rendered ineffective by the disabling 'I was about to speak'.

Shakespeare has shown the democratic implications of pastoral: and then betrayed them. It is hardly surprising that the motif is so widespread: prince loves shepherdess, and is allowed to marry her because she is really a king's daughter. It occurs in the story of Pastorella in *Faerie Queene* VI and in that of the Salvage Man; it is common enough in folk-tales. Its effect is to release a glow of satisfaction at the brushing aside of degree and wealth, of delight that true worth and beauty can be recognised in a cottage; but to set up a rule that quite clearly stops cottage lasses from getting ideas. It is a masterly confidence trick played by court upon country. They have to be kept out, and if the argument from environment won't do, then we have to use that from heredity.

VI

CITY TROUBLES:
PASTORAL AND SATIRE

I

THE Renaissance critics were all agreed that there was more than one kind of pastoral. 'For either they be plaintive', wrote E. K. in the General Argument of *The Shepherd's Calendar*,

> as the first, the sixth, the eleventh, and the twelfth; or Re-creative, such as all those be, which contain matter of love, or commendation of special personages; or Moral, which for the most part be mixed with some satyrical bitterness; namely, the second, of reverence due to old age; the fifth, of coloured deceit; the seventh and ninth, of dissolute shepherds and pastors; the tenth, of contempt of Poetry and pleasant wits.

E. K.'s distinctions need a little tidying up. The difference between plaintive and recreative is not important, or even consistent: two of the 'plaintive' Eclogues also 'conceive matter of love'. But the difference between them and the moral Eclogues is quite clear-cut. As well as being 'mixed with some satirical bitterness', they are all allegorical, and three (perhaps four) are concerned with church politics. True, the tenth Eclogue, which 'sets out the perfect pattern of a poet', is neither harsher nor more allegorical than the twelfth, in which Colin Clout 'proportioneth his life to the four seasons of the year'. But despite these borderline cases, an almost universal testimony of readers of pastoral has seen that there are two kinds, the idyllic (Sannazaro and Sidney; and, on the whole, Theocritus and Virgil) and the satiric. Hardly any poet wrote satiric pastorals all the time, but there are examples in Mantuan, in Marot, in Googe—and of course in Spenser.

Perhaps the most interesting of Spenser's satiric Eclogues is the ninth, which consists of a conversation between Hobbinol and his friend Diggon Davie, who 'in hope of more gain, drove his sheep into a far country', and has now returned, poor and disillusioned, to his home.

> *In foreign coasts, men said, was plenty,*
> *And so there is, but all of misery.*

In the countries he has been to, all is corruption and neglect:

> *The shepherds there robben one another,*
> *And layen baits to beguile her brother.*

Invited by Hobbinol, Diggon tells his story, which consists largely of an indignant account of the malpractices of the foreign shepherds, who are either 'idle and still' or 'false and full of covetise', and all efforts to improve matters seem only to make them worse.

> *Sike as the shepherds, sike been her sheep,*

who have fallen into mischief and been torn by wolves. Diggon then tells a story about Roffynn, his dog Lowder, and the wolf who slipped among the flock, and lured Lowder outside, and would have killed him if Rorry had not run to the rescue. He concludes with renewed exhortations to watchfulness and a lament over his own fallen fortunes ('my sheep been wasted; wae is me therefore!'), and is invited by Hobbinol to spend the night in his cottage.

The tone of this Eclogue is one of indignation, and it is easy to say what Spenser is indignant about. The shepherds are priests; the flocks they neglect are the English people; and the wolf is Popery. There are various speculations about the exact identity of Roffynn and Lowder, which are of no interest to the modern reader of poetry; no doubt Elizabethan readers argued about it too, and no doubt they realised that it didn't really matter.

Behind the poem lies the ninth Eclogue of Mantuan, in which a shepherd from North Italy comes to Rome, where he finds only corruption; a Roman companion takes him in, and they discuss the folly of leaving your home, the disappearance of once glorious cities, and the wickedness of contemporary life. In a central passage, Faustulus describes to Candidus how men kill and steal while others laugh; how the dogs who should protect the flocks have turned into wolves; how the *morbosa aestas* destroys the domestic animals while the wild beasts feast on the dead. It is no doubt intended as contemporary satire and a denunciation of the clergy.

But there is also another—and a different—poem behind the September Eclogue, the first Eclogue of Virgil. Diggon Davie and Hobbinol have obvious resemblances to Tityrus and Meliboeus. Tityrus like Diggon has been to a far country (also Rome, as it happens), and there he found help; but all the same, Rome is the source of evil in the poem, and Meliboeus, like Diggon, has been dispossessed. Spenser's conclusion, in which Hobbinol invites Diggon to his cottage

—*There mayst thou lie in a vetchy bed*
Till fairer Fortune show forth her head—

is clearly taken from Tityrus' invitation to Meliboeus to take shelter with him for at any rate one night.

Both Mantuan and Virgil lie behind Spenser's poem, and we can't completely separate them as influences, since Mantuan had also read Virgil, and must have had the *Eclogues* in mind when he wrote. All the same, there is a difference, for they are different sorts of poem. Mantuan uses the metaphor of the shepherd because it is appropriate for discussing ecclesiastical abuses: priests are called pastors. Virgil uses it (it's not altogether metaphor for him, of course) because of the contrast between *silvestrem Musam* and the great city that the yokels gape at.

Verum haec tantum alias inter caput extulit urbes
quantum lenta solent inter viburna cupressi.

(but this town rears its head above others as far as the cypresses among the supple osiers.)

Mantuan, in short, is using pastoral as convention; Virgil, pastoral as theme.

Now in the September Eclogue itself there is an ambiguity that corresponds to this double influence. Where has Diggon Davie been? I have assumed it is to Rome, but there may be some disguise here that we have to penetrate. The argument, after mentioning 'a far country', goes on to speak of 'the loose living of Popish prelates': this certainly suggests Rome. But when he mentions the danger which these flocks run from wolves, Hobbinol replies that everyone knows there are no wolves in England today. This suggests Diggon has not been abroad, but to London; and the second half of the poem does seem to assume that the abuses he saw on his journey are no different from those at home; Roffynn, for instance, is obviously known to the stay-at-home Hobbinol.

Part of the explanation may be that Spenser wrote an attack on the Church of England, and either he or E. K. thought it prudent to cover up by pretending that it was an attack on the Papists. What concerns us, however, is not the explanation but the fact. If Diggon stayed in England, then Spenser like Mantuan was using pastoral as convention; if he went to Rome and the poem is about the exhausted countryman's return from court, appalled by what he saw, and relieved to be back with his flock and his simple friends, then the poem is a satire simply because it is a pastoral.

To put this distinction into terminology, we can speak of satiric pastoral and pastoral satire. In a satiric pastoral—like Mantuan's —the speakers are shepherds, and there are all the obvious features of the form. Yet because the purpose is so different, this formal adherence may only be superficial: the poet's true interest will be in the church, or in politics. A pastoral satire, on the other hand, may look formally quite unlike an eclogue (some of the examples later in this essay have never been called pastorals), yet the similarity of attitude may be so important as to tell us (essentially) what the work is about. Indeed, the similarity may amount to identity: when the pastoral poet comes to court, he automatically becomes a satirist.

Spenser described his visit to court in *Colin Clout's Come Home Again*. It is a thinly allegorical version of his trip to London and his return to Ireland in 1591. Most of the poem consists of an account of the splendours of 'Cynthia's' court. Spenser's friendship with Raleigh prompted an account of the Shepherd of the Queen; his professional interests prompted a description of the poets he had met there (Harpalus, Corydon, Alcyon—good guessing ground for scholars, with no answers); and there is the usual praise of Queen Elizabeth:

> *Until that we to Cynthia's presence came:*
> *Whose glory greater than my simple thought,*
> *I found much greater than the former fame;*
> *Such greatness I cannot compare to ought:*
> *But if I her like ought on earth might read,*
> *I would her liken to a crown of lilies,*
> *Upon a virgin bride's adorned head,*
> *With roses dight and golds and daffodillies.*
>
> 332-339

If Cynthia is like that, how wonderful a court must be that is filled with her influence. A long passage describes the other 'ornaments of womankind' whom he met there; and so, not surprisingly,

his rural friends ask him why, if the court is so splendid, he ever
left it:

> *since thou foundst such grace*
> *With Cynthia and all her noble crew;*
> *Why didst thou ever leave that happy place,*
> *In which such wealth might unto thee accrue;*
> *And back return unto this barren soil,*
> *Where cold and care and penury do dwell?*
>
> 652-657

And now the poem changes startlingly. Now we are told about the
enormities of court, and how horrified a simple swain like him felt
at what he saw.

> *For, sooth to say, it is no sort of life,*
> *For shepheard fit to lead in that same place,*
> *Where each one seeks with malice, and with strife,*
> *To thrust down other into foul disgrace,*
> *Himself to raise.*   688-692

As well as ambition, there is calumny and betrayal:

> *Either by slandering his well-deemed name,*
> *Through leasings lewd and fained forgery;*
> *Or else by breeding him some blot of blame,*
> *By creeping close into his secrecy. . . .*
>
> 695-698

—as well as extravagance and boasting:

> *For each man's worth is measured by his weed,*
> *As harts by horns, or asses by their ears. . . .*
>
> 711-712

—and vanity and folly:

> *So they themselves for praise of fools do sell,*
> *And all their wealth for painting on a wall;*
> *With price whereof they buy a golden bell,*
> *And purchase highest rowmes in bower and hall.*

In contrast to these sophisticated evils

> *Single Truth and simple Honesty*
> *Do wander up and down despised of all.*
>
> 723-728

The inconsistency is obvious, and cannot be justified. There is no internal reason for it, we simply have a poem that retraces its steps. But if we look at the poet in his situation, it is very easy to explain; for we are seeing the tension between a literary and a social pressure. The social pressure was to make a career at court, if possible with the patronage of the Queen herself, if not, with that of some nobleman. This entailed accepting the social tone of the court, and its position in the culture; and it probably entailed flattering the Queen personally. The literary pressure was—as it always is—to use the dominant conventions, which included pastoral. As long as pastoral was only a convention, this did not matter; but as soon as the theme of court *v.* country appeared, an inconsistency had to follow. The court of Queen Elizabeth had to be seen as both glorious and corrupt. I know of no poem which shows this as blatantly as *Colin Clout's Come Home Again.*

Simple sociological theories of literature take a blow from this sort of case. If literary forms reflect the structure of their society, then the history of pastoral is incomprehensible. An urban form, it declined when urbanisation was reaching an unprecedented intensity; a rejection of court, it flourished in the heyday of absolute monarchy.

The last point does, of course, make some sociological sense if we use a less simple theory. An age when all culture is centred on the court is perhaps just the age when we should expect the pastoral dream to arise, a symbolic rejection of so much that the poet was forced to accept. If the result is mere contradiction, as in *Colin Clout,* the poem breaks in two. If it is a genuine tension, poetic power can be engendered. This is the case in *The Faerie Queene.*

II

One way—one of the many, many ways—in which *The Catcher in the Rye* has been discussed has been to ask what literary genre it belongs to. The usual answer is the child-hero- or adolescent-hero-novel, a sub-category of modern American fiction. A genre like this is of course *post factum.* No modern American novelist—or not many, and no good one—has set out to write a child-hero-novel in the deliberate way a Renaissance poet set out to write epic, knowing that it was expected of him, knowing the rules, measuring himself against accepted models. What we have instead

is a genre that has arisen because critics have noticed that a number
of books have children as heroes.

In a way, these are the best literary categories. European literature is littered with the brittle results of prescriptive criticism, and
there is much to be said for the critic who issues no orders, but waits
humbly to see what the writers have done. But though this may be
good for literature, it is too modest a task to produce the best
criticism: such categories are, after all, tautological. All we learn
from the classification is that the hero is a child, which we knew
already. It seems worth while to classify otherwise, perhaps in ways
the author himself had not thought of. If we extrapolate outwards
from the book's attitudes towards a literary form it has not
actually assumed, we may if we are lucky learn something central
about what it is doing. That, at any rate, must be my justification
for calling *The Catcher in the Rye* a pastoral satire.

It is obviously a satire. Holden cannot adjust to his society, and,
is not sure that he wants to. He looks at Pency Prep, at the boys
and the teachers and the parents, he looks at the Edmond Hotel,
at the Radio City Show, at Carl Luce, at almost everyone he meets,
and he finds them all phoney. He is the malcontent, who can leave
nothing alone, who picks at it sourly because he is maladjusted—
and who for this very reason is often right.

What kind of satirist is Holden? In the first place, a very inarticulate one. He is constantly offended by the coarseness of his environment, yet his vocabulary is as clumsy as what he is attacking:

> Then he said, 'I had the privilege of meeting your mother and
> dad when they had their little chat with Dr Thurmer some
> weeks ago. They're grand people.'
> 'Yes they are. They're very nice.'
> Grand. There's a word I really hate. It's a phoney. I could
> puke every time I hear it.   ch. 2

The terminology here could easily be reversed. Mr Spencer might
have said 'They're very nice people,' and Holden replied, 'Yes they
are. They're grand.' Then the last comment would have begun
'Nice. There's a word I really hate . . .' and nobody would have
known the difference. It seems a mere accident which word Holden
used, and which one he hated. Yet here as so often, Holden has
a point: Mr Spencer is being phoney, and where will it show if not
in his vocabulary? He might equally well—perhaps better—have

136

complained of 'had the privilege', especially in combination with 'little chat'—the formal gliding into the pseudo-friendly. Holden knows what Mr Spencer is like, all right.

It is one of the central paradoxes of *The Catcher* that Holden is and isn't part of the world he hates. Rejecting, passionately and shrewdly, the sophisticated adolescence of rich and kitsch New York, he has nowhere else to turn for his weapons when he flays it. He is even more inarticulate than Huckleberry Finn. Mark Twain had the same idea—a young man who could see through the society he still belonged to; but it needed more courage to deploy the inarticulateness of real speech in 1884 than in 1951, and so Huck's language is sometimes tempered, as Holden's never is.

> What really knocks me out is a book that, when you're all done reading it, you wish the author that wrote it was a terrific friend of yours and you could call him up on the phone whenever you felt like it. . . . You take that book *Of Human Bondage*, by Somerset Maugham, though. I read it last summer. It's a pretty good book and all, but I wouldn't want to call Somerset Maugham up. I don't know. He just isn't the kind of a guy I'd want to call up, that's all. I'd rather call old Thomas Hardy up. I like that Eustacia Vye. ch. 3

No teacher could give high marks for this, but it is the voice of a man of sensibility. The same shrewd eye that saw Mr Spencer picking his nose or Mrs Morrow making herself conspicuous in the train has seen the difference between Hardy's integrity and Maugham's competence. Yet he has no vocabulary to make his point with: 'he just isn't the kind of guy I'd want to call up, that's all'. *That's all*: this is a half-defiant admission that he has not really been able to make the point, and it too is inarticulate. Holden's language is a blunt instrument that he uses for precision tooling.

Because Holden is completely formed by the world he has grown to hate, the question so many critics have asked—is he society's judge or its victim?—is unanswerable. He is both. The question is a useful one, but only if we see that it is unanswerable.

I have called Holden a malcontent. We could also call him the wise fool, unable to hold his own in a tough world, yet for this very reason, able to see through its pretensions. Just as Lear's fool, who knows which side his bread is buttered ('Let go thy hold when a great wheel runs down a hill, lest it break thy neck with following') can do nothing but whimper for help when he is on the heath, so

Holden, who can see through and despise the sophistications of Carl Luce's sexual competence ('I like a mature person if that's what you mean. Certainly') is reduced to a figure of farce when the prostitute visits him. There are even one or two hints that Holden's judgement of society, as that of a fool should be, has a religious dimension:

> They had this Christmas thing they have at Radio City every year. All these angels start coming out of the boxes and everywhere, guys carrying crucifixes and stuff all over the place, and the whole bunch of them—thousands of them—singing 'Come all Ye Faithful' like mad. Big deal. . . . I saw it with old Sally Hayes the year before, and she kept saying how beautiful it was, the costumes and all. I said old Jesus probably would've puked if He could see it—all those fancy costumes and all. Sally said I was a sacrilegious atheist. I probably am.
>
> ch. 18

This is very tactfully done. Holden only mentioned Jesus in the first place because it was a Christmas show. He is embarrassed to use a religious standard; he hasn't the courage of his insight, and he thinks apologetically that the Grand Inquisitor really does represent religion. Yet it is left to us, if we wish, to agree that Jesus would have puked—though that might embarrass Holden even more. I admire this tact particularly when I think of what has happened to Salinger since, how grossly, in his descriptions of Seymour Glass, he thrusts the religious significance on to us.

Holden then is a satirist, or at least the mouthpiece of satire. To call it pastoral satire is to direct attention to the criterion against which New York and Pency Prep are judged, which is quite clearly—indeed explicitly—pastoral. Here a rather long quotation is needed.

> Then, all of a sudden, I got this idea.
> 'Look,' I said. 'Here's my idea. How would you like to get the hell out of here? Here's my idea. I know this guy down in Greenwich Village that we can borrow his car for a couple of weeks. He used to go to the same school I did and he still owes me ten bucks. What we could do is, tomorrow morning we could drive up to Massachusetts and Vermont, and all around there, see. It's beautiful as hell up there. It really is.' I was getting excited as hell, the more I thought about it, and I sort of reached over and took old Sally's goddam hand. What a goddam *fool*

I was. 'No kidding,' I said. 'I have about a hundred and eighty bucks in the bank. I can take it out when it opens in the morning, and then I could go down and get this guy's car. No kidding. We'll stay in these cabin camps and stuff like that till the dough runs out. Then, when the dough runs out, I could get a job somewhere and we could live somewhere with a brook and all, and, later on, we could get married or something. I could chop all our own wood in the winter-time and all. Honest to God, we could have a terrific time! Wuddaya say? C'mon! Wuddaya say? Will you do it with me? Please.'

'You can't just *do* something like that,' old Sally said. She sounded sore as hell.

'Why not? Why the hell not?'

'Stop screaming at me, please,' she said. Which was crap, because I wasn't even screaming at her.

'Why cantcha? Why not?'

'Because you can't, that's all. In the first place, we're both practically *children*. And did you ever stop to think what you'd do if you *didn't* get a job when your money ran out? We'd *starve* to death. The whole thing's so fantastic it isn't even—'

'It isn't fantastic. I'd get a job. Don't worry about that. You don't have to worry about that. What's the matter? Don't you want to go with me? *Say* so, if you don't.'

'It isn't *that*. It isn't that at all,' old Sally said. I was beginning to hate her, in a way. 'We'll have oodles of time to do those things—all those things. I mean after you go to college and all, and if we should get married and all. There'll be oodles of marvellous places to go to. You're just—'

'No, there wouldn't be. There wouldn't be oodles of places to go to at all. It'd be entirely different,' I said. I was getting depressed as hell again.

'What?' she said. 'I can't hear you. One minute you scream at me, and the next you—'

'I said no, there wouldn't be marvellous places to go to after I went to college and all. Open your ears. It'd be entirely different. We'd have to go downstairs in elevators with suitcases and stuff. We'd have to phone up everybody and tell 'em goodbye and send 'em postcards from hotels and all. And I'd be working in some office, making a lot of dough, and riding to work in cabs and Madison Avenue buses, and reading newspapers, and playing bridge all the time, and going to the movies and seeing a lot of stupid shorts and coming attractions and

newsreels. . . . It wouldn't be the same at all. You don't see what
I mean at all.'   ch. 17

These cabin camps are not in Vermont at all, but in Arcadia.
Holden knows this, rather uneasily, but he will not quite admit it.
He talks about how to get there, and how to live there, as if it was
a practical question he could deal with, yet his practical suggestions
are too vague even to convince himself with. Later in the book he
has the same pastoral vision, this time to himself alone, when walking down Fifth Avenue. He sits down on a bench and wonders what
to do; and he decides to go hitch-hiking out west. When he gets far
enough he'll take a job at a filling station, 'putting gas and oil in
people's cars. I didn't care what kind of job it was, though. Just so
people didn't know me, and I didn't know anybody.' He will
pretend to be a deaf-mute. He will build himself a cabin, and if he
wants to get married 'or something' he'll meet 'this beautiful girl
that was also a deaf-mute'. If they have children, they'll hide them
away somewhere.

It does not matter that there is a petrol pump in this Arcadia,
instead of a flock of sheep. Sheep and petrol may not have the
same relation to the urban economy (though emotionally they may
not be so far apart: Proust found petrol the most haunting of all
the rural odours); but Holden is here expressing the longing to find
an occupation that will allow him, like Daphnis and Tityrus, to
dwell at ease among the woods. He won't, alas, be able to *formosam
resonare doces Amaryllida silvas*, since he's going to act deaf-mute;
but the price seems to him worth while, in order to reject the
sophisticated world completely.

Holden admits, this time, that the sunny place out west is unattainable. 'You can never find a place that's nice and peaceful,'
he says, five pages later, 'because there isn't any.' Somebody will
always write '—you' where Phoebe can see it. Sally Hayes had
known this all the time. She was angry, because Holden made a
category mistake. He thought you could get to Arcadia by car—
and then was so obviously incompetent about getting the car.
Sally is a realist: she accepts society and wants it to accept her,
she knows that among its many gifts to the conforming is the right
to escape every now and then. There's no need to rush things. But
holidays are not what Holden wants: the suitcases and the postcards are signs that you have not rejected court, simply gone away

for a while. The Duke has to lose his dukedom to enter Arden, and Sally wants to get back to the cabs and the newsreels when the weekend is over.

If we ask who is right in this argument, we have to say that of course Sally is right: her shrewdest remark, though she doesn't realise how shrewd, is 'You can't just *do* something like that'. But this sentence has a shadow side, of which she is quite unaware: you can't just *do* it, you can dream it—and dreaming goes deeper than doing. To know that Arcadia is a fiction is to be an integrated courtier, but to possess the Arcadian dream is to see the court for what it is.

Holden possesses the dream, and in the most important moment of the book it comes to the surface, explicitly, as a dream. Perhaps even in this conversation he had an inkling of what he was offering. 'We could live somewhere with a brook and all, and, later on, we could get married or something.' When Sally says marriage, there is no 'or something' in her mind; just as she knows what a stream is, even though she doesn't care for them. Holden is only clumsily able to describe Arcadian love, and he has an uneasy awareness that he has got it all from books. 'A brook and all'—Holden's embarrassment is Salinger's tactful hint that the poor lad doesn't know what he is talking about. In Vermont there are streams: no doubt Sally will swim in them, or her husband fish. In Arcadia there are only brooks.

Even Phoebe thinks in terms of practical arrangements. 'Name something you'd like to be,' she says to Holden with the irritation of love. 'Like a scientist. Or a lawyer or something.' Holden can't answer a question like that: unless the 'one psychoanalyst guy' at the end of the book succeeds in doing something with him, he'll never be anything. That is, he'll never qualify or practise or follow a profession. The idiom that refers to a man's profession as what he *is* accepts a total identification between a man and his social role. This is what Holden cannot do, and when eventually he does answer Phoebe he describes not a profession but a dream. Perhaps he understands the meaning of 'is' better than she does:

> I wasn't listening, though. I was thinking about something else—something crazy. 'You know what I'd like to be? I mean if I had my goddam choice?'
> 'What? Stop swearing.'
> 'You know that song "If a body catch a body comin' through

the rye . . ." I keep picturing all these little kids playing some game in this big field of rye and all. Thousands of little kids, and nobody's around—nobody big, I mean—except me. And I'm standing on the edge of some crazy cliff. What I have to do, I have to catch everybody if they start to go over the cliff —I mean if they're running and they don't look where they're going I have to come out from somewhere and *catch* them. That's all I'd do all day. I'd just be the catcher in the rye and all. I know it's crazy, but that's the only thing I'd really like to be. I know it's crazy.'

Old Phoebe didn't say anything for a long time. Then when she said something, all she said was, 'Daddy's going to kill you'. ch. 22

Phoebe has accepted his vision: her long silence, followed by changing the subject, tells us this. But by changing the subject she tells him that this vision won't help, that in practical life he has still made a mess of everything.

As for the vision itself; there aren't even any sheep to look after, simply an open field and a carefree life. It is the extreme of idyllic idleness, complicated (indeed enriched) by the presence of the dreamer in his dream. The fact that the catcher is present symbolises the fact that it is all an illusion, a mediated vision; and what he has to do is keep the children in Arcadia.

A few critics have suggested that the crazy cliff is growing up, and that what Holden wants is to keep the kids in the field which is childhood. Psychologically, this is surely right. Holden is himself finding it so painful to grow up because he dislikes what he is meant to grow up into. Yet he is seventeen, and childhood is no longer available. His way of helping others (and he wants to do this, for he is a saintly as well as a wise fool) is to protect them from the same fate. If he comes as a protector, he will have an excuse to re-enter the field of rye, the only big person around. In another sense too this explanation seems correct: the very idea of the idyllic, so touchingly figured by this image, may be equated with childhood, and quite apart from Holden and his situation, we may say that the children are so carefree in the rye because they are children, and that the field must therefore be threatened, simply because childhood is temporary.

Yet both these remarks are psychological explanations, not, in the strict sense, literary interpretations. I don't believe the idea of growing up actually forms part of the image. Holden does after all say 'if they're running and don't look where they're going', which seems to suggest that falling over the cliff is not inevitable. Arcadia has always a double threat, sudden and arbitrary (the wanton troopers riding by may shoot the fawn) and gradual (had the fawn lived, it might have been like Sylvio), and this looks more like the former. What is essential to the image is simply that the children, for whatever reason, are in danger, and that Holden feels he has to protect them. In his dream, he is not sure that he will fail.

By taking his title from this passage, Salinger has shown how important it is. It is Holden's one positive moment of true self-expression. Most of the book is negative: Holden's bewildered attempt to cleanse the foul body of th'infected world. We have looked at the two occasions when he tried to set a positive alternative against this infected world, and seen that he made the mistake of situating them in reality, in Vermont or out west. In this passage he sees the truth: that what he wants to be can be perceived only in dream. A few hypercritics have accused the dream of softness, and found the passage sentimental in comparison with the astringent satire of the rest. I find them wrong, and am moved by the passage: but even if they were right, I could not blame Salinger for it. The dream is the basis of the satire: we needed to be shown Arcadia.

III

Nathaniel West's brilliant short novel *Miss Lonelyhearts* tells the story of a journalist who finds himself writing the advice column in a New York newspaper. The crude embarrassing suffering in the readers' letters finally becomes unbearable to him, and though he had begun the assignment cynically, 'he could not go on finding the same joke funny thirty times a day for months on end'. The book shows his neurotic disintegration, his struggle to accept a religious solution, and his final ironic death.

Though it is hard to imagine a bigger contrast in style, this book has much in common with *The Catcher in the Rye*. Both have a hero who is corrupted by, and trying to reject, the urban American world of advertising, snobbery and kitsch. It is hard to say which of them is more deeply corrupted: 'Miss Lonelyhearts' is older and therefore sicker, but has retained a vision of hatred to unleash on his own degradation, whereas Holden has lost the very weapons of invective, so much is he a part of the culture he hates.

From what standpoint does Miss Lonelyhearts see and judge his world? He never finds one, and the book is his futile, threshing quest. He cannot fully accept religion as a standard, for he is not proof enough against the contempt of his boss, Shrike, who refers to Christ as 'Miss Lonelyhearts of Miss Lonelyhearts'; the gibe has too much truth for him to shake it off. But there is only one other cure for him, and this is even less successful—his love for Betty, his goodhearted simple-minded girl friend. Betty is quite clear what is wrong with him:

> She told him about her childhood on a farm and of her love for animals, about country sounds and country smells and of how fresh and clean everything in the country is. She said that he ought to live there and that if he did, he would find that all his troubles were city troubles.

And Miss Lonelyhearts had already had one vision that suggests the same diagnosis as Betty's. Sitting in the speakeasy, he found himself remembering an incident of childhood:

> One winter evening, he had been waiting with his little sister for their father to come home from church. She was eight years old then, and he was twelve. Made sad by the pause between playing and eating, he had gone to the piano and begun a piece by Mozart. It was the first time he had ever voluntarily gone to the piano. His sister left her picture book to dance to his music. She had never danced before. She danced gravely and carefully, a simple dance yet formal. . . . As Miss Lonelyhearts stood at the bar, swaying slightly to the remembered music, he thought of children dancing. Square replacing oblong and being replaced by circle. Every child, everywhere; in the whole world there was not one child who was not gravely, sweetly dancing.

This is very close to Holden's rye field. The link between his own childhood and this vision of children is quite explicit: the passage starts as a memory, and goes on as a dream. So is the fact that this happiness is there as a contrast to his actual world: a moment later he accidentally collides with a man holding a glass of beer who, because he is real and adult, punches Miss Lonelyhearts in the mouth.

Unlike Holden, Miss Lonelyhearts actually goes to Arcadia, in the chapter called 'Miss Lonelyhearts in the country'. He and Betty go down to the farm in Connecticut where she was born, and live in idyllic solitude for a few days. The idyll is streaked with irony (the local at the Aw-Kum-On Garage tells them about the deer, and adds 'it wasn't the hunters who drove out the deer but the yids'), but at its heart it seems healthy. In Arcadia, Betty and he succeed in shedding the fumblings of city sex, and consummate their love on the grass. But none of it lasts: the moment they return to the city 'Miss Lonelyhearts knew that Betty had failed to cure him'. Further, he is glad of this, 'because he had begun to think himself a faker and a fool'. That is a truly bitter moment: the rejection of the pastoral standard. Miss Lonelyhearts is so corrupted by court, that he doesn't *want* to be able to dismiss his troubles as city troubles: he will lose too much of what has become his actual self.

> Prodded by his conscience, he began to generalise. Men have always fought their misery with dreams. Although dreams were once powerful, they have been made puerile by the movies, radio and newspapers. Among many betrayals, this one is the worst.

Miss Lonelyhearts, trying to be a pastoral satire, has to abandon the attempt: its standard of judgement is cut from beneath it. The ironic details in the idyll (they drank gin just before their love-making) were, we realise, essential. West had to make his hero sure of nothing: returning to the city he not only finds the dream deserting him, he finds it losing its truth as dream. It is a bitterer book than *The Catcher*.

IV

I have claimed that when the pastoralist goes to court he automatically becomes a satirist. A simple effect in *As You Like It* is based on this. It takes a good while for Rosalind and Celia to get to the Forest of Arden: and all theatre-goers are familiar with the feeling of delighted relief that their arrival brings. Once in Arden, we stay there—except for one brief scene. The return to Duke Frederick's Court in III.i is startlingly effective theatrically, for it is a reminder of what we have escaped from.

Duke F: ... Thy lands and all things that thou dost call thine
    Worth seizure, do we seize into our hands
    Till thou canst quit thee by thy brother's mouth
    Of what we think against thee.
Oliver: O that your highness knew my heart in this.
    I never loved my brother in my life.
Duke F: More villain thou. Well, push him out of doors.

The last line never fails to draw a laugh—or, better still, a gasp. Villainy has at any rate this usefulness, that it can smell villainy out, and destroy it in others. The brevity of this scene is part of its sharp, cutting effect. Just for a moment, we need a reminder of what the court is like: then we can be taken back to Arden. I have seen a production in which this scene was transposed, and given earlier, before Rosalind, Celia and Orlando are safely in Arden. This may have obvious conveniences for scene shifting—though not, of course, at the Globe, and not, as it happens, in this production either, which was in a very well-equipped theatre—but dramatically the loss is enormous. It is because we have been breathing the air of Arden that we gasp at this reminder of corruption.

If the pastoral poet is implicitly a satirist, is the reverse true? Is there a pastoralist locked up in every satirist, waiting only for a breath of country air to step out and announce himself? It seems rash to say yes: to claim satire as a by-product of pastoral is to erect an almost lunatic theory of *genres*. Yet there is a kind of truth in the claim none the less. Consistent satire—attacking the same institution for the same faults—must imply a contrasting standard of judgement; and since the satirist traditionally denounces the sophisticated vices—corruption, cheating, lying, sexual excesses or perversions, elaborate dishonesty—this standard will have a lot in common with the pastoral ideal. Much of the greatest satire, of course, like Swift's, is not consistent: we need as an example a work whose brilliance lies in its narrow emotional range, a work which anatomises corruption with unremitting fierceness.

The Revenger's Tragedy is such a work. Except for the opening, and the two scenes with Vindice's mother and sister, it is entirely set at court. Vindice establishes himself as a malcontent chorus before the action begins. Disguising himself as Piato, he deliberately enters the world of the corrupt court in order to clean it up; and he can only do this by being corrupted himself. His disguise is more

than a disguise: determining all his actions, it becomes a persona—
that is, not something put on externally, but the use as a mask of
something which is part of himself. We identify with Vindice's
vengeful passion, but we have also to be shown that it belongs to
the world he is destroying. 'We die after a nest of Dukes, adieu':
this superb line is really the play's climax: in it Vindice asserts
that he both does and does not belong to the court. If he belonged
completely he could not destroy it; if he was quite free of it he
could survive—but then he could not have destroyed it either.

Since Vindice's initial entry into the play was his decision to
come to court, it is natural for him to say 'let blushes dwell i' th'
country'. A pastoral standard is automatically implied. When he
is later introduced to Lussurioso under his real name, he greets
him in dialect: 'How don you? Gi' ye good den.' Lussurioso is
amused:

> *We thank thee.*
> *How strange such a coarse homely salute*
> *Shows in the place, where we greet in fire,*
> *Nimble and desperate tongues! Should we name*
> *God in a salutation, 'twould ne'er be stood on.*
>
> IV.ii.44

The amusement remarks, first that the court is not coarse and
homely; then, that it is not religious. Now there can be no doubt
that Tourneur was more interested in the second of these: his
rejection of sophistication is that of *contemptus mundi*, not that of
the simple rural swain. What touches of pastoral, therefore, we
find suggested can be attributed not to the author's interest but
to the form itself.

In the course of the action Vindice escapes from court once.
By a typical Elizabethan irony, absurd and brilliantly powerful,
he is employed by the Duke to seduce his own sister. He takes
convenient advantage of the Elizabethan convention that disguise
is impenetrable, and sets out, as Piato, to do this in order to test
her. Though he succeeds in corrupting his mother, his sister Castiza
resists, and he drops the disguise to praise her and threaten his
mother, till eventually she repents. Pastoral and religious implications mingle in these two scenes. The contempt for honesty is cast
in social terms:

And't has a good report, prettily commended,
But pray, by whom? Poor people, ignorant people;
The better sort, I'm sure, cannot abide it.
And by what rule should we square out our lives,
But by our betters' actions.   II.i.146

This is Touchstone's use of the term, when he refers to himself as 'thy better, sirrah', speaking to the rustic clown. But though the immediate undertone of moral rejection is pastoral (country folk, says the irony, are morally better than their 'betters'), the ultimate scheme of values is religious. 'Poor people, ignorant people' is not simply a social irony, it is an echo of New Testament language.

I don't therefore want to exaggerate the point. There isn't much pastoral imagery in the scenes with Castiza and Gratiana, but they give us the feel of a pastoral contrast. To this extent, *The Revenger's Tragedy* is a mirror image of *As You Like It*. Shakespeare takes us to Arden after a preliminary visit to court, and a brief reminder of it later; Tourneur takes us to court after a preliminary glance, and offers a short escape for contrast. The result is two utterly different plays: one delights, and one disgusts. But by attending, in each case, to the contrasting episode, we can see the continuity between them, and the fact that they assert the same preference.

This preference is the essential element in pastoral. It finds the winter wind less unkind than friends' ingratitude, the penalty of Adam preferable to flattery. This means it automatically has one face to praise rural delights, another face of satire.

PART II

SOME ARCADIANS

VII

SIR CALIDORE'S HOLIDAY

SPENSER made his bow as a pastoral poet; he never lost his taste for pastoral; and he lives in his readers' affections much more as the poet of 'Sweet Thames run softly', of 'The woods shall answer and your echo ring', than as the sophisticated allegorist. It is not therefore absurd or trivial to write about pastoral in *The Faerie Queene.*

Yet it is, in the literal sense of the word, eccentric. For we shall not find pastoral in the centre of this vast poem, but only in the corners. The moral centre of *The Faerie Queene* is the court of Gloriana, and Book XII would no doubt have shown it to be the structural centre as well. Above all, this ought to be true of Book VI, whose central virtue is actually named after the court.

> *Of Court, it seems, men Courtesy do call,*
> *For that it there most useth to abound;*
> *And well beseemeth that in Princes' hall*
> *That virtue should be plentifully found,*
> *Which of all goodly manners is the ground,*
> *And root of civil conversation.*

VI.i.1

Virtue, we see, depends on civilisation, and is found in Princes' hall: exactly the opposite view to the Duke Senior's. If he has to choose between courtesy and the pastoral preference, the epic poet cannot hesitate. Heroic poetry offers us action of vast scope, and a universal standard of value. To hold up an ideal of conduct to the world, it needs a moral centre—the court of Gloriana or of God, the hut of Agamemnon, the grandeur of a Rome risen from the ashes of Troy. No epic hero can be disillusioned with court, or can say

> *How much . . . more happy is the state*
> *In which ye, father, here do dwell at ease,*
> *Leading a life so free and fortunate,*
> *From all the tempests of these worldly seas,*
> *Which toss the rest in dangerous disease.*

VI.ix.19

This is Calidore's enthusiastic response to the pastoral quiet he finds with Meliboe—who, it turns out, had once been a courtier, but disillusioned with 'the world's gay shows' returned to the country:

> *Tho, back returning to my sheep againe,*
> *I from thenceforth have learn'd to love more deare*
> *This lowly quiet life which I inherit here.*

VI.ix.25

Meliboe can do this for he is a minor character whom the poem can spare (perhaps the only wholly virtuous character who is killed); but if Calidore does it, he is abandoning his quest. He ought to be hunting the Blatant Beast, not resting his bark which hath been beaten late, and as long as he stays among the shepherds he is neglecting the larger duties laid on him from the centre of the poem.

Pastoral can never be more than an interlude, a *locus amoenus*, in an epic: it flees the centre that the epic poet seeks, and casts doubts on the value of heroic action. On several occasions in *The Faerie Queene* the action pauses and we are led into a pastoral idyll: for instance, Una's sojourn among the satyrs in Book I, canto vi. Una is struggling in the grip of Sansloy when her cries bring a troop of fauns and satyrs, 'rude, misshapen, monstrous rabblement', who frighten him off. At first she is terrified of her rescuers, but her beauty and her distress soon awe them to submission, and falling prostrate they 'Do kiss her feet and faun on her with count'nance fain'. For a few idyllic stanzas she stays among them as their queen, but she knows that she doesn't belong there. Both her longing and her duty make her want to escape and go to the help of the Red-cross Knight, and so she persuades Satyrane (who is half-human, half-satyr) to help her. The episode is an interlude: its pastoral charm does not threaten the main story. And the poem's attitude towards the 'satyr nation' is curiously half-committed. They have a natural feeling for the good, and their reverence for Una contrasts very finely with the brutality of Sansloy; yet their natural goodness is naïve and even idolatrous, for they tried to worship her

> *And made her th' Image of Idolatries;*
> *But when their bootless zeale she did restrain*
> *From her own worship, they her Ass would worship fain.*

I.vi.10

Their devotion is excessive because the light of nature in them is untutored; and even their true light does not shine with a radical pastoral message, for it shows them their own inferiority. The goodness of a savage nation consists in their ability to know their place: Spenser's opinion of them is like Prospero's of Caliban, that they should recognise the virtue of the sophisticated, and in return they will be taught. When Satyrane finds Una she is

> *Teaching the Satyrs, which her sat around,*
> *True sacred lore, which from her sweet lips did redound,*
>
> I.vi.30

as Caliban was taught to endow his purposes with words by Prospero or (if we are to leave the Folio unamended and so make the parallel even closer) by Miranda. The story of Satyrane, and the story of the Salvage Man in Book VI, cantos iv and v, have the same moral. Satyrane is only half-satyr—his mother was human—but he was born out of wedlock and in the woods (a natural son in every sense), and was taught by his father to touch lions, to tear whelps from the bear, and to ride bulls. This is not the tamed nature of gardens, nor even the chilly but benevolent nature of the Forest of Arden, but a wild life that terrifies Satyrane's mother when she comes to see him. She finds him fleeing a lioness, clutching its cubs, and when she can summon the courage not to run away she begs him to 'leave off this dreadful play'. Satyrane is wild but not evil, as his origin was lawless but, in its primitivist way, attractive:

> *Till that with timely fruit her belly swelled,*
> *And bore a boy unto that salvage sire: . . . .*
> *Whom, till to riper years he gan aspire,*
> *He nousled up in life and manners wild,*
> *Amongst wild beasts and woods, from laws of men exiled.*
>
> I.vi.23

To be successful, Satyrane's history should be presented free of moralising—certainly free of moral terms whose basis is courtly and anti-pastoral. It is unfortunate, poetically, that Satyrane's father, when he captured Thyamis, 'the loyal links of wedlock did unbind'; every censure of the bastardy undermines the rugged but healthy primitivism that Satyrane represents. It is not easy to be sure how far Spenser has offended here. He tells us that the satyr had 'coals of lust in brutish eye', that he made Thyamis 'thrall unto his beastly kind', and 'captive to his sensual desire'. Brutish, beastly, sensual: if we surround these words with their natural modern overtones they sound like terms of censure, and it would be nice to be able to say that their content for Spenser was simply primitivism, implying no judgement. On such matters the Oxford Dictionary is no help. Of course 'beastly' can carry a judgement: it depends how the poem has led us to feel about beasts. We must move from context to word, and if the poem implies no censure, then 'what beasts do' need not be a pejorative idea.

When Satyrane meets Una he is already half-tamed: he is 'a noble warlike knight', already renowned through all Fairyland for 'strange adventures'—which seems to mean the same kind of adventures as other knights have—but with his heart in the woods still:

> *Yet evermore it was his manner fair,*
> *After long labours and adventures spent,*
> *Unto those native woods for to repair,*
> *To see his sire and offspring ancient.*

I.vi.30

When Una begins to instruct him, she tames him still further; and during the rest of his adventures he is known as Sir Satyrane, and he saves maidens, kills pagans and behaves like any other well brought-up knight. A pastoral figure has been integrated into the main action.

The same thing happens in Book VI. Sir Calidore's sojourn with Meliboe and his daughter Pastorella is the longest and finest pastoral passage in the poem; and in the end, it is not treated as a digression. Either Spenser (like Calidore) fell in love with Pastorella, and could not bear to abandon her when he returned to the main action, or else he intended from the beginning to promote her from pastoral to epic status. Whatever the reason, the result is clear. Material from the pastoral interludes can only rejoin the main action if it loses its special identity. The Pastorella of canto XII might as well have grown up with all the best teachers in castle or palace. In fact she almost did: it is no surprise when she turns out to be the long-lost daughter of Sir Bellamour and the Lady Claribell.

But the influence of epic on pastoral is subtler and more destructive still, for it works within the idyllic episodes themselves. When Calidore is among the shepherds he has to lay aside his 'knightly service' for 'shepherd's weed', but it is a change that Spenser finds it hard really to believe in. Calidore may change his clothes, but he can't lay aside his courtesy and polish, and it is these that win Pastorella in the end:

> *Thus did the gentle knight himself abear*
> *Amongst that rustic rout in all his deeds,*
> *That even they, the which his rivals were,*
> *Could not malign him, but commend him needs;*
> *For courtesie amongst the rudest breeds*
> *Good will and favour.*   VI.ix.45

In the very act of praising her simple beauty he is the courtier still. When he first sees Pastorella she is 'y-clad in homely green that her own hands had dyed', but as the description of her simple rural charm proceeds it is more and more infiltrated by another kind of praise. The shepherds esteem her as 'their sovereign goddess', and the poem assures us, 'Though mean her lot, yet higher did her mind ascend'. Not surprising then that in the next stanza Sir Calidore praises her not because she is a country lass, but because she looks as if she isn't:

> *As that he in his mind her worthy deemed*
> *To be a Prince's Paragon esteemed.*
>   VI.ix.11

One amusing touch of false learning offers a neat example of this switch in values. When a tiger attacks Pastorella and her friends as they are gathering strawberries (for the natural history of Fairyland is splendidly impossible), Corydon, the true rustic, soon runs away; after Calidore has defeated the beast and struck off his head (even though 'he had no weapon'), Pastorella finally chooses him and rejects Corydon, now described as 'fit to keep sheep'! And what made Corydon flee?

> *Through cowherd fear he fled away as fast,*
> *Ne durst abide the danger of the end.*
>   VI.x.35

There is no truth in this etymology. Onions derives 'coward' from Old French 'couard', presumably a 'turn-tail'. But 'cowherd' is revealing: it provides, in the very heart of the pastoral digression, the most anti-pastoral touch in the whole poem.

Renaissance pastoral was constantly tugged towards the anti-pastoral. We can see it in Sannazaro, most clearly at the moment when the narrator, Selvaggio, reveals that he is of noble birth, and is a disappointed lover who has taken refuge in the countryside. His real name is not Selvaggio (a rustic fiction) but, ironically, Sincero. He thinks about the pleasures of his *deliciosa patria*, among these Arcadian solitudes in which (and now he grows condescending, even insulting)

> I can hardly believe that the beasts of the woodlands can dwell with any pleasure, to say nothing of young men nurtured in noble cities.   *Arcadia*, Prosa Settima

Shortly before, he had already betrayed something of this feeling. Debating with himself whether to commit suicide out of unrequited love, he ran over various ways of killing himself, but his soul grew timid *da non so che viltá sovrapresa*. He is ashamed of the cowardice because it degrades him socially (it is cowherdly)—a point which the recent American translator craftily emphasises by rendering *viltá* as 'peasantish sentiment'.

Carino replies to Sincero's lament by asking him to sing, and offers him in reward a pipe of elder wood, with which he'll later sing the loves of fauns and nymphs *con più alto stile*. And so, having fruitlessly spent 'his adolescence among the simple and rustic songs of peasants, he will pass his happy youth among the sounding trumpets of the greatest poets of the age'. His career, in fact, is going to follow that of Virgil. The Virgil-career was so widely accepted as the norm by Renaissance poets that the young man who wrote pastoral found it difficult to forget that he ought later to pass to a higher style; and if this awareness finds its way into the poems, then it will be clear that the retirement from the world of court is not being taken quite seriously.

I suggested in Chapter VI the nearest thing to an explanation that I can find: that the social assumptions and pressures of the poet, being those of a courtier, are liable to come to the surface and pull against the form. The pastoral digression, then, is tugged from within back to the centre of the poem. This sets up tensions, and they in turn pose a poetic problem.

What does a long and complex heroic poem do with subversive elements inside it? Viewed schematically, such elements naturally do harm: the poem cannot both seek and flee the centre of its values. But what undermines the scheme may enrich the poem, not only quantitatively (some individual fine passages) but also in some more organic sense. Spenser tries three times, in the course of Book VI, to show what this enriching relationship is.

The first and most explicit attempt comes in the first four stanzas of canto **x**. 'Who now does follow the foul Blatant Beast?' they ask. Calidore has abandoned his quest, and 'entrapt of love' is following Pastorella instead, setting his rest 'among the rustick sort'. Then Spenser defends him for this defection:

> *Ne certes mote he greatly blamed be*
> *From so high step to stoop unto so low;*
> *For who had tasted once (as oft did he)*
> *The happy peace which there doth overflow,*
> *And prov'd the perfect pleasures which do grow*
> *Amongst poor hinds, in hills, in woods, in dales,*
> *Would never more delight in painted show*
> *Of such false bliss, as there is set for stales*
> *T'entrap unwary fools in their eternal bales.*
>
> VI.x.3

Seen from the pastoral shelter, the court of Gloriana is full of 'painted show', of 'shadows vain of courtly favour' that cannot compare with 'the happy peace . . . amongst poor hinds.' It is a neat statement of the epic-pastoral contrast, but poetically it is surely a mistake. In apologising so explicitly for Calidore's defection, Spenser has drawn our attention to his own inconsistency, he is forced to denounce what the poem is about. This lands him, in the next stanza, in an amusing embarrassment. To undermine his own poem may be excusable, but to detract from his compliment to the Queen is too much for any Elizabethan; so in the midst of insisting that the sunshine of court, in comparison with the sight of Pastorella, makes courtiers 'look askew', he adds hurriedly:

> *Save only Gloriana's heavenly hue,*
> *To which what can compare?*

The trouble with these stanzas is of course that they are too explicit. If a contradiction in the poem's scheme can be valuable, it must be because what would be contradiction in discourse can be enrichment in poetry. When the contradiction is spelt out in rhymed discourse, as here, there is nothing specifically poetic about its use, and the whole passage reads as clumsily as a footnote.

The opening of canto xii is more successful. Again Spenser is apologising, and again he is too explicit:

> *For all that hitherto hath long delayd*
> *This gentle knight from sewing his first quest,*
> *Though out of course, yet hath not been missayd.*

VI.xii.2

But this time he has found an image for what he is doing:

> *Like as a ship, that through the Ocean wide*
> *Directs her course unto one certain coast,*
> *Is met of many a counter wind and tide,*
> *With which her winged speed is let and crossed,*
> *And she her self in stormy surges tossed:*
> *Yet, making many a borde and many a bay,*
> *Still winneth way, ne hath her compass lost:*
> *Right so it fares with me in this long way,*
> *Whose course is often stayed, yet never is astray.*

VI.xii.1

It is a happy image: its sense of effort and apparent misdirection is beautifully appropriate, and the verse mimes the shape of the argument very effectively. The first five lines are impeded and clogged with clause after clause like counter winds and tides; then the movement picks up and gathers speed triumphantly for two lines:

> *Yet, making many a borde and many a bay,*
> *Still winneth way, ne hath her compass lost.*

Out of the whole emerges a sense of an overriding purpose, and the image has offered not apology but conviction. Even the second stanza, which as we have seen grows explicit once more, is not a complete failure, for when it comes to its pivotal line

> *But now I come into my course again*

it draws upon the same image; and the otherwise weak metaphor of 'course', coming so soon after the previous stanza, retains enough genuine metaphoric quality to charge the line—even the stanza—with something more than statement.

All the same, it is only a local image. It does not inform the canto, or radiate much beyond itself, it merely does more appropriately what x.1-4 did clumsily. Nor perhaps does it work with the power of a symbol that conveys more than could be spelt out. To use C. S. Lewis' useful distinction, it is more a magistral than a pupillary comparison, conveying to us an idea that the author was already fully possessed of before he thought of the image. This cannot be said of the third and most extended attempt to bring the pastoral and the courtly together, the vision of Calidore on Mount Acidale. Here we have a symbol that says far more than any commentary can spell out; that corresponds marvellously to the relation between court and country without ever mentioning them; and that turns a schematic difficulty into poetic enrichment because it uses it for pure poetic purposes. In looking at this passage we shall not merely be noticing the relationship between pastoral and epic; we shall be seeing the full possibilities of pastoral itself, in the hands of a learned poet, and also the greater richness and scope of *The Faerie Queene* in comparison with the mere pastoralism of *The Shepherd's Calendar*.

One day Calidore goes for a walk and comes upon a hill placed in an open plain and surrounded by a wood. It is called Mount Acidale, and is said to have been the favourite haunt of Venus. On the open hilltop he sees a hundred naked maidens dancing to a shepherd's pipe. In the centre of the ring are three other Ladies ('Those were the Graces, daughters of delight, Handmaids of Venus . . .'), and in the midst of it all another damsel, the sweetheart of Colin Clout. Colin Clout, the simple shepherd who was piping while the ladies danced, is usually taken to be Spenser himself—one of the two appearances he makes in the poem, both in Book VI. Since his preferred persona is that of a shepherd, this is clearly the right moment for him to appear. Calidore, 'rapt with pleasance', rushes out of the wood towards the dancers, whereupon they vanish. He asks the shepherd who they were, is first rebuked for driving them away 'whom by no means thou canst recall again', apologises, and is then told something of the Graces, their pedigree and their iconography. Finally, Colin Clout turns to praise the fourth maid, the 'country lass', who exceeds all other country lasses in beauty and virtue. This draws another apology from Calidore, who then returns to Pastorella.

Perhaps no episode in *The Faerie Queene* shows Spenser's strength and limitations as well as this. The paradox we are observing, of simplicity temporarily exalted above culture, or rusticity above learning, is perfectly embodied in the elaborate ritualistic graces of the image. Mount Acidale is sheltered from the complications of the world, and in that respect is like the pastoral community of Meliboe; but then it is further sheltered, this time from the wildness of nature:

> *And at the foot thereof a gentle flood*
> *His silver waves did softly tumble down,*
> *Unmarred with ragged moss or filthy mud;*
> *Ne mote wilde beasts, ne mote the ruder clown,*
> *Thereto approach . . .*   VI.x.7

By doubling back on itself in this way, the setting takes us further from court, and less far. The pattern of the dance has the same effect. The hundred naked maidens come from Spenser's classical learning, but with a certain vagueness: they are graces depending on Venus, but no further specified. The three graces in the centre are given a more precise pedigree:

> *They are the daughters of sky-ruling Jove,*
> *By him begot of fair Eurynome.*

                    VI.x.22

They are named, their iconography is given in a form recognisable to the learned, they are linked with the courtly virtue of Civility, which is described with a courtly deference towards heirarchy:

> *They teach us how to each degree and kind*
> *We should our selves demean, to low, to high,*
> *To friends, to foes; which skill men call Civility.*
>   VI.x.23

As we move inward, then, from the hundred to the three, we find a greater elegance, a greater learning, a more sophisticated myth. Then we move further in, to the climax, and what we find is a simple country lass. Again, the description has mimed the poem's paradox. By far surpassing all other country lasses, the girl has earned a place at the pinnacle of this civilised dream.

To conclude, I want to draw from the discussion a suggestion about the strength and the weakness of Spenser's poetry. I have already tried to show the strength—the beautiful appropriateness of the intricate image to the state of the poem at that point. The weakness concerns not the conception but the words. It is amazing that a poet with so rich an invention should sometimes show so trite a verbal command. That the first mention of Mount Acidale should simply tell us of its 'pleasance', without description, is perhaps defensible; but not, surely, that it should tell us in two lines of such utter banality as that it was

> . . . a place, who pleasance did appear
> To pass all others, on the earth which were.

VI.x.5

At the touching moment when the maidens have vanished and Colin Clout is heartbroken, Spenser tells us that he broke his bagpipe,

> And made great moan for that unhappy turn

VI.x.18

Could language more signally fail to rise to situation?

Spenser is a poet of undistinguished adjectives. When the satyrs rescue Una they 'find the virgin doleful desolate'. In the same stanza (I.vi.9) her foe is 'outrageous', her state is 'unhappy' her beauty is 'bright' and is 'in their rude eyes unworthy of so woeful plight'. It is usually dangerous to stop and look at Spenser's adjectives. There are so many of them, and they are all so conventional—yet without ever belonging so deeply to their nouns that they take on the unpretentious ritual quality of stock epithets.

The old saw that claimed Spenser as the poet's poet, though one can see how it arose, was quite mistaken. No doubt it was based on the idea that forests and enchantments drear, knights, maidens, battles, long descriptions and drowsy caves are especially poetic. We no longer hold such simple ideas on subject-matter, and therefore are only likely to confer the title of poet's poet on someone whose verse has great technical interest, who is likely to be read by other poets more than by the reading public, who is more eager to use language creatively than to write a successful poem. Mallarmé is the most obvious example; among the living, perhaps William Empson is a poet's poet. Now in both the episodes we have looked at there is nothing like this, but there is a genius of invention that recalls some other art. Una among the satyrs, and Satyrane's youth, seem the work of a painter's poet. Hazlitt compared Satyrane among the wild beasts to Rubens; and old Sylvanus tottering forth, leaning on a cypress, ivy twined round his waist (the lines lose little by being turned into prose) hangs, painted by Rubens, in a score of European galleries. The vision on Mount Acidale, with its interweaving dance, its graceful disposition of figures, seems to belong more to Botticelli. The tenderness of the savage Nation, or of the birth of Amoret and Belphoebe in Book III, with the odd feel of closeness to wild nature, belong to Piero di Cosimo. And the maidens on Mount Acidale suggest not only the painter but the choreographer: the brilliance consists in its interweaving movements, its way of apparently thrusting an image further while also drawing it back, its turning of a paradox of ideas into an elegance of pattern. Pictures, procession and dances, not verbal splendours, || are Spenser's gift to us.

VIII

FAREWELL, REWARDS AND FAIRIES

I

PAGANISM has always been a problem for Christianity. Only
with the secularisation of the world—with the loss of the belief
that to cut down a tree is to destroy a nymph—has the problem
been finally solved. As long as men saw nature as animate and full
of spirits which they were prepared to appease, even worship,
Christianity had a problem. Since the culture of Christendom was
permeated with a pagan mythology that came to it from the
ancient world, the problem of what to do about paganism was the
problem of what to do about antiquity.

There were two solutions, syncretist and Puritan. The former
claimed that the ancient world, though without the benefit of
revelation, did through the light of nature find out a good deal of
truth. The pagan gods, interpreted allegorically, can then be seen
as foreshadowings of Christianity: Apollo is a figure for Christ,
Daphne for the Virgin Mary, Deucalion and Pyrrha for Noah, and
so on: it is astonishing to discover how ingenious the Middle Ages
could be in giving a Christian interpretation to everything—
as in the extracts from Ovid compiled for the enlightenment
of nuns, or the vast and influential *Ovid Moralisé* of about 1300. In
the sixteenth century there was a good deal of respect for Greek
mythology among humanists who believed that all religions were
ultimately one; whose Christianity was no doubt sincere, but who
thought, like Dolce in his *Transformationi* (1554), that

> those who will take the trouble to look with discernment not at
> the surface of the fables . . . but at the motives which brought
> about their invention, and the ends to which they were directed
> by those early Masters, will see beneath the rind of fiction, all
> the sap of moral and sacred Philosophy.
>
> Quoted by Seznec, *The Survival of the Pagan Gods*, II.2

As late as 1672 Theophilus Gale, in *The Court of the Gentiles*, found
no less than seventeen points of resemblance between Bacchus and
Moses, and at least one between Bacchus and Christ:

Bacchus (the son of God) falling from Jupiter's throne was torn
by the Titans: and his members being again composed, he
ascended alive up to Heaven. Which fable the Greeks interpreted figuratively of the soul; but it seems rather to be a
shadow of Christ his Descent, Passion and Ascension.

This syncretist tradition was the dominant one, but there was
always an opposition. *The Ovid Moralisé* was put on the Index in
the sixteenth century; Luther attacked and Rabelais made fun of
the allegorisers; and Seznec quotes several stern rejections of the
lying stories of the Greeks, such as the following:

All these things are not only vanity, but in the mouth of a
worshipper of Christ they are almost blasphemy, and an unconscious cult (*ignota cultura*) of idols; they befoul the mind like
horrible monsters, and overthrow morals.

The quarrel goes back to the early Fathers, and was re-animated
by the Reformation. Ultimately, it hinges on how seriously you
take the Fall of Man. If man is depraved in all his faculties, as
Calvin held; if the light of Nature was extinguished by the Fall,
so that the wisdom of unredeemed man is devilish counsel at
best, then the Christian must have no truck with the wisdom of
antiquity. Pan is not an emblem of Christ, but his enemy.

In no poet was this conflict more painfully enacted than in
Milton. That Milton was both Puritan and Humanist has become
a textbook commonplace: for him it was no commonplace, but a
long struggle between the deepest elements of his being. The
inevitable contradictions it issued in are present in his work from
the beginning. In stanza 8 of the *Ode on the Morning of Christ's
Nativity*, the shepherds sit 'simply chatting':

> *Full little thought they then*
> *That the mighty* Pan
> *Was kindly come to live with them below.*

If Christ is the mighty Pan—if pagan mythology was an anticipa-
tion of Christianity—why were the old gods so fiercely banished
on his arrival?

> *From haunted spring, and dale*
> *Edg'd with poplar pale,*
> *The parting Genius is with sighing sent,*

With flower-inwov'n tresses torn
The Nymphs in twilight shade of tangled thickets mourn.

You could hardly be more illogical than this: Pan is accepted into
Christian terminology, while his nymphs, pagan to the last, grieve
for the coming of Christ. It is not a dilemma Milton ever solved,
though he dragged himself out of it in *Paradise Regained*. Considering the poetry that resulted, we should feel only gratitude for
his confusion.

good

II

To ask what kind of world we are shown in *Comus*, let us look
first at the Attendant Spirit. He has come down to earth from 'the
starry threshold of Jove's court', and his opening lines are a sad
explanation of the contrast between 'this dim spot which men call
earth' and his own serene dwelling. That dwelling may be on
Olympus, but it has Christian elements too. Most men live

> *Unmindful of the crown that Virtue gives*
> *After this mortal change, to her true Servants.*

That is no crown given by Jove, who did not allow the spirits of
the blest to join him on Olympus. And, a few lines later,

> *the Golden Key*
> *That opes the Palace of Eternity*

seems to derive more from St Peter than from Jove. The double
origin of these opening lines is quite clear in their conclusion, the
Spirit saying that but for the truly virtuous

> *I would not soil these pure Ambrosial weeds*
> *With the rank vapours of this Sin-worn mould.*
> II.9-17

'Ambrosial'/'Sin-worn': the terms don't belong together. They
come, as we say nowadays, from quite different universes of
discourse.

The Attendant Spirit moves through the action of the play like
a benevolent power, at home in the world. There is something
very pagan about him—he seems to belong in that particular

place, and naturally disguises himself as Thyrsis, the local shepherd. The protection he offers the brothers is an extension of the Elder Brother's scholarly interest in the possibilities of magic. The speech in which the Elder Brother asserts the power of chastity to protect his sister is pagan in both the common senses of the term. It is the speech of a classical scholar, filled with learned references to Greek mythology—quaintly explicit at one point:

> *Do ye believe me yet, or shall I call*
> *Antiquity from the old Schools of Greece*
> *To testify the arms of Chastity?*
>
> 438-440

And it is suffused too with a sense of the magical powers of the earth, a feeling that we walk surrounded by presences that should be propitiated:

> *Some say no evil thing that walks by night*
> *In fog, or fire, by lake, or moorish fen,*
> *Blue meagre Hag, or stubborn unlaid ghost,*
> *That breaks his magic chains at curfew time,*
> *No goblin, or swart faëry of the mine,*
> *Hath hurtful power o'er true virginity.*
>
> 432-437

This is the poetry that Milton learned from Spenser and Shakespeare, the feeling for country superstitions, the fascination of the half-seen and almost-believed-in:

> *Ne let hob Goblins, names whose sense we see not,*
> *Fray us with things that be not . . .*
> Spenser, *Epithalamion*, 344

> *And then (they say) no spirit can walk abroad,*
> *The nights are wholesome, then no planets strike,*
> *No fairy takes, nor witch hath power to charm . . .*
> *Hamlet*, I.i.161

This is the world to which the Attendant Spirit belongs: not to believe in it, is not to believe in his powers:

> *I'll tell ye, 'tis not vain or fabulous,*
> *(Though so esteemed by shallow ignorance)*
> *What the sage Poets taught by th'heav'nly Muse,*
> *Storied of old in high immortal verse*
> *Of dire Chimeras and inchanted Isles,*

> *And rifted Rocks, whose entrance leads to hell,*
> *For such there be, but unbelief is blind.*
>
> 519-525

The Elder Brother is one of the sage poets: he is telling us the same kind of tale, of a world filled with natural magic.

The Attendant Spirit has, of course, various magic powers at command; and in particular he has a plant which he describes at length:

> *Care and utmost shifts*
> *How to secure the Lady from surprisal,*
> *Brought to my mind a certain Shepherd Lad*
> *Of small regard to see to, yet well skilled*
> *In every virtuous plant and healing herb*
> *That spreads her verdant leaf to th'morning ray . . .*
> *. . . a small unsightly root*
> *But of divine effect, he culled me out;*
> *The leaf was darkish, and had prickles on it,*
> *But in another country, as he said,*
> *Bore a bright golden flower, but not in this soil:*
> *Unknown, and like esteemed, and the dull swain*
> *Treads on it daily with his clouted shoon,*
> *And yet more med'cinal is it that* Moly
> *That* Hermes *once to wise* Ulysses *gave;*
> *He call'd it* Haemony, *and gave it me,*
> *And bad me keep it as of sov'ran use*
> *'Gainst all inchantments, mildew blast, or damp*
> *Or ghastly furies' apparition.*
>
> 617-641

This passage too is pagan. The shepherd lad loves the earth and has learned its lore; the root is compared with something famous in mythology; it is effective like a country simple or a wise woman's charm. Yet there are hints too that paganism is being transcended. The 'other country' sounds a little like Heaven; the root would then be God's grace, neglected in this world, blossoming in the next. Christ, we remember, is the good shepherd: not much has been done to emphasise this meaning, but the possibility is there.

What we have here is a pagan world reaching out to Christianity. None of its paganism is rejected (it is, in the end, Sabrina, the *genius loci*, who has to be called up to free the Lady), but there is a Christian overtone. After reading these beautifully controlled lines, we can see that the same balance was being struck at the

beginning. The Attendant Spirit has descended to a world ready
for Christianity, rather than to a Christian world; and at the end,
he leaves for a paradise that is almost purely pagan: the Garden
of the Hesperides, merged with the Garden of Adonis (this passage
too is by the Milton who learned from Spenser)—a paradise of
sexual fulfilment. It is probably the purest bit of paganism in the
play, perhaps in Milton, yet even that paradise is offered as the
reward of virtue:

> *Mortals that would follow me,*
> *Love virtue, she alone is free.*

1018-1019

All this is the sheerest syncretism. It assumes the view that ancient
fables have a rind of fiction, and a sap of moral and sacred
philosophy.

> What can *Adonis horti* among the Poets mean other than
> Moses his Eden, or terrestiall Paradise,—the Hebrew
> Eden being Voluptas or Delitiae . . .
>> Henry Reynolds, *Mythomystes* (1632)

Milton goes even further, for his 'Adonis horti' are a figure for
Heaven itself. We are a long way from Christ's eventual rejection
of all classical culture in *Paradise Regained*.

Such is the world of *Comus* if we look through the eyes of the
Attendant Spirit. How different it looks to the Lady. For her, the
world is a test: she is faced with stark alternatives, in which she is
required to choose right. Offered sensual indulgence, she chooses
chastity; offered riches, she chooses austere socialism ('Nature's
full blessings would be well dispensed In unsuperfluous even
proportion'). Her world is shaped by morality. And so when
Comus approaches her from the fascinating half-light of pagan dance
and magic spell, she regards him simply as temptation. For her,
the wonderful creatures who surround him—the oughly-headed
monsters—are simply a sign of his power and danger. She thinks
in simple contrasts: credulous innocence and base forgery, 'lickerish
baits fit to ensnare a brute' and 'a well-governed and wise appetite'.

We cannot of course distinguish between Attendant Spirit and
Lady by their reaction to Comus: both are against him. But the
nature of their resistance is quite different, and perhaps the best
way to describe it is to say that the Spirit (and to a lesser extent
the Elder Brother) fights Comus with his own weapons. For

Comus is pagan too—the most deeply pagan figure in the play. He loves the earth, he loves the life of the senses, he loves moonlight as if he had stepped out of *A Midsummer Night's Dream*. His speech on nature's bounty has quite rightly become the most famous in the play:

> *Wherefore did Nature pour her bounties forth,*
> *With such a full and unwithdrawing hand,*
> *Covering the earth with odours, fruits and flocks . . .*
>
> 710-713

This is a hymn of praise to the world for what it is, not as the gateway to another.

Chastity has two meanings in *Comus*. For the Lady it means, quite literally, what it says: renunciation, resistance to temptation, virtue. For her brother it is a magic spell, a way of taking on some of the very powers it is combating. It is the dread bow of Diana, the 'fair silver-shafted Queen', it is the 'snaky-headed Gorgon shield'—images as exciting as those of the enchanter himself, and with a similar beauty. The Lady's chastity, in contrast, is a simple rejection. She understands 'the sage And serious doctrine of Virginity', and calmly tells Comus that he doesn't: 'Thou hast nor Ear, nor Soul to apprehend'.

I am tempted to describe all this by saying that the Lady has simply walked out of the play. All readers notice that there is no real conflict when she encounters Comus, and have usually felt that this makes the scene undramatic. No doubt it is, but how could it have been done differently? How *could* there be conflict between her and Comus, for conflict implies communication. She has no interest in Comus' twilight speells; she lives in the daylight.

III

At the time Milton was performing, through the Lady, this huge act of rejection, a whole segment of the population was doing something very similar. It had been building up for a century, and we can find it described as early as 1579, in the fifth Eclogue of *The Shepherd's Calendar*. This is a dialogue between two shepherds, Piers and Palinode, two shepherds under whose persons, the Argument tells us, 'be represented two forms of pastors or Ministers, or the Protestant and the Catholic'. To Palinode, May is the month of pagan celebrations, 'girt in gawdy green':

Tho to the green Wood they speeden them all,
To fetchen home May with their musical:
And home they bringen in a royal throne,
Crowned as king: and his Queene attone
Was Lady Flora, on whom did attend
A Fair flock of Faeries, and a fresh band
Of lovely Nymphs . . .

Shepherd's Calendar, V.27

Piers reacts to this as the Lady reacts to Comus:

Thilke same been shepeherds for the Devils stead,
That playen while their flocks be unfed.

V.43

To Piers, the world is divided, quite simply, into two parties:

Shepherd, I list none accordance make
With shepherd that does the right way forsake:
And of the twain, if choice were to me,
Had lever my foe my friend he be.

V.163

He who is not with us is against us: a natural attitude to any-one who sees the world as a battlefield between God and the devil, the stern necessity of choosing the right side hanging continually over us.

The Reformation acted slowly on English culture. Hamlet's father could return from purgatory after two generations of Protestantism with—as far as we know—no protest from the audience. The true cultural impact of the Reformation had to wait for the great upsurge of Puritanism in the seventeenth century, and its fierce disentangling of true Christianity from the relics of barbarism, the rags of Rome, the devilish superstitions it was held to have got entwined with.

Most poets of the sixteenth and seventeenth centuries were in no hurry to disentwine. The *Hymne des Daimons* of Ronsard (1555) describes the various kinds of pagan and popular spirit (*Incubes, Larves, Lares, Lémurs, Pénates et Succubes*) with the loving curiosity of an antiquary (the tone rather resembles that of *The Anatomy of Melancholy*). It includes his own personal ghost-story, an encounter with the skeleton of a usurer who had recently died and

Que le peuple pensait pour sa vie méchante
Etre puni là-bas des mains de Rhadamante.

Whom the people believed to be punished down there at the
hands of Rhadamanthus for his wicked life.

This is a very neat mingling of all three elements we have been discussing: Christianity, popular superstitution and learned paganism.
The shape of the thought is Christian and popular, the splendid
rhyming word (is Ronsard smiling slightly?) is learned. There may
be irony, too, in the way the story continues:

> *Si fussé-je étouffé d'une crainte pressée*
> *Sans Dieu, qui promptement me mit en la pensée*
> *De tirer mon épée et de couper menu*
> *L'air tout autour de moi avecque le fer nu:*
> *Ce que je fis soudain, et sitot ils n'ouïrent*
> *Siffler l'épée en l'air que tous s'évanouirent . . .*

I would have been choked by a pressing fear had it not been
for God, who promptly put it into my head to draw my sword
to chop the air around me with the bare blade—which I did
without delay, and as soon as they heard the sword whistle in
the air they all vanished.

God came to his aid: that is to say, God put into his head the very
thought that would first have come into anyone's head, to draw
his sword. With it he performed the thoroughly useless action of
cutting the air into bits—and the ghosts vanished. Because ghosts
are frightened of swords? Or of God—even though no outsider
would have thought God had much to do with it? Or because they
weren't there in the first place?

A hundred years later, Herrick has an attitude to paganism
that may not be very different from Ronsard's. In the last resort,
Herrick renounces his pagan attitudes and sets his hopes on
heaven, but most of his poetry was written without this choice
being forced into attention:

> *And* Titan *on the Eastern hill*
> *Retires himself, or else stands still*
> *Till you come forth. Wash, dress, be brief, in praying:*
> *Few Beads are best, when once we go a Maying.*
>
> *Some have dispatched their Cakes and Cream,*
> *Before that we have left to dream:*

And some have wept, and wooed, and plighted Troth,
And chose their priest, ere we can cast off sloth:
   Many a green gown has been given;
   Many a kiss, both odd and even:
   Many a glance too has been sent
   From out the eye, Love's Firmament:
Many a jest told of the Keys betraying
This night, and Locks picked, yet w'are not a Maying.
          Corinna's Going a-maying, ll. 26-29, 47-56

The first of these passages is a passing Christian reference: he hurries Corinna through her prayers as rapidly as decency permits. The second is mock religious. The 'priest' is clearly an imitation May-day priest: for if these are real marriages, they are shockingly hurried—wooing, plighting troth and choosing the priest are not likely to happen all in one morning except in a May-day parody of a wedding. Both 'odd and even kisses' and 'the key's betraying' suggest sexual meanings, though unfortunately the OED gives no clear evidence for these. All in all, the passage is clearly pagan; and to juxtapose it with the earlier and so much hastier one is to do more good to Herrick's reputation as poet than as parson.

I suppose it is no longer possible for us to know how far Herrick's paganism is literary and nostalgic, and how far he is describing what is actually going on.

    Some prank them up with Oaken leaves:
    Some cross the Fill-horse; some with great
    Devotion, stroke the home-borne wheat:
    While other rustics, less attent
    To Prayers, than to Merriment,
    Run after with their breeches rent.
          The Hock-Cart, l. 20

These 'prayers' must be country customs, not real prayers; and the literal tone of the poem suggests that it may be describing actuality. What is quite clear is that there is no opposition between these prayers and this merriment: they are certainly not prayers of renunciation, and they are certainly not Christian.

Perhaps the most interesting exploration in seventeenth-century poetry of the world of paganism and country superstition is *The Sad Shepherd* of Ben Jonson. As with Herrick, we cannot really tell what is literary and what is immediate: certainly there

is a good deal that is literary—the love of Aeglamour, the sad
shepherd, for his lost Earine, and the string of pathetic fallacies in
which he delivers it; or the virginal love of Amie for Karol ('His
lip is softer, sweeter than the rose . . .'). Most of this is frigid stuff,
and what gives the play its interest today is the story of Robin
Hood, Maid Marian and Maudlin the witch.

Because *The Sad Shepherd* is unfinished, we don't know how
that story would have developed: presumably Maudlin would
have continued, by disguising, to outwit Robin—stealing venison,
keeping Earine prisoner, egging her son and daughter on to sexual
misdemeanours (she does all these in the two and a half acts we
have)—until she was finally outwitted in Act V. Maudlin is clearly
the character who corresponds to Comus: she too can change her
shape, and though she has no attendant menagerie, she makes up
for it by turning into a raven herself. Like Comus, she is proud of
her ancestry, and of the provenance of her magic properties:

> *A Gypsan lady, and a right beldame,*
> *Wrought it by moonshine for me, and starlight,*
> *Upon your grannam's grave, that very night*
> *We earthed her in the shades . . .*
>
> II.i

She is in favour of sexual freedom—and says so, in coarser language
than Comus ever uses:

> *I know well*
> *It is a witty part sometimes to give;*
> *But what? to whom? no monsters, nor to maidens.*
> *He should present them with more pleasant things,*
> *Things natural, and what all women covet*
> *To see, the common parent of us all,*
> *Which maids will twire at 'tween their fingers thus!*
>
> II.i

There is no character in *The Sad Shepherd* who corresponds to
the Lady—no virtuous Puritan. Puritanism appears only in the
angry remarks of Robin Hood's followers about 'the sourer sort of
shepherds' who complain, in the same terms as Piers (or as Milton
in *Lycidas*) of the neglect of flocks, 'when with such vanities the
swains are led'.

> *They call ours Pagan pastimes, that infect*
> *Our blood with ease, our youth with all neglect;*
> *Our tongues with wantonness, our thoughts with lust. . . .*
>
> I.ii

Tuck and Lionel—the speakers here—are describing the same
world of country pleasures as Herrick. To speak of these as pagan
pastimes is to put them with Maudlin's—and certainly there are
resemblances. Maudlin's coarseness is paralleled by Robin's, in the
scene of the lovers' meeting:

> *. . . The moon's at full, the happy pair are met.*
> Marian: *How hath this morning paid me for my rising!*
> *First, with my sports; but most with meeting you.*
> *I did not half so well reward my hounds,*
> *As she hath me today; although I gave them*
> *All the sweet morsels called tongue, ears and dowcets!*
> Robin: *What, and the inch-pin?*
> M: *Yes.*
> R: *Your sports then pleased you?*
> M: *You are a wanton.*
> R: *One I do confess,*
> *I want-ed till you came; but now I have you,*
> *I'll grow to your embraces till two souls*
> *Distilled into kisses through our lips,*
> *Do make one spirit of love.*
> M: *O Robin, Robin!*
> R: *Breathe, breathe awhile. . . .*
>
> I.ii

Robin's feeble pun, and his image of the souls distilling, are
literary and commonplace; but the touch of coarseness sounds
rural and genuine, and is quite as typically Jonsonian. Jonson—
who always found technical processes fascinating as sources of
imagery—describes the dismemberment of the deer at great and
careful length. The dowcets are the deer's testicles; the inchpin is
explained by the OED as 'the lower gut', but the bawdy quibble is
obvious. 'Things natural,' as Maudlin said, are 'what all women
covet to see.'

Robin Hood and his followers, then, belong partly to the world
of Maudlin the witch: she is their enemy, but not in the uncompromising way that Comus was the Lady's enemy. Their main
weapon against her is the hunt, and we see them preparing for it

in Act II: 'Rare sport, I swear, this hunting of the witch Will make us.' They are guided by the old shepherd Alken, who is the nearest equivalent to the Attendant Spirit. He knows all about Maudlin, and describes her den in creepy poetry:

> *Within a gloomy dimble she doth dwell,*
> *Down in a pit, o'ergrown with brakes and briars,*
> *Close by the ruins of a shaken abbey,*
> *Torn with an earthquake down unto the ground,*
> *'Mongst graces and grots, near an old charnel-house,*
> *Where you shall find her sitting in her fourm,*
> *As fearful and melancholic as that*
> *She is about; with caterpillars' kells,*
> *And knotty cobwebs, rounded in with spells.*
> *Then she steals forth to relief in the fogs,*
> *And rotten mists, upon the fens and bogs,*
> *Down to the drowned lands of Lincolnshire:*
> *To make ewes cast their lambs, swine eat their farrow,*
> *The housewives tun not work, nor the milk churn.*

II.ii

Describing the soul that had been 'clotted' by defilement, the Elder Brother says:

> *Such are those thick and gloomy shadows damp*
> *Oft seen in Charnell vaults, and sepulchers*
> *Lingering, and sitting by a new made grave*

—held there, surely, by the same fascination with bodily decay that keeps Maudlin near *her* charnel house.

Alken, like the Attendant Spirit, fights the witch with her own weapons. He obviously enjoys knowing all about her: when Scarlet remarks 'He knows her shifts and haunts', Alken proudly adds 'And all her wiles and turns', and goes on to describe 'the baneful schedule of her nocent charms' with something of the scholar's enjoyment we saw in Ronsard. Alken, of course, like Shakespeare's Friar Lawrence and the Attendant Spirit's shepherd lad, knows the virtuous plants and healing herbs as well, but we can be sure that the sourer sort of shepherds would have lumped the two impatiently together—and they would not have been altogether wrong.

The ambivalence of Robin and his followers—enemies of witch-craft yet accused of paganism themselves—may be inherent in the story. Maid Marian may derive both from the Virgin Mary and

175

from Mary Magdalen: the paradoxical fusion does not seem implausible. Her very name—Maid Marian, when she is also clearly Robin's mistress—suggests ambivalence (for it is obviously not simple sarcasm); and Maudlin the witch may be etymologically the same person. Robin Hood too may have something in common with Robin Goodfellow (who appears in *The Sad Shepherd* as Puck Hairy, the familiar of Maudlin). All this would give a special appropriateness to the scene in which Maudlin impersonates Marian, leaving Robin and his followers astounded at her change of mood and character; and to the later scene in which she repeats the trick but is spotted by Robin, who seizes her girdle and so turns her back into her own shape again. If the ambivalence of Marian was somehow present in Jonson's consciousness, or that of the audience he was writing for (and who did not, alas, ever see the play), then he has found a dramatic device that recalls it with apt and mysterious power. Here we have something much more interesting than the elegantly turned laments of Aeglamour.

The Sad Shepherd belongs to a world of half-lights, a world in which the frightening and the fascinating merge into each other, in which the earth has magical powers that might be used for good or evil. It is quite different from the stern world which is a battlefield between God and the devil, in which everything which is not on one side is on the other, in which 'all these things are not only vanity, but in the mouth of a worshipper of Christ they are almost blasphemy'. In the mid-seventeenth century, these worlds, the old and the new, were struggling for the English soul; and Bishop Corbet, in a poem which is also a superb piece of cultural history, sadly records the victory of the new:

> Lament, lament, old Abbies,
>   The Fairies lost command;
> They did but change Priests babies,
>   But some have changed your land:
> And all your children stolen from thence
>   Are now grown puritans;
> Who live as changelings ever since
>   For love of your domains. . . .
>
> When Tom came home from labour,
>   Or Cisse to milking rose,
> Then merrily merrily went their Tabour,
>   And nimble went their Toes.

Witness those rings and roundelays
Of theirs, which yet remain,
Were footed in Queene Mary's days
On many a grassy plain;
But since of late, Elizabeth,
And later James came in,
They never daunc'd on any heath
As when the time hath been.

By which we note the Fairies
Were of the old profession;
Their songs were Ave Maryes,
Their dances were procession. . . .

What most distresses Corbet is not the effect of Puritanism on religion, the stern theology of justification by faith alone, of arbitrary election by a fierce God; nor even the economic basis, of which he seems quite aware; but its effect on popular culture. Corbet was an Anglican Bishop, and we can assume that his protestantism was genuine: in so far as Popery meant transubstantiation or papal authority, he no doubt preferred the Established Church. But in so far as it was 'the old religion', he sees it as a happier, richer way of life than the constant battle with sin.

IV

We are now able to say succinctly what happens in *Comus*: it enacts the cultural change that came over England in the seventeenth century. The world of the Attendant Spirit is the old world, and it only rejects Comus as Robin and Marian reject Maud—on the level of action. But the Lady belongs with the sourer shepherds, and her rejection is total: she doesn't want to listen, or to unlock her lips in that unhallow'd air. She feels only distaste.

One last point remains to be made: poetically, the most important of all. What makes *Comus* so beautiful? Its marvellous poetry is based on darkness, suggestiveness, mystery. The Lady is most haunting when she is expressing her fear of the unknown:

And airy tongues that syllable men's names
On Sands, and Shores, and desert Wildernesses

208-209

The Elder Brother, we have already seen, lingers in his speech among 'grots and caverns shagged with horrid shades', and I must now say explicitly, what was previously assumed, that it is at such moments that he becomes a true poet. The contrast with Jonson is marked. True, Jonson can also begin a speech 'Within a gloomy dimble she doth dwell', and for a few lines sound like Milton, but he continues

> *Then she steals forth to relief in the fogs,*
> *And rotten mists, upon the fens and bogs,*
> *Down to the drowned lands of Lincolnshire.*

That last line could never have been by Milton. Its humdrum, concrete topographical feel is very Jonsonian: Maud is located in a part of England he has been to, or read about recently and incidentally brought into one of his plays, for Meercraft, the Projector in *The Devil is an Ass*, had a scheme for the recovery of the drown'd lands—one of a hundred very Jonsonian schemes:

> *Sir, money is a whore, a bawd, a drudge . . .*
> *I'll never want her! Coin her out of cobwebs,*
> *Dust, but I'll have her! raise wool upon eggshells*
> *Sir, and make grass grow out of marrow-bones,*
> *To make her come.*
> *The Devil is an Ass*, II.i

Topicality, ingenuity, commercial and technical liveliness fired Jonson's imagination; darkness, mystery and magic fired Milton's. It is not anachronistic, I believe, to sum this up by calling Milton a romantic.

I have claimed that the Attendant Spirit still belongs in the world of Comus; and now we must add that we owe his poetry to this. This world of fog or fire or lake or moorish fen, of 'Dark-veild Cotytto, t'whom the secret flame Of mid-night Torches burns', which the Lady rejects, is also the world of the play's beauty. The deepest paradox of *Comus* is that the moral rejects the poetry.

Milton realised this: and at one point he tried to do something about it. This makes perhaps the most moving and interesting moment of the play. The Lady has just sung her song; and Comus, before speaking to her, has a soliloquy in which he describes how moved he has been:

Sure something holy lodges in that breast,
And with these raptures moves the vocal air
To testify his hidden residence. . . .
I have oft heard
My mother Circe with the Sirens three,
Amidst the flowery kirtl'd Naiades
Culling their potent herbs, and baleful drugs,
Who as they sung, would take the prisoned soul,
And lap it in Elysium, Scylla wept,
And chid her barking waves into attention,
And fell Charybdis murmured soft applause:
Yet they in pleasing slumber lulled the sense,
And in sweet madness robbed it of itself,
But such a sacred, and home-felt delight,
Such sober certainty of waking bliss
I never heard till now.   246-264

Here Milton is trying to say that the poetry of light is finer than
the poetry of darkness: he is urging us to prefer the Lady on
aesthetic as well as on moral grounds. Quite rightly, he has done
this through the mouth of Comus: her song ravishes even the
very apostle of dark-veiled Cotytto. The crucial line is 'Such sober
certainty of waking bliss'. Here is the new experience she has
offered to Comus, and he tells us it is more splendid than anything
he had known before. She has done for him what only a true poet
can do, enlarged the range of his sensibility.

But even here we are dragged back from daylight to darkness.
How does Comus praise the Lady's song? Naturally, by telling us
that it is finer than the songs he knows—which he describes in
ravishing terms. A line like 'Culling their potent herbs, and baleful
drugs' is really a struggle between moral meaning and romantic
suggestiveness: the drugs are baleful, yes, but the line is haunting.
Comus is moved by the memory even as he speaks of it.

We have here the familiar rhetorical method of praising the
experience you know in order to add that another experience
surpasses it. It is used in religious poetry, of course, but the Lady
is an earthly creature; and one thing is certain about using this
method to talk about the earthly, that you can only use it once.
To put in front of us the beauty of the Naiades' song, and then say
that the Lady's is even finer, will do very well to record the delighted
shock of hearing the Lady for the first time: but it must then be
followed by a new kind of poetry, which needs to be as beautiful,

179

but in a new, daylight way. If it can only be described in terms of 'even finer than', then it has not, in the end, had a transfiguring effect on the sensibility. And in *Comus* there is no such follow-up: there is this one superb moment of rejection, and then we sink back to a simple contrast between the beauty and the moral. Milton—the Milton of *Comus* at any rate—was too incurably romantic.

In the course of the 1640s the Lady won. The victory did not last long politically, but its effect on English culture was deep and lasting. It had many splendid consequences, but Bishop Corbet was surely right: the cultural price was heavy. *Comus* is the most eloquent admission of this fact in English Literature.

IX

PASTORAL *VERSUS* CHRISTIANITY

For all the Puritanism of his life, Marvell wrote thoroughly un-Puritan poetry: for his poems do not treat of the Fall. Or rather, two do: and before going on to consider Marvell's prelapsarian pastoral world, I must say something about these two exceptions. One of them, the 'Dialogue between the Resolved Soul and Created Pleasure', is not very interesting poetically—and in any case not a pastoral. It divides the world clearly into temptation and virtue, and enacts a simple clash between them. Such unhesitating rejection of pleasure as a distraction from Heaven is no doubt Puritan—though stylistically the poem has a rhetorical extravagance that would do credit to a Bernini saint:

> *Close on thy Head thy Helmet bright.*
> *Balance thy sword against the Fight . . .*

Only occasionally does Pleasure offer a subtler charm, as when she describes music

> *Which the posting winds recall,*
> *And suspend the Rivers Fall.*

If the whole poem had such delicacy, the uncompromising rejection of the resolved soul might make us feel that Marvell was betraying his own best self—that he was as bad as Milton's Lady. But for the most part the poem exists not in Marvell's world but in Crashaw's, and the simple rhetoric of the conclusion ('Triumph, triumph, victorious Soul') is hardly cruder than the sophisticated offers of Pleasure.

'The Coronet' is more interesting—and a much better poem. This time it is not Crashaw but Herbert we are reminded of, and there is nothing in Herbert subtler than its psychological probings and twisted rhythms:

> *When for the Thorns with which I long, too long,*
> *With many a piercing wound,*
> *My saviour's head have crowned,*
> *I seek with garlands to redress with wrong;*
> *Through every garden, every mead,*

181

I gather flowers (my fruits are only flowers)
Dismantling all the fragrant towers
That once adorned my shepherdesses head . . .

Like so much of Herbert, the poem ruefully confesses a love of the world, tries to rise above this, and then confesses the difficulty of that. Even his poem to the Saviour turns out to be overlaid 'with wreaths of fame and interest'. It would be rash to insist that Herbert could never have written this poem; but one point seems to reveal the poetic identity of Marvell. 'The Coronet' is about the rejection of secular, pastoral poetry, yet its form and its central image are still pastoral. In the course of trying to transform his world, he still needs that world, for it gives him the language to write in: 'my fruits are only flowers'. The two enchanting lines at the end of the quotation above describe what the poem is doing, and if it is to dismantle under our eyes it must first have built.

This is the great paradox of religious poetry: its content is rejection, and its form retains what is rejected. Out of this paradox came some of the great religious poems of the age, and all of them have a feeling of uniqueness, as if that was the one poem left to write before subsiding into silence. One world is being rejected for another, and when the rejection is complete there will be nothing to say, only the Word of God to hear. Donne, Herbert and a host of minor poets wrote this same poem over and over, obsessively and with rich variety. 'Leave me O love, which reachest but to dust', they kept saying; 'Aaron's drest'; 'I did sit and eat'. Marvell wrote this poem only once.

That this religious poem should be in pastoral form is a paradox, but a paradox that is appropriate, perhaps even essential to the act of writing. We cannot say the same of two other 'religious' pastorals, 'Thyrsis and Dorinda' and 'Clorinda and Damon'. They are both rather conventional poems, but I want for the moment to approach them as if they were unique.

'Thyrsis and Dorinda' is obviously a religious allegory. Thyrsis describes the joys of Elysium/Heaven so eloquently that he fires Dorinda with enthusiasm: she loses interest in worldly pleasure, and grows impatient for death. Religious? Let us notice what Heaven/Elysium is like.

Oh, there's neither hope nor fear
There's no world, no fox, nor bear.

No need of dog to fetch our stray,
Our Lightfoot we may give away.

. . . . . .

Then I'll go on: there, sheep are full
Of sweetest grass, and softest wool;
There, birds sing consorts, garlands grow.
Cool winds do whisper, springs do flow.
There, always is a rising sun,
And day is ever, but begun.
Shepherds there, bear equal sway,
And every nymph's a Queen of May.

This is the Golden Age again, when there was no need of hard work, even of agriculture. Here we have an Arcadian egalitarianism ('every nymph's a Queen of May'), no hierarchy of 'Thrones, Dominations, Virtues, Princes, Powers'. This is not the Christian heaven at all: it is not strenuously won, it is not preceded by a Day of Judgement, it involves no rejection of this world—in short, it is not morally conceived. Clorinda's final suggestion that they should commit suicide in order to reach Elysium would be outrageous in a Christian poem: in this idyll it is acceptable, for the death is made to seem so natural:

Then let us give Carillo charge o' th' sheep,
And thou and I'll pick poppies and them steep
In wine, and drink on't even till we weep,
So shall we smoothly pass away in sleep.

If we wish, we can even take these lines as a hint that Heaven is found in dreams—or in narcotics.

There is no contrast between nature and grace in 'Thyrsis and Dorinda', and its idea of Heaven is correctly named 'Elysium'. It does not merely use the pastoral form, it fills it with pastoral content. The same is true of 'Clorinda and Damon', but before looking at that we can seek out Marvell's conception of nature in one or two other poems.

In *Appleton House* to begin with. Though this long miscellaneous compliment to the Fairfax family lacks unity in a rather obvious way, it is easily enough divided into a number of independent verse essays, all loosely about Appleton House, and each with its own unity. There is an Introduction (i-x), a history of the house (xi-xxxv), the Garden (xxxvii-xlvi), the Meadow (xlvii-lx), the

Forest (lxi-lxxxi), Maria Fairfax (lxxxii-xcv), and a short conclusion. The section that will now concern us is that on the Forest.

In it Marvell describes a withdrawal into nature of a kind that has become familiar since Wordsworth. The strangeness of the sense-experiences as he enters the forest cause him to look around in awe:

> *When first the eye this forest sees*
> *It seems indeed as wood not trees:*
> *As if their neighbourhood so old*
> *To one great trunk them all did mould.*
> *There the huge bulk takes place, as meant*
> *To thrust up a fifth element;*
> *And stretches still so closely wedged*
> *As if the night within were hedged.*

All natural creatures seem friendly, both to one another and to him; and he begins to feel himself a part of nature:

> *And little now to make me, wants*
> *Or of the fowls, or of the plants.*

He has learned the language of the creatures; he can read in nature's mystic book; he is secure from the distractions of the world, and would like to stay there for ever.

To describe it like this is to make Marvell sound like a Romantic —like J. M. Synge, for instance:

> *Still south I went and west and south again,*
> *Through Wicklow from the morning till the night,*
> *And far from cities, and the sight of men*
> *Lived with the sunshine, and the moon's delight.*
>
> *I knew the stars, the flowers, and the birds,*
> *The grey and wintry sides of many glens,*
> *And did but half remember human words*
> *In converse with the mountains, moors and fens.*
>
> 'Prelude'

Synge too withdraws into nature, replaces human language with that of the landscape itself, feels himself absorbed into his surroundings. Yet Marvell could never be mistaken for Synge, and to put the two together is to see, first of all, how completely *Appleton House* belongs to its time. First, because of the wit. Synge might have felt he was seeing wood not trees, but he would not have gone on to call wood a 'fifth element'; Synge has become part of nature, but not in a way that can lead him to say

> Or turn me but, and you will see
> I was but an inverted tree.

Marvell, we observe, has *not* become part of nature: he is standing watching himself, his intellect is looking for ever more ingenious ways to show that he is 'but a tree'. Compared with this, Synge *is* a tree. Both poets tell us they have learned the language of nature, but only Marvell has his attention caught by the idea of learning a language—hence the conceits about Mexique paintings and reading books. What impresses about Synge's poem, when it stands next to Marvell's, is its quietness. It sets out to have no style, to sound like the glens themselves. Its language is as ordinary as rock.

Other comparisons with the nineteenth century are possible. Keats saw the same oaks as Marvell:

> As when upon a tranced summer night
> Those green-robed senators of antique woods,
> Tall oaks, branch-charmed by the earnest stars,
> Dream—and so dream all night without a stir.

The comparison with senators could well have come from Marvell; but the trance, the charm, the air of magic, suggest that the sensual swoon of summer has invaded Keats' lines more than they ever did Marvell's. Keats' dreaming and Synge's self-forgetfulness lie behind Marvell's language, but he has not set out to recapture them with the same intensity: he has built on them.

We have here two radically different conceptions of how language is related to experience. We may regard language as a bridge between experience and tradition: between the particularity of one man seeing a forest, and the rich apparatus of interpretation provided by centuries of thinking. The nineteenth-century poets were concerned to shed a good bit of that thinking, so that the experience itself could in all its particularity figure in their poems. In the twentieth century this has, as we all know, gone further still, till even rational comprehensibility is sometimes thrown out because it generalises. The seventeenth-century poet, standing nearer the other end of the bridge, used his language to retain a great deal of interpretative possibility.

For instance, he retained the idea of the Fall. Keats, we may say, could not mention an apple without thinking of the sensation of stroking its smooth curves, or biting into its tart juiciness. Marvell could not mention an apple without thinking of Adam and Eve.

> *Bind me ye woodbines in your twines,*
> *Curl me about ye gadding vines,*
> *And oh so close your circles lace,*
> *That I may never leave this place,*
> *But lest your fetters prove too weak,*
> *Ere I your silken bondage break,*
> *Do you, O brambles, chain me too,*
> *And courteous briars nail me through.*

The reference to the Fall is very slight here: perhaps only in the last two lines. The rest of the stanza is, indirectly, about sex. Having escaped from human society, he would like to stay where he is: instead of being bound in women's arms, instead of being encircled and laced by them, he wants the forest to do its own entangling. In *The Garden* there is the same movement from sex to the Fall:

> *What wondrous life in this I lead!*
> *Ripe apples drop about my head;*
> *The luscious clusters of the vine*
> *Upon my mouth do crush their wine;*
> *The nectarine and curious peach*
> *Into my hands themselves do reach;*
> *Stumbling on melons as I pass,*
> *Insnared with flowers, I fall on grass.*

Once again, nature offers him an equivalent to sex, and he prefers it: the garden is love's 'best retreat', and instead of women, he has fruit to kiss. Appropriately, then, he finds that nature also offers an equivalent to the Fall. To appreciate the point of the final couplet, we must realise that the emphatic word in the last clause is not 'fall' but 'grass'. Nature smothers him with gifts; she is so kind that the only snare is one made of flowers (not serpents). The last couplet is a sigh of relief: if there's a fall in *this* garden it's a harmless one, even an attractive one. The briars are courteous.

The fact that Marvell likes to mention the Fall in this playful way makes it clearer than ever that for him nature is unfallen.

Nature is friendly, and offers only a harmless parody of the Fall.
Escaping into Arcadia turns out to be like escape into Eden:
unspoilt by cities, man is prelapsarian.

'The Mower against Gardens' shows this clearly. It is a poem on
how man has corrupted the world, and is therefore easy to compare
with religious poems of the time—Vaughan's 'Corruption' for
instance. Marvell contrasts the sophistication of gardens with the
simplicity of wild nature:

> *With strange perfumes he did the Roses taint,*
> *And flowers themselves were taught to paint . . .*
>
> *Tis all enforc'd: the Fountain and the Grot;*
> *While the sweet fields do lie forgot.*

Vaughan's poem describes how shortly after the Fall man still 'had
some glimpse of his birth', and was able to contrast the thorn and
weed of his actual world with Paradise, still to be glimpsed 'in
some sweet shade and fountain'. At times the two poems are very
close: Marvell's opening:

> *Luxurious Man, to bring his Vice in use*
> *Did after him the World seduce,*

makes exactly the same point as Vaughan's:

> *He drew the Curse upon the world, and crackt*
> *The whole frame with his fall.*

Each has its peculiar beauty, too. Vaughan's lies in the colloquial
vividness with which we are given Adam's nostalgia, like any old
man reminiscing:

> *He sigh'd for Eden, and would often say*
> *Ah! What bright days were those?*

And Marvell's lies in the haunting power that sees a garden, in
contrast to the liveliness of the fields, as

> *A dead and standing pool of air.*

When all this is said, however, what concerns us is the difference
between the two poems. Vaughan's is about the Fall, and it
contrasts the 'thorn and weed' with Eden itself. Marvell has only
the one cursory reference to the Fall, which begins his poem, and
even that is oblique: it is all contained, really, in the words 'after
him'. When he turns at the end of the poem to give an extended
contrast to the 'luxury' of gardens he finds it in the fields:

Where willing Nature does to all dispense
A wild and fragrant Innocence.

Marvell has reversed Vaughan's contrast. In 'Corruption', nature was fallen, and the garden (being Eden) was unfallen; in 'The Mower against Gardens', Nature is innocent, and the garden (being man-made) is corrupt. The contrast is a neat one, but it is not the reversal of the garden image that really matters to us. Gardens are after all ambivalent symbols in pastoral: they can be contrasted with the town (as elsewhere in Marvell) or with wild nature, as here. What matters is that in each case we are offered the pastoral contrast between the sophisticated and the natural, and in each case Marvell (it is the pastoral reference) prefers the natural. For his nature, unlike Vaughan's, unlike that of any Christian poet, is unfallen. Hence the end of the *Mower* poem:

And Fauns *and* Fairies *do the Meadows till,*
More by their presence than their skill,
Their Statues polish'd by some ancient hand,
May to adorn the Gardens stand:
But howso'ere the Figures do excel,
The Gods *themselves with us do dwell.*

This is the elegant paganism of the classical scholar, and also a more haunting paganism, announced in the second line, and beautifully suggested in the hushed movement of the last—an almost animistic feeling for the presence of local deities, perceived more as a sense of place than as human 'skill'.

A very different poem suggests a very similar feeling. The paradise offered to the English emigrés in Bermuda looks magical and innocent:

He gave us this eternal spring,
Which here enamels everything;
And sends the fowls to us in care,
On daily visits through the air.
He hangs in shades the orange bright,
Like golden lamps in a green night.
And does in the pomegranates close,
Jewels more rich than Ormus shows.
He makes the figs our mouths to meet;
And throws the melons at our feet.
But apples plants of such a price,
No tree could ever bear them twice.

This again is the imagery of the Golden Age: nature offers us her bounty, no use of metal, corn, or wine, or oil. But where can this Paradise be? When the forbidden fruit was eaten, nature fell with man, and there can be no unfallen spot on earth.

> *He cast (of which we rather boast)*
> *The gospel pearl upon our coast.*
> *And in these rocks for us did frame*
> *A temple where to sound his name.*

The song grows religious, but without losing its once-born quality. There is no contrast between the delight of the senses in this world, and the same soul's delight in God. Marvell is running counter to the whole tradition that emphasises man's corrupt state, and his poem is one no Puritan ought to write, for a Puritan ought not to think in such terms.

Yet plenty of Puritans did. A fascinating piece of research by Rosalie L. Collie ('Marvell's *Bermudas* and the Puritan Paradise', *Renaissance News*, X, p. 75) has gathered together some of the records left by Puritan travellers of their first impression of the Bermudas. 'There seems to be a continual spring', wrote Captain John Smith. Lewis Hughes felt they were an earthly paradise, another Eden, and praised the goodness of the Lord Jesus in leading them there, showing them that far from being the Island of devils they were 'the vineyard of the Lord Jesus'.

It is refreshing to see that the sternest men of the seventeenth century could be so human, but though it may change our view of the men, it cannot prevent us wondering how they could say it all. To cross the Atlantic and find Eden ought not to be possible in a sinful world. These Puritan travellers were joining 'those Franciscan and Dominican friars' (cited by Poggioli in 'Naboth's Vineyard') 'who took it upon themselves to safeguard the rights of the Indians of all the New Spains of the Americas', and who found themselves led to a belief in the natural goodness of man. The American natives, according to Bartolomé de las Casas, were 'people of the Golden Age, which has been so greatly praised by the poets and historians'.

The pastoral element in 'Bermudas' is only peripheral: a few images suggest the Arcadian tradition. But 'Clorinda and Damon' is pastoral from start to finish. It is so polished a poem, so perfect in decorum, that it almost seems distinctive: as someone in an impeccably conventional suit might, if he carried it with enough assurance, seem the most strikingly dressed man in the room:

> C: *Damon come drive thy flocks this way.*
> D: *No: 'tis too late they went astray.*
> C: *I have a grassy Scutcheon spy'd,*
> *Where Flora blazons all her pride.*
> *The grass I aim to feast thy Sheep:*
> *The Flow'rs I for thy Temples keep.*
> D: *Grass withers; and the Flowers too fade.*
> C: *Seize the short Joyes then, ere they vade.*
> *Seest thou that unfrequented cave?*
> D: *That den?*
> C: *Love's Shrine.*
> D: *But Virtue's Grave.*

The modulation is so tactful as to be a delight. Polished pastoral description for six lines; then a generalising step to the *carpe diem* theme; then another step to moral rebuke, in the same polished diction. The poem has now turned into a moral debate, unexpectedly, but without ruffling its surface. Clorinda urges 'seize the short joys', but Damon no longer wants them. The other day great Pan met him, and

> *He ere since my songs does fill:*
> *And His Name swells my slender Oat.*

It is a debate but not really a conflict; imperceptibly, Clorinda drops her temptation, and joins in the praise of Pan. The final chorus runs:

> *Of* Pan *the flowry Pastures sing,*
> *Caves echo, and the Fountains ring.*
> *Sing then while he doth us inspire;*
> *For all the World is our* Pan's *Quire.*

The brilliant ordinariness of this poem is so striking that one does not, at first, notice its two unusual features. The first is the reversal of the sexes: nymphs don't often woo reluctant shepherds in pastoral. I have to admit critical defeat here. I'm sure this reversal is significant, and in some way deeply right, yet it is hard to say why. Is it because it makes sex seem more natural, more completely accepted? The world Damon has forsaken had no coyness in its nymphs: all the more drastic then is his rejection of it.

190

In rejecting it, he never ceases to speak the language of pastoral: 'Grass withers; and the Flowers too fade'. Most interesting, he speaks of Christ as Pan.

The equating of Christ with Pan is of course an example of the syncretist attitude to pagan mythology, which was discussed in the last chapter. 'Sage and serious Spenser' uses the same figure in the May Eclogue of *The Shepherd's Calendar*, and the prose gloss on this (could it really be by the otherwise so pedantic E. K.?) is one of the most haunting discussions in the Renaissance of the clash between Puritan and syncretist views. The note tells the story of the voice that was heard crying, at the time of the Crucifixion, that Pan was dead

> wherewithall there was heard such piteous outcries, and dreadful shrieking, as hath not been the like. By which Pan, though of some be understood the great Satanas, whose kingdom at that time was by Christ conquered, the gates of hell broken up, and death by death delivered to eternal death, (for at that time, as he saith, all Oracles surceased, and enchanted spirits, that were wont to delude the people, thenceforth held their peace;) and also at the demand of the Emperor Tiberius, who that Pan should be, answer was made him by the wisest and best learned, that it was the son of Mercury and Penelope: yet I think it more properly meant of the death of Christ, the only and very Pan, then suffering for his flock.

How strange that the rejected interpretation should be set forth so eloquently, with such evident passion, learning and understanding; and the accepted one so cursorily stated at the end. In a way, it is another, and better kind of eloquence, and I find the last sentence very moving; but its simplicity seems the right eloquence for the Puritan view, and the fascination with oracles and Tiberius seems to belong to the view that Christ is the only and very Pan. Perhaps these very complications enact some of the interweaving of the two views in the mind of the sixteenth century.

Usually, the syncretist tradition is explicit: commenting on, or translating, ancient literature, it mentions both Christ and Pan, both Noah and Deucalion, and asserts that they are really the same. But if the pagan name only is used, with allegorical intent, we have quite a different effect. It may, as in Marot, be a sign that the poem is pastoral in convention only (this is not true of Spenser or Marvell). In Spenser it is part of a rich world, full of significances

191

and layers of meaning: the birth of Chrysogone's children in *The Faerie Queene*, Book III, is a parallel to the immaculate conception, in which both ideas seem to enrich each other. But the classical, poised Marvell is very different from the rich muddle of Spenser and Golding. This cool, lapidary poem seems to talk of Pan but mean Christ. And for all the explicit Puritanism of Damon's rejection, it does not reject the pastoral tradition. It is imbued with an almost numinous sense of the pagan magic of the world, and as a poem it is utterly un-Puritan.

'The Nymph Complaining for the Death of her Fawn' is less conventionally pastoral, but it explores much more deeply what pastoral is. Once we get used to the quaintness of the subject, and the naïvety, even occasional clumsiness, of the couplets, it is one of the most beautiful of Marvell's poems. Its interpretation is not without controversy: a good deal of learned commentary has disputed whether the poem is Ovidian or Christian, and whether the deer is a symbol for Christ. The controversy matters, since it concerns the poem's view of evil, and this is clearly a poem about innocence and experience. The nymph, who is obviously a figure of innocence, has encountered evil in two ways. One opens the poem:

> *The wanton troopers riding by*
> *Have shot my Faun and it will die.*

The other is more gradually revealed: it is the deceit of Sylvio, who 'left me his Faun, but took his Heart'.

Innocence is represented by the fawn in the garden, playing on roses and lilies.

> *I have a Garden of my own,*
> *But so with Roses over grown,*
> *And Lillies, that you would it guess*
> *To be a little wilderness . . .*
> *For, in the flaxen Lillies shade,*
> *It like a bank of Lillies laid.*
> *Upon the Roses it would feed*
> *Until its Lips even seem'd to bleed . . .*
> *Had it lived long it would have been*
> *Lillies without, Roses within.*

I don't think it matters whether this is a real garden or the *hortus mentis*, the 'garden of the mind'. The latter makes good sense of the structure of the poem: it has surely been set in the nymph's garden from the beginning, and if she is turning now to a garden of her own she must be turning inwards. But it does not make such good sense of the lines themselves, since it seems to be the real fawn who

> all the Spring time of the year
> Only loved to be there.

(why should a mental image of the fawn change its habits with the seasons?); and there is an obvious clumsiness in making the nymph herself ('I have sought it oft . . .') an inhabitant of her *hortus mentis*. But the reason it doesn't matter is that in so symbolic a poem, fawn and garden obviously represent innocence; and a symbol of them will represent innocence too.

Thematically then this passage is the beginning of the poem: she was happy with her fawn in her garden. The garden contrasts with the town, not with the woods and fields—so much so that it is half turned into a wilderness, to prevent us taking it like the mower's 'dead and standing pool of air'. The lilies and roses clearly symbolise innocence, though there is of course an irony in 'lillies without, Roses within'. When the nymph discovers evil, she will feel the garden to be white, the world outside scarlet. The red of the roses contrasts with the symbolic red of the sinful world.

Next (still thinking thematically) comes the first betrayal:

> But Sylvio soon had me beguil'd,
> This waxed tame; while he grew wild,
> And quite regardless of my Smart,
> Left me his Faun, but took his Heart.

Commentaries disagree whether 'beguil'd' means 'seduced', 'deserted', or both. 'Deserted' is certainly the most plausible meaning, especially if 'nymph' means 'virgin', and it makes good sense of the poem's movement; but it does remove from the poem all the haunting suggestions that innocence is pre-sexual:

> Thy love was far more better than
> The love of false and cruel men.

It is tempting to take this as regression: the 'ruined' maid reverting to childhood love, to playing with animals because of the unsexual love she feels for them. In that case her fear that the fawn might, had it lived, have turned out as false as Sylvio is a fear of growing up, transferred from herself to the fawn, and the poem is a pure song of innocence and experience. (For the alternative we do not need to choose between 'seduced' and 'seduced and deserted': it is simply a question of whether 'grew wild and . . . took' is an amplification of the meaning, or the next thing he did.)

Such an equation of innocence with presexuality is certainly plausible, since it is the very theme of at least one of Marvell's poems, 'The Picture of Little TC in a Prospect of Flowers'. The charm of this poem lies in its playful tone, but the material is serious, if not urgent: the relation of childhood to love and death. The second and third stanzas say, elegantly, that the nymph's charm is that she is not yet taking part in the sex war.

Whether or not the beguiling of the fawn's nymph was directly sexual, we are surely right to associate it with growing up. Her paradise was destroyed from within; happiness is by its nature frail, like childhood. The other danger comes from without. She never discovered whether the fawn would grow up as false as Sylvio, because it was killed, quite arbitrarily, by the troopers. And this fact opens the poem, which (we can see now) is written back to front: first the irruption from outside that destroyed innocence, then the danger of innocence itself corrupting, and only after that the description of innocence itself. The last section ('Oh help! O help! I see it faint') is a kind of epilogue, describing the actual death of the fawn and her subsequent grief. The style changes in it: only in this part are we given the baroque images of the brotherless Heliades and their amber tears, or the stone statue that will continue to weep. The poem having made its point, it can end on this more elaborate flourish.

As for the point, it is an important one for pastoral. There are always these two threats to Arcadia, from within and from without. The threat from within is not certain: the pastoral lovers could remain in unchanging bliss, the 'shepherd boy piping as if he never would be old', the lover and his mistress never growing old or ugly:

> She cannot fade, though thou hast not thy bliss,
> For ever wilt thou love, and she be fair.

But the price of this is that they be frozen on a Grecian urn. If Arcadia is to seem alive it will have forces of change: ironies that remind us of the world outside, vitality that will bring ageing, or even simply the sadness of knowing its own frailty. The threat from without is not certain either: since it is arbitrary, its nature is that it always threatens but may never strike. But Sir Calidore has only to ride off on a fresh adventure, and he will find, on his return, Melibee killed and Pastorella captured by bandits: the wanton troopers have shot his fawn.

The argument of this chapter is that Marvell's view of nature is not Christian, since he regards nature as innocent and unfallen; and that this is appropriate for a pastoral poet. The hints that associate natural innocence with childhood are appropriate, too, to the view of pastoral I have advanced. To conclude, we should take a look at the poem in which Marvell explicitly discusses his view of nature, the 'Dialogue between the Soul and the Body'.

It is also a dialogue between two views of man, the once-born and the twice-born. The Soul finds the mortal state one of suffering and conflict, and looks forward to its liberation with the traditional Christian paradoxes:

> *And all my Care itself employs*
> *That to preserve, which me destroys . . .*
> *And ready oft the Port to gain,*
> *Am Shipwrecked into Health again.*

'Our only health is the disease': the Soul speaks like the sinner who has to lose his life to find it. His lines are fascinating in their ability to turn the very facts of corporeal existence into a torture.

> *O who shall from this Dungeon, raise*
> *A Soul inslaved so many ways?*
> *With bolts of Bones, that fettered stands*
> *In Feet; and manacled in Hands.*

The puns are completely justified, since the Soul's point is that the very fact of having hands and feet is a burden. He therefore suggests that the language itself contains what he is saying: he is bringing out a point, not making one.

The Body uses the Soul's rhetoric in reverse. In the first of his stanzas, he maintains that the very fact of the Soul is his burden, and the central image is that of the fever. One by one emotions are named, and equated with diseases. Now if 'possession' by a soul is unnatural, what is natural? Only in the last lines does the Body hint at an answer:

What but a Soul could have the wit
To build me up for Sin so fit?
So Architects do square and hew,
Green Trees that in the Forest grew.

Sin is unnatural: left alone, the Body would then be in harmony with itself. This is the doctrine of the once-born man, at home in the world, accepting his own nature as healthy. Hence the final, marvellously ambivalent image of the green trees. Does the architect destroy what is natural, to create the sophisticated, even the corrupt? Or does he improve the mere wood of the forest by putting it to use? The lines are carefully poised between asserting corruption and asserting improvement: 'square and hew' could be creative or could be destructive. The Body means it as destructive, of course; but there is a sense in which the lines don't altogether belong to the Body: in their ambivalence, they are Marvell's own comment. They remind us that the poem is a dialogue.

Pastoral *versus* Christianity: it is the same contrast as that of Body and Soul. The poem is a dialogue between Fallen Man and Natural Man, between Man divided against himself and Man who believes himself innocent. As if to confirm the point of this essay, Marvell gives to his Natural Man a concluding image of the forest.

THE LOSS OF PARADISE

P ASTORAL and Christianity conflict because of the Fall; and so the Christian poet has one way of avoiding the conflict. If he writes about the time when man was unfallen, he can with good conscience use pastoral imagery and the feeling of innocence. The Christian Arcadia was Eden.

The Fall is both like and unlike the loss of the Golden Age, as we have seen in Chapter III; and a poetic treatment of it can emphasise either the likeness (with sadness, as loss) or the difference (with anger or guilt, as corruption). And of one thing we can be certain: that by discussing *Paradise Lost* in this way, we are looking at the poem as Milton intended us to. He could, after all, have called it *Adam's Fall*, or *Mankind's Corruption*, or at least *Adam Unparadis'd*. He has invited us to place Paradise, rather than Adam or God, at the centre of our thoughts.

How does Milton depict life in Eden? The task has one intrinsic difficulty, that might at first seem insuperable. The happiness of Paradise was beyond any happiness we can know; how then can it be described? If it can be described, how does it differ from ordinary, post-lapsarian happiness? Must our praise of Paradise be merely Benthamite, that its joys lasted longer, recurred more often, were felt more intensely than ours, but were not of an unimaginably different kind? The only alternative would be to describe Eden by negatives, to keep assuring ourselves that this or that joy is inadequate for understanding what it was like. Rhetorically, the trick stales easily: none the less, we shall see that Milton did make one use, and a very powerful use, of it.

The most acute manifestation of this problem concerns the love of Adam and Eve. This is because Milton departs from tradition and makes that love carnal, thus maintaining that the Fall did not cause sexuality, but corrupted it. This gives him one enormous advantage in his poem: when he describes pre-lapsarian love, he really has something to write about. It puts him among the poets of free, not chaste Arcadia (and in this Arcadia the problem of profligacy does not arise!). His material is not shadowy and unreal, but has the richness of love as we know it.

Such was the poetic opportunity he gave himself. To see the results, we can turn to the hymn to wedded love in Book IV:

> *This said unanimous, and other Rites*
> *Observing none, but adoration pure*
> *Which God likes best, into their inmost bower*
> *Handed they went; and eas'd the putting off*
> *These troublesome disguises which we wear,*
> *Straight side by side were laid, nor turnd I ween*
> *Adam from his fair Spouse, nor Eve the rites*
> *Mysterious of connubial love refus'd:*
> *Whatever Hypocrites austerely talk*
> *Of purity and place and innocence,*
> *Defaming as impure what God declares*
> *Pure, and commands to some, leaves free to all.*
> *Our Maker bids increase, who bids abstain*
> *But our Destroyer, foe to God and Man?*
> *Hail wedded Love, mysterious law, true source*
> *Of human offspring, sole propriety*
> *In paradise of all things common else . . .*
> *Here Love his golden shafts employs, here lights*
> *His constant lamp, and waves his purple wings,*
> *Reigns here and revels; not in the bought smile*
> *Of Harlots, loveless, joyless, unindeared,*
> *Casual fruition, nor in Court amours,*
> *Mixt dance, or wanton masque, or midnight ball,*
> *Or Serenade, which the starv'd lover sings*
> *To his proud fair, best quitted with disdain.*
> *These lulld by Nightingales imbracing slept,*
> *And on their naked limbs the flowery roof*
> *Showered Roses, which the morn repair'd. Sleep on*
> *Blest pair; and O yet happiest if ye seek*
> *No happier state, and know to know no more.*

> IV.736-752, 763-776

Three styles are distinguishable in this passage. There is the formal eloquence of 'Hail wedded Love, mysterious Law. . .', the deliberately solemn invocation of a concept the poet wishes us to reverence. This is the style that twentieth-century readers will have most difficulty with, since the extreme formality seems to us like stiffness, the complete lack of speech rhythm suggests a lack

198

of genuine feeling. I suspect it must have been difficult for the seventeenth-century reader too, when faced with this style, to distinguish empty eloquence from the solemn voice of formalised emotion; and it is as wrong for us, in an excess of historical con-scientiousness, to concede the invariable beauty of such passages, as it would be to disparage their invariable emptiness. Perhaps all we can say of this example is that the eloquence will powerfully underwrite the beauty of any lines that move us by less obviously rhetorical means.

Secondly, there is the very personal voice of Milton the contro-versialist, angry with the obstinacy of his opponents, shouting louder than them, not above insulting them ('whatever hypocrites austerely talk . . .'). It is a voice very familiar to the reader of Milton's pamphlets; poetically, it seems to belong to satire rather than epic, and it was surely controversial zeal rather than poetic judgement that brought it in here. It comes, we can notice, not once but twice in this short passage: in the lines against the hypocrites (744-749) and in the outburst against harlots and court amours (766-770).

These lines are hardly to modern taste, yet their occurrence here is interesting and even, in a way, effective. The second passage is a direct statement of pastoralism: the innocence of love in Eden is so attractive because of the contrast with courtly sophistication, with its

> Serenade, which the starv'd lover sings
> To his proud fair, best quitted with disdain,

where a surprising new touch is introduced, not indignation now but contempt, and contempt because the sophisticated lover has to do without sex! 'Starv'd' (a sexual meaning is surely the most probable here) is a brilliant touch, and makes, in this personal style, the same point as the earlier passage made argumentatively:

> Our Maker bids increase, who bids abstain
> But our destroyer, foe to God and man.

If we think what has happened to the meaning of 'puritan' since, or if we think of Comus, it is instructive to find the great Puritan poet telling us angrily that sex comes from God and abstinence comes from the devil.

The third style of the passage is the tender lyricism of its close, which enlists the nature imagery on the side of sexuality, and movingly hints at the fragility of their happiness. If this is an Arcadia of sexual fulfilment, it has a new note of moral earnestness added, and a more direct threat than usual of impending destruction.

For all its unevenness, the passage is memorable, and gives life to Eden; but the poetic price to be paid for all this is clear when the Fall has taken place. For the first result of eating the apple was lust; and next to the account of pre-lapsarian sex, we must now put this account of post-lapsarian:

> *but that false fruit*
> *Far other operation first displaid,*
> *Carnal desire inflaming, he on Eve*
> *Began to cast lascivious eyes, she him*
> *As wantonly repaid; in lust they burn:*
> *Till Adam thus 'gan Eve to dalliance move.*
>
> *Eve, now I see thou art exact of taste,*
> *And elegant, of Sapience no small part,*
> *Since to each meaning savour we apply,*
> *And Palate call judicious; I the praise*
> *Yield thee, so well this day thou has purvey'd.*
> *Much pleasure we have lost, while we abstain'd*
> *From this delightful fruit, nor known till now*
> *True relish, tasting; if such pleasure be*
> *In things to us forbidden, it might be wish'd*
> *For this one tree had been forbidden ten.*
> *But come, so well refresh't, now let us play,*
> *As meet is, after such delicious fare;*
> *For never did thy beauty since the day*
> *I saw thee first and wedded thee, adorn'd*
> *With all perfections, so enflame my sense*
> *With ardor to enjoy thee, fairer now*
> *Than ever, bounty of this virtuous tree.*
>
> *So said he, and forbore not glance or toy*
> *Or amorous intent, well understood*
> *Of Eve, whose Eye darted contagious fire.*
> *Her hand he seiz'd, and to a shady bank,*
> *Thick overhead with verdant roof embower'd*
> *He led her nothing loth; flowers were the couch,*
> *Pansies and violets and asphodel,*
> *And hyacinth, earth's freshest softest lap.*
> *There they their fill of love and love's disport*

Took largely, of their mutual guilt the seal,
The solace of their sin, till dewy sleep
Oppressed them, wearied with their amorous play.

IX.1010-1045

These marvellous lines are impregnated with that feverish quality
that distinguishes lust from love. At the climax of his invitation, Adam uses the highly ambiguous, charged word 'play'; Milton
spits out some of his contempt in 'nothing loth'; and the lines
culminate in a brilliant impression of sexual exhaustion. It is
interesting too that the first effect of the fruit is not only to in-
flame lust but to corrupt the intellect: the two go hand in hand,
for Adam's seduction speech carefully justified his invitation with
a good deal of neo-Platonic sophistry. His first four lines, finding
correspondences between excellence of intellect and the cultivation
of the various senses, sounds like something which a Renaissance
intellectual might—just—have said seriously. Perhaps some of our
modern scepticism at Renaissance Platonism is bolstered by
observing that Milton gives this kind of reasoning to Adam as the
first consequence of the Fall.

These two passages, dealing with pre- and post-lapsarian sex,
are clearly parallel, and some of the differences are subtle and
effective. In both cases, the setting is one of flowers: in the later
passage, of course, for the sake of the contrast between 'earth's
freshest, softest lap' and 'love's disport'. But the earlier passage
also has a hint of a contrast. The showering of roses is an echo and
a crowning of their love-making, but it is difficult not to feel that
they belong so perfectly in Eden because they are asleep. What
they will wake to is the amorous play of Book IX.

Here we have two love scenes: are we more struck by their
difference, or their resemblance? The problem is obvious: if by
their resemblance, then what is the difference between fallen and
unfallen sex? If by their difference, then is the earlier scene really
about sex? Or (the same question) if it is, was Paradisal sex so
unimaginable, that we mislead ourselves by calling it sex at all?

Certainly the difference between the two scenes is obvious and
violent. It is the difference between the two kinds of love in Keats'
Lamia: the unfallen love of Hermes and the nymph, set in Arcadia:

> *Upon a time, before the faery broods*
> *Drove nymph and satyr from the prosperous woods,*

201

and the deeply tainted sexuality of Lycius and Lamia, that enriches the senses but destroys the man, and can lead only to
self-deception or death. Keats offers us the same contrast in the
Ode on a Grecian Urn, where the unheard melodies and unfelt
sexuality are set against something very like Adam's seduction
of Eve:

> *All breathing human passion far above,*
> *That leaves a heart high sorrowful and cloyed,*
> *A burning forehead and a parching tongue.*

Now the contrast in the *Grecian Urn* is between human passion
and a perfection that depends on catching the moment before fulfilment and freezing it out of existence, and into the substitute
existence of art. Perfection and existence are incompatible.

The application to *Paradise Lost* is irresistible: fallen sexuality
differs from unfallen by being *real*. Its immediacy is compelling:
this is breathing human passion as we know it. What is there in
the earlier passage that corresponds to this sexual realism? The
answer is, nothing. Milton has simply omitted details that in
Book IX he mentioned. Sex is not here described in equivalent
but uncorrupted detail, it is merely mentioned in general terms
and not described at all. It is hard not to conclude that we have
here a contrast between the unreal and the real.

II

Most of Milton's account of Paradise describes not the behaviour
of Adam and Eve, but the Garden itself, and on this too there is
much to say. The most important descriptive passage is Book IV,
lines 131-287, and what strikes us most strongly, perhaps, is how
conventional its details are:

> *And higher than that wall a circling row*
> *Of goodliest trees, loaden with fairest fruit,*
> *Blossoms and fruits at once of golden hue,*
> *Appeared, with gay enamelled colours mixed;*
> *On which the sun more glad impressed his beams*
> *Than in fair evening cloud, or humid bow,*
> *When God hath showered the earth: so lovely seemed*
> *That landskip.*

All the epithets are general: the trees are 'goodly', the fruit 'fairest',
the colours 'gay' and 'enamelled'. It is a passage we could easily
match in contemporary descriptive verse:

> Upon this mount there stood a stately grove,
> Whose reaching arms, to clip the welkin strove,
> Of tufted cedars, and the branching pine. . . .
> Imbraudering these in curious trails along,
> The clustered grapes, the golden citrons hung,
> More glorious than the previous fruits were these,
> Kept by the dragon in Hesperides . . .
> Out of this soil sweet bubbling fountains crept,
> As though for joy the senseless stones had wept;
> With straying channels dancing sundry ways,
> With often turns, like to a curious maze:
> Which breaking forth, the tender grass bedewed,
> Whose silver sand with orient pearls was strewed . . .
>
> Drayton: *Endimion and Phoebe*

Drayton has none of Milton's rhythmic magic, but he has most of
his diction: his 'stately grove' and 'tufted cedars' belong on the
same canvas as Milton's goodliest trees. There is only one touch in
the Milton that has no parallel whatever in the Drayton; that is the
last five words. 'So lovely seemed that landskip': this sounds more
like someone's comment than part of the description proper—as if,
having carried out his conventional task, the poet has to assure
us, in his own person, that he really means it. Though the tone is
quite different, this irruption of the personal has something in
common with the irruption of Puritan anger we noticed in the
Wedded Love passage.

A little later in Book IV we are told about the fountain:

> How from that sapphire fount the crisped brooks
> Rolling on orient pearl and sands of gold,
> With mazy error under pendant shades
> Ran nectar, visiting each plant, and fed
> Flowers worthy of Paradise, which not nice Art
> In beds and curious knots, but Nature boon
> Poured forth profuse on hill, and dale, and plain,
> Both where the morning sun first warmly smote
> The open field, and where the unpierced shade
> Imbrowned the noontide bowers. Thus was this place,
> A happy rural seat of various view:

Groves whose rich trees wept odorous gums and balm;
Others whose fruit, burnished with golden rind,
Hung amiable,—Hesperian fables true,
If true, here only—and of delicious taste.

Once again, this is the descriptive world of Drayton: for 'curious maze' and 'golden citrons' we have 'curious knots' and 'golden rind', and both poets have (inevitably) 'orient pearl'. These epithets offer neither the particularity of sense-experiences, nor a subtlety of meaning that corresponds to the poem's needs at the moment; their function is to assert poetic habit, to remind the reader of certain accepted ways of describing. When Milton adds touches of individuality that outgo Drayton, what he offers is not perceptual but linguistic vigour: he resurrects an etymology ('mazy error') or displays a Latinism ('pendant shades'). And then once again, in the midst of all this, a personal note intrudes:

—Hesperian fables true,
If true, here only—and of delicious taste.

There is nothing unusual in mentioning the Gardens of the Hesperides: Drayton did the same, we notice. Indeed, Milton offers classical parallels all through Book IV: one of his main rhetorical devices is to tell us that this Paradise surpasses all the classical paradises.

not that fair field
Of Enna, where Proserpine gathering flowers,
Herself a fairer flower, by gloomy Dis
Was gathered—which cost Ceres all that pain
To seek her through the world—nor that sweet grove
Of Daphne, by Orontes and the inspired
Castalian spring, might with this Paradise
Of Eden strive.

There is no higher compliment in Milton's power, as many commentators have pointed out, than to offer up in sacrifice a whole lifetime's dedication to classical studies. Nothing in this marvellous list, he tells us, was as fine as Eden: and it hurts to say it. Surely it is not far-fetched to find that hurt, that personal pain of the poet at what he is writing, in the wonderful rhythm of

might with this Paradise
Of Eden strive,

204

and also in the so strangely moving familiarity of 'all that pain', which *means* 'Ceres' pain', but takes its poignancy from the hidden sorrow of the poet himself. And it is fitting too that he cannot leave the point alone, that he must go on and on for another ten lines, piling on more and more out of the way references, giving it all away for God. So far from being a wanton display of Milton's monstrous learning, it is a piece of triumphant relevance: the more he can find to dazzle us with, the greater is the compliment he is paying to Eden.

And in a quaintly intimate way, we can see the same struggle compressed into the eleven words quoted earlier. Imagine that Milton has written:

> *Hesperian fables true*
> *And of delicious taste—*

(it is metrically plausible, and I like to think this is how it happened). This would be a gesture of supreme eloquence by Milton the humanist, an extravagance of classically-based compliment. And then into this he inserts a parenthesis: 'if true, here only'. Perhaps it is a nostalgic touch: how sad that the pagan stories are not, after all, true. Or perhaps it is angry, a rebuke by the Puritan to the humanist. The words can be read either way: what is certain is that they sound like a personal irruption.

Such irruptions are scattered through the description, as if Milton the man felt he had to keep breaking in on Milton the poet to add something in his own voice. Often they come during the classical allusions, or are used to introduce them.

> *In shadier bower*
> *More sacred or sequestered, though but feigned,*
> *Pan or Sylvanus never slept, nor Nymph*
> *Nor Faunus haunted.*

> IV.706

Here the parenthesis, 'though but feigned' (humanist-nostalgic this time, or Puritan-angry?) is more smoothly integrated, and there is a note of personal urgency all through the lines, springing (such technique must be quite unconscious here) from the way the sentence balances on adverbs and conjunctions that all can be emphasised in the reading, and that all concern the same renunciation: 'more . . . though . . . never . . . nor . . . nor'.

Unpoetic and even quaint as they are, these touches of direct intervention seem oddly welcome when we read. No doubt modern taste is speaking in this comment—we like the irruption of the unpoetic, and a few crisped brooks go a long way with us—but I think there is also a reason for accepting them that the seventeenth-century reader could not fail to accept. The smooth descriptions needed breaking up because they are in a serious way inappropriate to their subject. There is a large discrepancy between style and content in Book IV.

Gardens, as we saw in the last chapter, form the centre of a threefold contrast: natural when compared with the town, artificial when compared with woods and fields. There can be no doubt which way Milton saw Eden. His garden is almost nature herself: it grows luxuriantly, it can't be controlled (this is useful proleptically, since it shows Adam and Eve their need for offspring to help them prune and lop), it bursts with abundance and fertility. This is how it appears to Raphael when he arrives on earth in Book V. Raphael himself is a source of life and energy:

> *like Maia's son he stood,*
> *And shook his plumes, that heavenly fragrance filled*
> *The circuit wide*

(No Puritan parenthesis there!); and as he walks through Eden, this is what he sees:

> *Their glittering tents he passed, and now is come*
> *Into the blissful field, through groves of myrrh,*
> *And flowering odours, cassia, nard, and balm,*
> *A wilderness of sweets; for Nature here*
> *Wantoned as in her prime, and played at will*
> *Her virgin fancies, pouring forth more sweet,*
> *Wild above rule or art, enormous bliss.*
>
> V.285-7, 291-7

Slight sexual hints have been added here to an account of fertility that can be matched from innumerable other passages. One such has already been quoted:

> *. . . fed*
> *Flowers worthy of Paradise, which not nice Art*
> *In beds and curious knots, but Nature boon*
> *Poured forth profuse on hill, and dale, and plain . . .*

The contradiction between style and content is simply this: that the style, as we have seen, is full of nice art. The careful polish of

the decorous epithets is a world away from the enormous, un-
restrained bliss of Eden.

The lines about ambrosial fruit and pendant shades could have
been written by Drayton—or by a score of others. The genius of
Milton appears not in them but in the moments at which they are
pushed aside for something else—even for the clumsy personal
interventions we have glanced at. Sometimes they are pushed
aside by something easier and less obvious—the simple removal
of polish. In the crucial line of this short passage there are no
adjectives:

> *Poured forth profuse on hill, and dale, and plain.*

'Hill, and dale, and plain'; a simple emphatic reading will convey
the point of the line, that the profusion was everywhere, that these
are not enamelled plains, for we are not now stopping to nod and
admire them, but the list of three nouns means 'all over the place'.
The long emphatic syllable of 'poured', starting the line, helps us
to get the right gesture of extravagance into our voice. Here as so
often, Milton's rhythm works on a profounder level than his
epithets.

III

There is one last point to be made about Eden, the most important of all. Indeed, it is a point about the whole poem, and
shows us its profoundest link with the pastoral tradition. It concerns the fact that Eden is doomed.

That Adam is going to fall has been told us over and over again,
from the very first line of the poem. We know all along that Adam
and Eve must be banished, and it is a fair guess that the garden
will be destroyed. The sadness of this loss is almost unbearable:

> *O unexpected stroke, worse than of Death!*
> *Must I thus leave thee, Paradise? thus leave*
> *Thee, native soil, these happy walks and shades,*
> *Fit haunt of Gods? where I had hope to spend,*
> *Quiet though sad, the respite of that day*
> *That must be mortal to us both. O flowers,*
> *That never will in other climate grow,*
> *My early visitation, and my last*
> *At ev'n, which I bred up with tender hand*
> *From the first op'ning bud, and gave ye names,*

Who now shall rear ye to the sun, or rank
Your tribes, and water from th'ambrosial fount?
Thee lastly nuptial bower, by me adorned
With what to sight or smell was sweet; from thee
How shall I part, and whither wander down
Into a lower world, to this obscure
And wild, how shall we breath in other air
Less pure, accustomed to immortal fruits?

XI.268-286

This is Eve's lament on learning that they must leave Eden. After its rhetorical opening, it turns into some of Milton's tenderest poetry. It is, to begin with, beautifully feminine: what will happen to the house when I am away? No one else can be trusted to look after things: 'who now shall rear ye . . .'. One would have thought the angels could perform so simple a task—but not to the anxious housewife. And as she thinks of Eden now, we see that Eve has already adjusted to the Fall, if only she could stay there. It is not hard for her to picture a 'quiet though sad' life there, and the loss of home seems to teach her the meaning of the Fall afresh. One of the most haunting touches in these lines is one which Milton probably never intended, though it is hard to think he did not feel it: 'My early visitation and my last—'. The line seems completely self-contained, associating finality and loss with the first task of her life. It is only reading on that we see the enjambment, and are forced to attach a less resonant meaning to 'last', as it becomes 'last at even'—just as 'Nymphs and shepherds dance no more' grows less resonant as we move to the Countess Dowager of Derby's house at Harefield (see Chapter XI). The line shrinks a little, but it has already made its nostalgic point.

The point was that Eden is tinged with sadness. Of course it is easy for Eve to think this now, and to read her new feelings back into her old home. Has Milton charged pre-lapsarian Eden with sadness too?

Thus saying, from her husband's hand her hand
Soft she withdrew, and like a Woodnymph light
Oread or Dryad, or of Delia's train,
Betook her to the groves, but Delia's self
In gait surpass'd and goddess-like deport,
Though not as she with bow and quiver arm'd,
But with such gardening tools as art yet rude,

Guiltless of fire had form'd, or angels brought.
To Pales or Pomona, thus adorn'd,
Likest she seemed, Pomona when she fled
Vertumnus, or to Ceres in her prime,
Yet virgin of Proserpina from Jove.

IX.385-396

It is a deservedly famous passage: our last glimpse of Eve while still innocent. Perhaps surprisingly, it does not use a proleptic simile to hint at the Fall. The description of the nuptial bower in Book IV, for instance, paused to mention the beauty of Eve when she was brought to Adam:

> *More lovely than Pandora, whom the gods*
> *Endowed with all their gifts, and O too like*
> *In sad event . . .*

IV.714-6

That is an especially explicit example of a favourite method of Milton's, spinning out the details of the simile to hint at what is to come. In this description of Eve in Book IX, however, prolepsis is used very delicately, hardly more than hinted at. Ceres in her prime was 'yet virgin of Proserpina from Jove': this reminds us that Eve has not yet had children, but doesn't suggest sin. The art that wrought Eve's tools is 'Guiltless of fire': the word is metaphorical, of course, but its literal meaning, hovering as a shadow, may touch Eve herself.

The rejection of the classical allusions, too, is very delicate, consisting of one line only ('but Delia's self In gait surpass'd and goddess-like deport'). It is the milder kind of rejection: it does not rebuke the classical, it does not tell us harshly that Delia is a fiction, is but feigned, it simply tells us that Eve was more beautiful. And Pales or Pomona are not put down at all.

I am not sure I can account for the strange beauty of these lines. They contain a hint of doom, haunting and mysterious, hard to locate, harder to describe. In some way, it must be due to the classical allusions; and it is striking that they are used so abundantly at this moment.

Eden, as we have seen, is the one subject on which a Christian poet can use pastoral imagery. Milton is sometimes uneasy about such imagery, because it is pagan and therefore wicked, but if the classical myths are really accepted then it is appropriate, but only up to the Fall. After that it will be not too wicked but too innocent. We are here at the very verge of the Fall, and at this moment Milton smothers Eve in suggestions of pastoral freshness and purity—and he almost refrains from his usual stern warnings that the comparisons are not fine enough. The frailty belongs to the act of comparison; and to insert, at this point, too open a rebuke to idolatry would quite destroy its strange magic.

IV

Finally, what are we to think of the loss of Eden? Could we have lived there forever, or did we have to leave? Was it even desirable that we should leave? Was it inevitable *and* desirable, like the proletarian revolution? The view that our greatest woe led to our greatest blessing is certainly present in the poem. Thus Adam in the last book rejoices over the Fall:

> *O Goodness infinite, Goodness immense,*
> *That all this good of evil shall produce*
> *And evil turn to good—more wonderful*
> *Than that which by creation first brought forth*
> *Light out of darkness! Full of doubt I stand*
> *Whether I should repent me now of sin*
> *By me done and occasioned, or rejoice*
> *Much more that much more good thereof shall spring.*
> XII.469-476

As Lovejoy has pointed out in his well-known article ('Milton and the Paradox of the Fortunate Fall', *Essays in the History of Ideas*, 1948) this joy of Adam's is not really unorthodox: *O felix culpa, quae talem ac tantum meruit habere Redemptorem.* Theologians may not have liked to dwell on the thought that the Fall was a blessing in the end, since it seems to take away its wickedness; but those who did point it out were willing to accept the paradox. Lovejoy quotes Gregory the Great:

What greater fault than that by which we all die? And what greater goodness than that by which we are freed from death? And certainly, unless Adam had sinned, it would not have behooved our Redeemer to take on our flesh. Almighty God saw beforehand that from that evil because of which men were to die, He would bring about a good which would overcome that evil. How wonderfully the good surpasses that evil, what faithful believer can fail to see? Great, indeed, are the evils we deservedly suffer in consequence of the first sin; but who of the elect would not willingly endure still worse evils, rather than not have so great a Redeemer?

To say this is certainly to say that the Fall was desirable. Is it also to say that it was inevitable? Yes, but only in a completely external sense. If God has given us so great a blessing as the Redemption, he must have done it deliberately; he must therefore have intended it from the beginning, and since there can be no Redemption without sin, he must have intended us to sin. There can be no way of avoiding what God has intended, therefore the Fall was inevitable.

No orthodox theologian can quite reject this reasoning, unless he is prepared to question God's omnipotence (and thus cease to be orthodox). So the Fall was inevitable: but with a special kind of inevitability, one that we deduce from studying what seem to have been God's intentions, not one which follows from the very nature of Adam's situation. An undeduced, immediate inevitability would be quite different: it would say that you obviously can't live in Eden forever, but must emerge into the world: pastoral poetry must change its notes to tragic. It would also say that the loss of Eden is a disaster, but inevitable and, yes, in the end desirable: not for an external reason, but because Eden is like that. And if that is the nature of Eden, it is also the nature of childhood: its loss is inevitable, desirable, and—in retrospect—unutterably sad. This then is the view which regards the Fall as growing up.

Whereas the Fortunate Fall, as St Gregory saw it, was an orthodox if disquieting doctrine, this version would be thoroughly heretical. That the Fall *in itself* was a gain must be unimaginable for a Christian. 'If the circumstances of this crime are duly considered, it will be acknowledged to have been a most heinous offence, and a transgression of the whole law. For what sin can be named, which was not included in this one act?'

So we need hardly ask which version of the Fortunate Fall Milton held—or need we? Doctrinally and officially he naturally held St Gregory's, and the fierce sentences I have just quoted are in fact by Milton (from the *De Doctrina Christiana*). But is there poetry in the orthodox view? There could be tragic poetry, and there could be heroic hope in it, but no pastoral. It is not a view that could suffuse Eden with sadness, shadow its landscape with

211

the inevitability of doom, or lead to any of the effects this chapter has tried to describe. It is not a view that tells us anything at all about Eden.

Milton would no doubt have been properly horrified at the suggestion that the apple had to be eaten in the same way that we have to grow up: yet it was in some sense a suggestion that fed his imagination. It saw Eve hovering on the edge of her doom like a wood-nymph light; and it saw Eden as Hesperian fables true. It closed the poem, too:

> *In either hand the hastening Angel caught*
> *Our lingering parents, and to the eastern gate*
> *Led them direct. . . .*
> *Some natural tears they dropped, but wiped them soon;*
> *The world was all before them, where to choose*
> *Their place of rest, and Providence their guide.*
> *They, hand in hand, with wandering steps and slow,*
> *Through Eden took their solitary way.*

XII.637-9, 645-9

These lines are built on a contrast between grief and comfort. Adam and Eve grieve because they realise their sin; they are strengthened because God has promised his providence. Now the beauty of the lines springs entirely from the grief. It is presented as inescapable, muted—and natural. The comfort appears rather stiffly ('and Providence their guide') and is then forgotten for the slow, sad close. Instead of ending his poem on a note of struggle and contrast, Milton has turned guilt and repentance into sad acceptance. 'The world was all before them': it is one of the richest lines in poetry, and I do not want to exclude any of its reverberations of meaning. But its very presence at the end of this poem testifies to the second, unorthodox feeling about the Fortunate Fall. These are two beginners setting out on life's journey. The scene is shown with a tremulous hope (that is their own) and a deep sadness (that is ours).

The last line of all tells us nothing about the Incarnation or the Redemption or even about sin. It does not justify the ways of God, and is not even specifically Christian. It takes us back to where the title started us from, it directs our attention to Paradise and the fact that it must be left behind. It is suffused not with the doctrine Milton believed in, but with the vision of Arcadia that he loved, that shaped his imagination and coloured his poem.

XI

OLYMPUS' FADED HIERARCHY

I

'WHAT is it in these six simple words of Milton,' asked Housman in his famous lecture, 'that can draw tears, as I know it can, to the eyes of more readers than one? . . . I can only say, because they are poetry, and find their way to something in man which is obscure and latent, something older than the present organisation of his nature.' The six words are the opening line of the last song in *Arcades*, but we shall need to quote at least half a dozen lines:

> *Nymphs and shepherds dance no more*
> *By sandy Ladons lillied banks.*
> *On old Lycaeus or Cyllene hoar,*
> *Trip no more in twilight ranks,*
> *Though Erymanth your loss deplore,*
> *A better soil shall give ye thanks.*

Housman's tears seem to have caused him, on the literal level, to ignore Milton's point (I will not say to miss it, since he remarks that the 'sense' of the line is gay). And so Mr F. W. Bateson has riposted:

> Milton's injunction to the nymphs and shepherds was not, in fact, to stop dancing, but to 'dance no more "By sandy Ladons lillied banks"'. The nymphs were only to transfer their dances from Arcadia to Harefield in Middlesex. . . . Housman's tears came from taking Milton's line out of context and giving it a meaning it was never intended to have.

I know few neater examples than this of the difference between a poet's reading and a scholar's reading. Would Milton—who after all was both—have treated Housman's tears with such learned disdain? Is it, for instance, an accident that his first line sounds so self-contained? Or that it has such a delicate ambiguity, between personal and historical regret—any given group of nymphs and shepherds will cease dancing, for death, too, is in Arcadia; and in this late age of the world the woods of Arcady are dead, and the dancing over. It is very like the ambiguity of Eliot's line in *The*

Waste Land, 'the nymphs are departed', which means either 'the young ladies have gone home' or 'who would describe *this* landscape in pastoral terms?' Eliot's point is the same as Milton's, and so is his technique; only his mood is different, for his anti-romanticism has renounced the plangent overtones of 'no more' —he doesn't care to bring tears to anyone.

All this is achieved by Milton in one line; and it reverberates through four more before it is finally pushed aside. These four lines list the places in which the dance has ceased, now Greece has lost her pastoral tradition. With cumulative sadness they make it clear that the historical and not the personal meaning is the one that matters, building up a sense of loss that line 6 can now push aside into a graceful compliment—indeed, if we really feel the pathos of Erymanth's loss, an almost desperate compliment—to the Countess of Derby. The dispute between Housman and Bateson is actually enacted by the movement of the song.

Milton's line asserts unquestioningly that the pastoral landscape is impregnated with loss. Arcadia is the happy place, but you cannot think about it without sadness. Wanton troopers riding by will shoot the fawn; the apple will be eaten and the great gates shut; the Golden Age will give place to silver, to bronze, to iron. All this is concerned not with what the poet has lost, but with what the world has lost. It says not 'nymphs depart' but 'the woods of Arcady are dead: the nymphs are departed'. The nostalgia of *Arcades* is impersonal.

This historical nostalgia is the theme of the ensuing discussion of Keats. For Keats is, in Schiller's famous terminology, a sentimental and not a naïve poet. A poet, according to Schiller, is either nature, or will search for it. The naïve poet moves us through the natural, through his dry truthfulness, through the living present; the sentimental is concerned with the clash between two conflicting concepts and sensibilities, with reality as a frontier and his ideas as the infinite. Homer is the supreme naïve poet, for the Greeks were in direct touch with nature in a way no longer possible for us. But we who are civilised and live in a later age have lost this innocence, and our feeling for nature is like that of the invalid for health. Our ancestor is not Homer but Horace, the poet of a cultivated and decadent age, who in consequence values peace and contentment in his country retreat. What makes Horace pastoral is, for Schiller, what makes him sentimental.

Keats' central poem of historical nostalgia is the *Ode to Psyche*. Certainly it seems one of his most personal poems, both extrinsically and internally. By 'extrinsically' I mean that its themes and concerns are those which haunted Keats. The possibility of sexual love that is free from sorrow and sick after-taste is almost an obsession in some of the poems, *Lamia, La Belle Dame, Ode on a Grecian Urn*; that possibility appears for a moving instant to be realised here:

> *Their arms embraced, and their pinions too;*
> *Their lips touch'd not, but had not bade adieu,*
> *As if disjoined by soft-handed slumber,*
> *And ready still past kisses to outnumber*
> *At ready eye-dawn of aurorean love . . .*

This time it is not explicitly set against a version of corrupt and human sexuality, as in the *Grecian Urn*; but there is an equivalent to that contrast in the question (another recurring obsession of Keats) whether this vision is to be trusted:

> *Surely I dreamt today, or did I see*
> *The winged Psyche with awakened eyes?*

He did dream of course, but it was Adam's dream: you awake and find it true. Or at least—this is the Keatsian desperation—you tell yourself this.

But it is not necessary to look at Keats' other poems and letters in order to see this as a deeply personal poem. It is after all personal in the most literal sense—the poet enters in his own person at the end. Clamouring for the honour of being the priest of Psyche, he offers to do more than honour her:

> *Yes, I will be thy priest, and build a fane*
> *In some untrodden region of my mind,*
> *Where branched thoughts, new grown with pleasant pain,*
> *Instead of pines shall murmur in the wind.*

This last stanza is one of the most astonishing in English poetry: a unique meeting-point of the metaphysical and the Romantic. It is an elaborate conceit on the nature of mental experience, in which the mind is described in physical terms, and an act of homage which consists of feelings not of actions is described through the image of building a temple. It has all the cool detachment needed for the elaboration of this conceit, yet at the same time it has, magically, an urgent personal involvement.

> *And there shall be for thee all soft delight*
> *That shadowy thought can win,*
> *A bright torch, and a casement ope at night,*
> *To let the warm Love in!*

Why is this passage so haunting? Partly, the power comes from the last line, which for all its apparent simplicity seems to be saying something mysterious, even weird. The mystery derives from the uncertain status of 'Love'. If we isolate the lines from their context for a moment, we could imagine that they belonged in a direct and literal love-poem, addressed to a woman: in that case 'Love' would refer to the emotion. Only if we put them back in the context of the poem's extended conceit is it clear that they refer to the God. There is a tension between the particular (a literal love-poem, an actual figure of a God) and the abstract (a conceit, an emotion): if it is particular in one respect, it is abstract in the other.

But personal as the poem is, it has a wider subject: title and argument both tell us that it is a poem about mythology. It asserts a double loss, both caused by the passage of time. There is, first, the fact (a fact that reverberates through Keats' poetry) that we live in a late day. Perhaps nothing in *Endymion* is as moving as the last lines of its Preface:

> I hope I have not in too late a day touched the beautiful mythology of Greece, and dulled its brightness: for I wish to try once more, before I bid it farewell.

There are really only four lines in the *Ode to Psyche* on this theme but they are crucial:

> *Yet even in these days so far retir'd*
> *From happy pieties, thy lucent fans*
> *Fluttering among the faint Olympians,*
> *I see and sing, by my own eyes inspired.*

There is much more on another historical gap, not that between ancient Greece and Italy, but that between classical Greece and late antiquity, which produced the tale of Cupid and Psyche, the

> *latest born and lovliest vision far*
> *Of all Olympus' faded hierarchy!*

We know this theme was in Keats' mind from the long journal letter to George and Georgiana, into which he transcribed the poem:

> You must recollect that Psyche was not embodied as a goddess before the time of Apuleius the Platonist who lived after the Augustan age and consequently the Goddess was never worshipped or sacrificed to with any of the ancient fervour—and perhaps never thought of in the old religion—I am more orthodox than to let a heathen Goddess be so neglected.

The third and fourth stanzas take their whole point from this theme; for their purpose is actually to *comfort* Psyche, born too late for real worship. The concern expressed with such gracious irony in the letter appears with intense sadness in the poem:

> *Too, too late for the fond believing lyre,*
> *When holy were the haunted forest boughs,*
> *Holy the air, the water and the fire.*

The holiness of these boughs is seen with a double nostalgia, Psyche's and our own. This can be seen in the poem's most beautiful ambiguity, so perfectly poised that to be moved by it almost requires that we do not notice it: 'all Olympus' *faded* hierarchy'. The ambiguity, of course, depends on whether they are now faded, or were already faded when the story of Psyche was invented, and the lines can be read either way with great power.

What this ambiguity does is to assume a special bond between Keats in the nineteenth century and Psyche in late antiquity, for both look back sadly to a simpler time of natural piety—to the time when Maia was worshipped, or old Homer's Helicon was not yet darkened. This theme is present in Keats from the beginning. Two invocations that appear suddenly and clumsily in the first book of *Endymion* associate the feebleness of the poet's powers with the fact that he lives in a late day of the world:

> *O kindly muse! let not my weak tongue falter*
> *In telling of this goodly company,*
> *Of their old piety and of their glee:*
> *But let a portion of ethereal dew*
> *Fall on my head, and presently unmew*
> *My soul; that I may dare, in wayfaring,*
> *To stammer, where old Chaucer used to sing . . .*
>
> I.128

217

There is not much to be said for these lines. They come in clumsily, and Chaucer comes clumsily into them. The rhymes are awkward, even for early Keats. They do not even say what he means, since they are a lament that his account of the pagan progression is too unreal: so the dew he wants is *not* ethereal. Yet the discontent they so awkwardly express was to be astonishingly fruitful.

A little later, in Book I, comes what is probably the finest thing in *Endymion*, the Hymn to Pan (which Wordsworth dismissed as 'a pretty piece of paganism'). It addresses Pan as an earth-deity, whose temple is the forest, whose worship is the processes of nature:

> *O thou, to whom*
> *Broad-leaved fig-trees even now foredoom*
> *Their ripen'd fruitage; yellow girted bees*
> *Their golden honeycombs . . .*

I.251

What Keats had to learn was to join the apology and the hymn; to realise that for a poet of latter-day paganism, the true subject-matter was a lost unity, of men with the earth (as in the hymn), of poetry with the community. It is not Chaucer he should have been sighing for, but the voice of that 'vulnerable priest' who led the hymn. That was the ideal he longed for as the invalid longs for health; and since it was an ideal of health, it could not be attained in mawkish diction.

All this he achieved in the *Ode to Maia*:

> *Mother of Hermes! and still youthful Maia!*
> >*May I sing to thee*
> *As thou wast hymnéd on the shores of Baiae?*
> >*Or may I woo thee*
> *In earlier Sicilian? Or thy smiles*
> *Seek, as they once were sought, in Grecian isles,*
> *By bards who died content on pleasant sward,*
> >*Leaving great verse unto a little clan?*
> *O, give me their old vigour, and unheard*
> >*Save of the quiet Primrose, and the span*
> >*Of Heaven and few ears,*
> *Rounded by thee, my song should die away*
> >*Content as theirs,*
> *Rich in the simple worship of a day.*

Perhaps this is the most perfect pastoral poem ever written. It is an expression of the deepest nostalgia, yet there is nothing sad or explicitly nostalgic about it. It is a delighted celebration of an early simple age, an age that was truly pagan, when goddesses who are now literary were merely local, when poetry was in dialect, was heard by everyone in the community and by no one else. It is the pure dream of Arcadia, and nothing betrays that it is a longing for the impossible: the nostalgia is altogether implicit, it made the poem and has dissolved in it—unless we want to betray it as we read, by a tremor in the repeated 'may I'.

And for an account of the kind of poem this is, we can turn back to Schiller. In his discussion of elegiac poetry, Schiller inserts a long, interesting footnote defending a classification of poetry based not on formal genres but on *Empfindungsweise* (the kind of sensibility involved). This enables us to find the elegiac note in epic and in lyric poems, and to classify as elegies one kind of lyric poem,

> welche eine Spezies der sentimentalischen Dichtung ist, zu deren Wesen es gehört, dass die Natur der Kunst und das Ideal der Wirklichkeit entgegengesetzt werde. Geschieht diese auch nicht ausdrücklich von dem Dichter, und stellt er das Gemälde der unverdorbenen Natur oder der erfüllten Ideales rein und selbständing vor unsere Augen, so ist jeder Gegensatz doch in seinem Herzen und wird sich auch ohne seinen Willen in jedem Pinselstreich verraten.

> (which is a species of sentimental poetry, part of whose essence it is to contrast Nature with Art, the ideal with reality. Even if this isn't explicitly done by the poet, even if he places his picture of unspoilt Nature or the fulfilled ideal pure and independent in front of our eyes, this contrast is none the less in his heart, and betrays itself, willy nilly, in every brush stroke.)

Dissolved nostalgia: that is the secret of the *Ode to Maia*, as of so much pastoral. In the *Ode to Psyche* the nostalgia is explicit, and indeed is used as the organising principle of the poem. The bond that Keats shares with Psyche is made explicit in the fourth stanza. Because she never had a priest or virgin choir, she knew from the first the state to which all the gods have now sunk—a faded hierarchy, they have only the poetry-lovers for worshippers. This means that the only worship Keats can offer—the fane within his mind, instead of in the world—is especially appropriate for her.

There is a comparable effect at the end of *The Eve of St Agnes*. The wonderful distancing effect of the last stanza of this poem has been praised by everyone.

And they are gone: aye, ages long ago
These lovers fled away into the storm.
That night the Baron dreamt of many a woe,
And all his warrior-guests, with shade and form
Of witch, and demon, and large coffin-worm,
Were long be-nightmar'd. Angela the old
Died palsy-twitch'd, with meagre face deform;
The Beadsman, after thousand aves told
For aye unsought for slept among his ashes cold.

The whole poem has been suffused with an atmosphere of fairy-tale and magic: it is clear that the union of the lovers has the perfection of dream, that even when Madeline sees the real Porphyro, awake and corporeal, it is only real because the poem is unreal. We might expect it all to conclude with a reminder of this, a reminder that said, for instance, 'it did not last, Madeline died, Porphyro grew cross or unfaithful'—or, if that sounds too direct, a reminder of the rare, frail beauty of their happiness, a hint that they are symbols of love, not mortal lovers. But Keats has not said all this: instead, he tells us at the end that all this happened a long time ago. We have had a slight hint of this earlier, but so subtle that no reader could take it—this is the fact that the poem begins in the past tense, in the opening stanza that sets the scene, and then, as it begins to tell the story, moves to the present. The shift of tense at the end is none the less a great surprise, and by this simple detail Keats achieves a marvellous effect: he gives a historical dimension to the world of the poem. Instead of telling us something about the lovers, he tells us something about the way he has told the story. That is why it was appropriate to finish with the Baron's nightmares and Angela's death: we now take these details as confirmation of what we've suddenly been made aware of, that all this is the world of once upon a time. Instead of concluding 'Nymphs and shepherds will not dance long, for they are mortal', he concludes 'nymphs and shepherds dance no more, for the world is older now'.

All this is only a part of Keats, of course; but an important part. Nostalgia is not his only emotion, but it is prominent; and it is nearly always linked, often very subtly, with his love for antiquity and legend. Keats loved ancient legends in part because they were old and dead; and this enabled him to write about what he had lost by writing about myth and legend. At its best, Keats' nostalgia is historical.

220

III

A prolific, uneven, unbalanced writer of memoirs, travelogues, confused and haunting stories, wrote a handful of sonnets at the end of his life that have reverberated through European poetry. No one can quite explain *Les Chimères* of Gerard de Nerval; no one who is sensitive to poetry is proof against their power. The most hard-hearted critic cannot talk about them without using terms like 'word-magic': they are poems that drive criticism to despair, and this is their glory.

Yet they are the sort of poems that challenge criticism. Though they anticipate symbolism, they don't quite sound like modern poems. They so obviously have the air of meaning something— their mysterious proper names so clearly adhere to some scheme —that they almost demand that we know what is going on. To state the argument of *Delfica*, or *El Desdichado*, is to state something that is and is not central to the poems. Their wonderful resonance eludes the argument; yet how could it ever arise if they *didn't* give such an air of control, of a meaning they are about to yield up?

I am not able to 'solve' these mysterious poems, but I want to point to one theme. For it seems clear that they show an obsession with faded mythologies that is comparable with Keats': they are poems of historical nostalgia. In one or two, this is patently the main subject—in *Delfica*, for instance.

> *La connais-tu, Dafné, cette ancienne romance,*
> *Au pied du sycomore, ou sous les lauriers blancs,*
> *Sous l'olivier, le myrte, ou les saules tremblants,*
> *Cette chanson d'amour qui toujours recommence?* . . .
>
> *Reconnais-tu le temple au péristyle immense,*
> *Et les citrons amers où s'imprimaient tes dents,*
> *Et la grotte, fatale aux hôtes imprudents,*
> *Où du dragon vaincu dort l'antique semence?* . . .
>
> *Ils reviendront, ces Dieux que tu pleures toujours!*
> *Le temps va ramener l'ordre des anciens jours;*
> *La terre a tressailli d'un souffle prophétique* . . .
>
> *Cependant la sibylle au visage latin*
> *Est endormie encore sous l'arc de Constantin*
> *—Et rien n'a dérangé le sévère portique.*

Daphne, do you know that old romance, at the foot of the sycamore, or under the white laurels, under the olive tree, the myrtle, or the quivering willows, that love song, eternally beginning anew? . . .

Do you recognise the temple with the huge peristyle, and the bitter lemons that your teeth sank into, and the cave fatal to imprudent visitors, where sleeps the old seed of the conquered dragon? . . .

They will return, those Gods you are always weeping for. Time will bring back the cycle of the old days; the earth has trembled with a breath of prophecy.

And yet the sybil with the Latin countenance is still asleep under the arch of Constantine—and nothing has disturbed the severe portico.

A race of gods has passed away, but will return. Will return: but there is no sign of it yet. It is clear that the poem balances hope against resignation, but the exact flavour is hard to be sure of. It depends largely on the way we take the octave: who is really talking to Daphne, and what is he showing her. *Cette ancienne romance*; *reconnais-tu*—the phrasing suggests something they are actually hearing and seeing, as if the *souffle prophétique* has already taken effect, as if the gods are actually returning. But the sestet doesn't fit this at all: there the return of the Gods is in the future, and the final lines firmly tell us that nothing is happening yet. So the definiteness of the details in the octave can only refer to a picture, or a song, or a dream, not an actual manifestation of the return. The poem is more nostalgic than prophetic: the marvellous tercet (*Ils reviendront* . . .) expresses longing as much as confidence, and indeed its resonance surely comes from a blend of these emotions.

Who are the gods whom Daphne is grieving for, and who has replaced them? There is something very primitive about the *chanson d'amour* and the fatal cave. The *dragon vaincu* may well be the python whom Apollo slew (appropriately lamented by Daphne, herself Apollo's victim). Daphne may be a kind of earth-goddess; the sibyl too is something very old and close to the earth. All this suggests a pre-Olympic theogony, driven out perhaps by the efficient *arrivistes* of classical Greek mythology. But the *arc de Constantin* seems to bring us into Christendom; and the most natural way to take the present tense of the poem is to refer it to today. This would give us a contrast between a lost primitive religion, and the modern world of Christianity—and in that contrast the position of the classical Olympians is ambivalent. They seem to pervade the poem, but are never mentioned; this is surely one source of its haunting power.

Delfica makes a kind of portal to the *Chimères*. It is the most straightforward, and its themes are the themes of the whole series. They are all poems of historical nostalgia, and they are all charged with ambiguity about the actual identity of each wave of gods that drives out the last.

Myrtho announces its historical nostalgia in a line that sounds like pure Keats: '*Car la Muse m'a fait un des fils de la Grèce*'. But the line is thrown out in passing, almost as a point too obvious to need dwelling on, in the course of explaining that his allegiance extends to Myrtho as well. It is hard to identify Myrtho precisely, but she too seems very old and not altogether Greek. In this poem too there is a promise that the defeated gods will return, and a new order is mentioned that broke but has not abolished them:

> *Je sais pourquoi là-bas le volcan c'est rouvert . . .*
> *C'est qu'hier tu l'avais touché d'un pied agile,*
> *Et de cendres soudain l'horizon s'est couvert.*

> *Depuis qu'un duc normand brisa tes dieux d'argile,*
> *Toujours, sous les rameaux du laurier de Virgile,*
> *Le pâle hortensia s'unit au myrthe vert!*

I know why the volcano over there has stirred into life . . . It's because you touched it yesterday with your agile foot, and suddenly the horizon is covered with ashes.

Ever since the time a Norman duke broke your clay gods, the pale hortensia joins itself to the green myrtle, under the boughs of Virgil's laurel tree.

In *Horus* one mythology is dying and another is coming into being:

> *Le dieu Kneph en tremblant ébranlait l'univers:*
> *Isis, la mère, alors, se leva sur sa couche,*
> *Fit un geste de haine à son époux farouche,*
> *Et l'ardeur d'autrefois brilla dans ses yeux verts.*

> '*Le voyez-vous, dit-elle, il meurt, ce vieux pervers,*
> *Tous les frimas du monde ont passé par sa bouche,*
> *Attachez son pied tors, éteignez son œil louche,*
> *C'est le dieu des volcans et le roi des hivers!*

'L'aigle a déjà passé, l'esprit nouveau m'appelle,
J'ai revêtu pour lui la robe de Cybèle . . .
C'est l'enfant bien-aimé d'Hermes et d'Osiris!'

La déesse avait fui sur sa conque dorée,
La mer nous renvoyait son image adorée,
Et les cieux rayonnait sous l'écharpe d'Iris.

The shivers of the god Kneph were shaking the universe: then Isis, the mother, rose on her couch, and made a gesture of hate towards her fierce husband, while the ardour of long ago shone in her green eyes.

Look at him, she said, he's dying, the old pervert. All the world's frost has passed through his mouth. Tie him by his twisted foot, put out his squinting eye, he is the god of volcanoes, and the king of all winters.

The eagle has passed already, the new spirit calls me. For him I have donned the robe of Cybele. He is the well-beloved child of Hermes and Osiris.

The goddess had fled on her gilded conch, the sea mirrored for us her adored image, and the skies shone under the scarf of Iris.

Kneph is dying in fury; Isis triumphs over his death, and greets the new order with delight: 'L'esprit nouveau m'appelle'. The new order issues from a mingling of Greek and Egyptian, and is symbolised by the *écharpe d'Iris*. It is something like Apollo's 'dying into life' in Keats' *Hyperion*. That too is the birth of a new order: probably it was to emerge as the central theme of the poem when it was finished. The theme is anticipated in Book II, when Oceanus, the old god of the sea, describes his successor Neptune:

> *I saw him on the calmed waters scud*
> *With such a glow of beauty in his eyes*
> *That it enforced me to bid sad farewell*
> *To all my empire.*

The transfiguration of Apollo in Book III is also witnessed—even caused—by the strange figure of Mnemosyne, the old that brings the new to birth:

> *Mute thou remainest—mute! Yet I can read*
> *A wondrous lesson in thy silent face:*
> *Knowledge enormous makes a god of me.*

224

In the context of Keats' poetry as a whole, *Hyperion* is moving in a special and ambivalent way. It tells of the birth of that 'beautiful mythology of Greece' which Keats usually regarded as tinged with the sadness of a dead past. What is here a glorious future is usually a past heavy with nostalgia. Of course the nostalgia is present in the poem—not in the picture of the Titans, who are warlike and defiant, but in that of the deposed Saturn, 'deep in the shady sadness of a vale', in the beautiful opening lines. The whole process of loss and defeat has been shifted back one stage.

In Nerval's *Horus* this tension, which in Keats exists between *Hyperion* and other poems, is part of the poem itself. The new is here older than the old. Isis who salutes the new order is the most primitive element in the poem: she is *la mère*, her delight is *l'ardeur d'autrefois*, she has *revêtu . . . la robe de Cybèle*. She sounds like the earth itself, shaking off a usurper. The final tranquil lines suggest both the new and the old—as the rainbow so often does. It is *Iris*, that is, it bears the name of (we presume) one of the new goddesses; but it is also the calm of sky and sea themselves, older than any gods.

Nerval's view of mythology (not always consistently held or stated) seems to be more or less as follows: One race of gods drives out another; the defeated do not altogether submit, for they are waiting for the day when they will return; and the revival of an old religion is a kind of reassertion of the poetry of earth itself. In his prose works, Nerval often seems more interested in the revival of the ancient gods than in antiquity itself. The fête in Chapter IV of *Sylvie* is named after the sophisticated, nervous, nostalgic Watteau, the greatest of eighteenth-century pastoralists; the modern ruin on the island to which the party sails *appartenait au paganisme de Boufflers ou de Chaulieu plutôt qu'à celui d'Horace*. There seems nothing perjorative here in attributing it to the paganism of two minor neo-classic poets, just as there is a genuine admiration in the description in *Isis* of the party given by an ambassador at Pompeii, in which the whole life of the ancient city was reconstructed.

Nerval was fascinated by the idea of the past being in layers: what once was, still exists, mingled with and overlaid by what comes after. In a haunting passage in *Aurelia* he describes a primitive race of people, with simple customs, preserving the

virtues of the first days of the world. They are very like the
extinct 'pastoral people' whom Shelley located on his island 'in
the far Eden of the purple East' (the passage, from *Epipsychidion*,
is discussed in Chapter I). But Nerval's race, unlike Shelley's, is
neither extinct nor living in seclusion: they mingle with the other
inhabitants of a populous city, preserving their distinct identity,
and respected by those around them. Meeting them brings to
the narrator the central pastoral emotion: *Je me mis à pleurer à
chaudes larmes, comme au souvenir d'un paradis perdu.* To weep at
the memory of a lost paradise: these are the tears Housman shed
over *Arcades*. What is unusual is that they are caused by something still extant, still to be found mingled with the living world.
This quality is precisely captured in one peculiar, dreamlike image.
As the narrator enters a house,

> il me semblait que mes pied s'enfonçait dans les couches suc-
> cessives des édifices de différents ages.

> It seemed as if my feet were sinking into the successive layers
> of the buildings of different periods.

In this picture of change and intermingling, every religion has an
ambivalent status, including Christianity. Christianity is the new,
conquering religion that will have to be displaced in its turn; it can
be seen as victor or as vanquished. This point is made in *Isis*.
Christianity once, in the name of a higher reason, unpeopled the
skies; now in its turn it is being deposed in the name of reason.
This is the fate reserved for the last of the sons of heaven; mortals
will find that what they've unveiled is simply death.

This is the theme of the set of five related sonnets, *Le Christ aux
Oliviers*. Jesus, praying just before his death, feels the universe
totally empty: abandoned by God, he turns to Judas (*qui du moins
as la force du crime*) but finds him, like Pilate, slumped in in-
difference, unaware of the vast significance of the death of God.
The death of Christianity two thousand years later has here been
transposed back into Jesus' agony. Christianity is dying at the
very moment of its birth: and in the last sonnet we see both a
victory and a defeat—the defeat described as a series of parallels
with all the other defeated gods and heroes, Icarus, Phaeton, Atys.

Longing for a lost contact with the earth, resentment at the
dieux vainqueurs, a feeling that the cycle of defeat and return has
happened before and will happen again, produces much of the

atmosphere of *Les Chimères*. Sometimes paganism is preferred to Christianity, sometimes they are seen as parallels,

> *Modulant tout à tour sur la lyre d'Orphée*
> *Les soupirs de la Sainte et les cris de la Fée*

Modulating in turn on Orpheus' lyre the sighs of the Saint and the cries of the Fairy

—and sometimes (as we have seen) classical paganism is itself the conqueror. In *Anteros* it is immediately and movingly clear that one race of gods has been conquered by another, but the identity of each is shifting and uncertain. The sides of the conflict change their identity; the emotion itself is constant.

What is the relation of this historical nostalgia to the personal emotional life of the poet? It is a fascinating and unanswerable question. Some scholars claim to be able to trace Nerval's longing for his mother and his hostility to his father in the images of the poems, and the pattern, in general terms, is not hard to make out. It is less easy with Keats, if only because we know less of his childhood.

If the poems of Keats and Nerval have their origin in a pattern of loss and regret in their own lives, then we can certainly claim that they have found a wonderful poetic equivalent for that pattern. The love of Olympus' faded hierarchy is a generalised emotion waiting to be colonised by the personal emotion of the poet: the result will be that substance and body are given to an emotional relationship that might have lain disentangled in the poet's private language. If the poet transcribes his emotion direct, the result may be sprawling and embarrassing; if his own emotion is not there, the result may be dry or theoretic, like the merely mechanical disposing of mythological names in Nerval's less successful sonnets, such as 'Λ Mme Ida Dumas'.

None of this is part of the experience of reading the poems. As readers, we can know of no one's emotion except our own. The power of a poem clearly cannot depend on researches into the childhood of the poet. Such researches are part of the discussion on how poems come into being. Since these poems are now written, and so marvellously written, we ought primarily to discuss what they are. And what they are, is poems about history.

XII

THE PROPER PLACE OF NOSTALGIA

MATTHEW ARNOLD'S two great elegies are contemporary in their preoccupations but old-fashioned in form. They are pastoral elegies but by the nineteenth century pastoral was no longer a living poetic tradition: the poems are modelled on great masters of the past, and *Thyrsis* at least uses conventions that Arnold has disinterred. Yet their theme is natural enough for a Victorian. The story of the poor lad who left Oxford and joined himself to a company of vagabond gipsies naturally attracted the melancholy inspector of schools whose imagination chafed at industrial society and his busy middle age: it was to be expected that the Scholar Gipsy on his endless quest should turn into a Romantic solitary, an Alastor, a Pedlar, an Ancient Mariner, holding aloof from his fellows, wandering the countryside in eternal search after wisdom. It was natural too that the figure of the gipsy should be contrasted with the actual life of the poet:

> *O born in days when wits were fresh and clear*
> *And life ran gaily as the sparkling Thames,*
> *Before this strange disease of modern life,*
> *With its sick hurry, its divided aims,*
> *Its heads o'ertaxed, its palsied hearts, was rife.*

This poem lays the pastoral mechanism completely clear. The gipsy may be dissatisfied, but it is a positive dissatisfaction: he waits for the spark from Heaven. To Arnold this quest is a refuge from the strange disease of modern life: on to the Scholar Gipsy's life he projects what is missing from his own. The whole structure of the poem is designed to show that its vision of 'retired ground' is a mediated one, a symbol for all we lack.

So much is obvious. It has one technical consequence in Arnold's art, that may be obvious too, but I have not seen it remarked. How is the idyllic life of the gipsy rendered to us?

> *Children, who early range these slopes and late*
> *For cresses from the rills,*
> *Have known thee watching, all an April day,*

228

> *The springing pastures and the feeding kine;*
> *And marked thee, when the stars come out and shine,*
> *Through the long dewy grass move slow away.*

Melancholy and hope, loneliness and a still-lingering belief in his quest, are combined in the figure of the Scholar Gipsy. It is a figure drenched in emotion—haunting, unutterably sad, yet possessed of a strength we lack:

> *Thee at the ferry, Oxford riders blithe,*
> *Returning home on summer nights, have met*
> *Crossing the stripling Thames at Bablock-hithe,*
> *Trailing in the cool stream thy fingers wet,*
> *As the slow punt swings round:*
> *And leaning backwards in a pensive dream,*
> *And fostering in thy lap a heap of flowers*
> *Plucked in shy fields and distant Wychwood bowers,*
> *And thine eyes resting on the moonlit stream.*

How is this deep, paradoxical emotion conveyed? Arnold, like most nineteenth-century poets, has two ways of conveying emotion.

> *And a look of passionate desire*
> *O'er the sea and to the stars I send:*
> *Ye who from my childhood up have calm'd me,*
> *Calm me, ah compose me to the end . . .*
>
> *And with joy the stars perform their shining,*
> *And the sea its long moon-silvered roll,*
> *For alone they live, nor pine with noting*
> *All the fever of some differing soul—*

This poem ('Self-Dependence') alternates between direct statement of emotion, and its rendering through the description of landscape or natural objects. On the one hand, Arnold tells us of his look of passionate desire: it is not possible to be more explicit than that in thrusting your emotion on the reader. In the same poem, he longs for the peace of sea and stars, yet in talking about them he cannot easily forget to mention his own feelings: telling us that they don't pine with noting the fever of some differing soul, he is really almost as explicit as ever—'pine', 'fever' or (earlier) 'compose me' are words about himself and his own feelings. And then in the midst of this comes

> *And with joy the stars perform their shining,*
> *And the sea its long, moon-silvered roll.*

The first line has broken half-free of the insistent poet: 'with joy' is perhaps too obvious a way of not mentioning his own lack of joy, but all the same there is a strength of rhythm in the line that begins to shift our attention from the poet's plaint to the stars. And then in the next line he has broken quite free, and the poem achieves its finest moment: the poet's emotion is completely dissolved in the image, the line rolls like the sea, the joy glows in the moon's silvering, we don't have to be told all about it.

Nineteenth-century poetry had, built into it, a need to be oblique and a tendency to be direct. Almost every Victorian poet had to *tell* his readers, over and over, of his grief, his melancholy, his joys; and they all did so as if they knew that was no way to write poetry, that their emotion ought not to be talked about, ought to emerge from the passion with which they showed us images to represent it. This finding of an object that embodies the emotion has come to be called, recently, the objective correlative (though Eliot may originally have meant something rather different by the phrase). We hardly need the phrase, really, since the difference between direct statement of emotion, and its oblique or symbolic rendering, is an old and familiar one. None the less it points usefully to the nineteenth-century habit of choosing landscape or physical description to embody emotion, rather than traditional symbols or conventional figures; and it emphasises too the fact that the nineteenth-century poet *starts from* his personal emotion (hence the temptation to be direct) and then has to look for something that correlates with it. The phrase does seem to tell us something about how Arnold wrote. For him, as it happens, the objective correlative is very often the same: over and over, he uses the sea, and it can stand for a rich range of emotion. We have seen it in this example; the waiting sea at the end of *Sohrab and Rustum* conveys a sense of healing and reconciliation; the 'melancholy long withdrawing roar' of 'Dover Beach' conveys the sadness of loss and spiritual emptiness; the waves in the midmost ocean of 'Rugby Chapel' convey futility. And each time the poem moves with strength and confidence: if we accept Arnold's explicitness, it is because we see it is leading him to an image that will silence his talk about his feelings. We can watch his poems as they cease to mean, and begin to be.

Now *The Scholar Gipsy*, too, uses the objective correlative when it wants to convey the gipsy's feelings: only the objective correla-

230

tive is the Scholar Gipsy himself. Instead of telling us about the loneliness, the hope, he describes—but describes not the landscape, not the flowers (or not these only), he describes the taciturn, haunting, remote figure of the Scholar Gipsy.

> *And marked thee, when the stars come out and shine*
> *Through the long dewy grass move slow away.*

This is wonderfully objective: we turn to the gipsy as we turn to the sea, to get away from the poet's emotion and to see it plain before us. Arnold never wrote with more command than there.

In contrast to the Scholar Gipsy, the strange disease: and in contrast to the slow beauty of its imagery, total explicitness:

> *Thou waitest for the spark from Heaven: and we,*
> *Light half-believers in our casual creeds,*
> *Who never deeply felt, nor clearly will'd,*
> *Whose insight never has borne fruit in deeds,*
> *Whose vague resolves never have been fulfilled;*
> *For whom each year we see*
> *Breeds new beginnings, disappointments new;*
> *Who hesitate and falter life away,*
> *And lose tomorrow the ground won today—*
> *Ah do not we, Wanderer, await it too?*

It is a moving stanza, yet it shouldn't be: it does all that a Victorian poem ought not to do. No one could say of this stanza

> *For grief*
> *An empty doorway and a maple leaf,*

for words like 'grief' have utterly driven the imagery out. Except for the spark from Heaven, a perfunctory enough metaphor, picked up anyway from the other part of the poem, the stanza has not a single concrete comparison or descriptive detail. It thrusts its personal feelings on us in handfuls: it insists. No poem could survive if it were written entirely like this, but *The Scholar Gipsy* can carry it. Partly because the change of style itself has its place in the overall contrast of the poem (this is how to deal with modern life), partly because its rhythm retains a strength that might otherwise have been lost, partly because the formal pattern of the polished stanzas carries us along. To and fro the poem moves, from glimpses of the Scholar Gipsy, ever fresh with images ('the sparkling Thames', the gesture of Dido, the nightingales), to sad lingerings on modern life, the language as jaded as the theme, jaded in a way we can hardly rebuke:

> *and we others pine*
> *And wish the long unhappy dream would end.*

Arnold was too wise to end the poem like this. At the end, it was necessary to find an image that embodied both halves of his contrast; and to do so he fell back on his classical learning, and elaborated a long, leisurely Homeric simile. For the first time in the poem both the Scholar Gipsy's feelings and 'ours' have found an objective correlative (if that is still the term for this simile). After the strange disease has been so painfully shown from within, it is now seen by the Tyrian—that is, the Scholar Gipsy—in the form of the intruders on his ancient home. Or is it? 'The young light-hearted masters of the waves': are they *us*? It could be: these could be the liberal believers in doing as one likes whom Arnold so constantly mocked, their coaster could be freighted with the material wealth of Victorian England—but at this point we have to pause and say that we are pressing the simile further than it will go. Arnold has not planned a detailed correspondence in these final stanzas, he has opened a bottle and loosed a geni. As we look, the geni keeps changing shape. The Greeks are merry, irreverent —the Greeks of Juvenal, perhaps, and the key word suddenly becomes 'indignant', the Tyrian taking on a marvellous angry dignity. But they are also the creators of that Hellenic culture that meant everything to Arnold; the grave Tyrian, fleeing them, is a fool—a stately fool but none the less a fool, choosing the wild Atlantic instead of the world's greatest civilisation. Is *that* the final comment on the Scholar Gipsy? We cannot hold the simile still, and its metamorphoses are part of its magic: in its last act, the gravely moral poem has relaxed into the open-ended, into something very near to decoration. Its stylistic triumph is a relaxation of purpose, and what reader wishes it different?

II

The stylistic contrast we have seen in *The Scholar Gipsy* is also present in Thyrsis. With this poem, of course, we are in the world of pastoral quite explicitly: the poem is a declared follower of *Adonais*, of *Lycidas*, and behind them of Virgil and Theocritus.

We shall need to look at it even more carefully than *The Scholar Gipsy*, for it can tell us a good deal both about the pastoral elegy and about Arnold.

There can hardly be a more nostalgic poem in English than *Thyrsis*. It is impregnated with a sense of loss; and when we pause to ask what has been lost we find ourselves overwhelmed with answers. It is an elegy for at least four losses.

First, the historical loss. We are no longer in Sicily, and the poet can no longer use the conventions of ancient literature with assurance;

> *O easy access to the hearer's grace*
> *When Dorian shepherds sang to Proserpine!*
> *For she herself had trod Sicilian fields,*
> *She knew the Dorian water's gush divine,*
> *She knew each lily white which Enna yields,*
> *Each rose with blushing face;*
> *She loved the Dorian pipe, the Dorian strain.*
> *But ah, of our poor Thames she never heard!*
> *Her foot the Cumnor cowslips never stirred!*
> *And we should tease her with our plaint in vain.*

'Our poor Thames'. The apology has a function in the poem, of course: this stanza, like the one before (quoted below), is based on the 'Lament for Bion', in which the Greek poet imagines that he will be able to bring back his friend from the Underworld, since the 'Maiden' who presides there (Proserpine) is Sicilian like him, and will respond to his songs. Ingeniously, Arnold sighs that he has lost that 'easy access', and the sigh of regret becomes an apology, that England is not Sicily—and so becomes untypical of Arnold, who never felt that his beloved Oxfordshire needed any apology. But that is because when he is lavish in praise for its beauty (as he is elsewhere in this poem) he is looking at it direct when he remembers other landscapes, nearer to the ancient literature he loved, he grows apologetic. His attitude is the exact opposite of Du Bellay's famous sonnet, *Heureux qui comme Ulysse, a fait un beau voyage*, in which the moment to praise the Loire most eloquently is when he is comparing it to the Tiber, and with defiant provinciality preferring his own culture, with its *douceur Angevine*, to the splendours of Rome. Arnold, however, is never a provincial. He loves the Thames for itself, or because it contrasts

with his busy urban life; but he would never dream of preferring
it to the world of Theocritus and Proserpine—least of all in the
middle of a pastoral elegy. In this stanza we are hearing not
Arnold the Englishman but Arnold the Hellenist, and he is mourning the passing of the ancient world.

The second loss is that of Clough; and this is a double loss.
Clough left Oxford and the academic life; and now he is dead:

> *It irked him to be here, he could not rest.*
> *He loved each simple joy the country yields,*
>   *He loved his mates; but yet he could not keep,*
> *For that a shadow lowered on the fields,*
> *Here with the shepherds and the silly sheep.*
>   *Some life of men unblest*
> *He knew, which made him droop, and filled his head.*
>   *He went; his piping took a troubled sound*
>   *Of storms that rage outside our happy ground;*
> *He could not wait their passing, he is dead!*

At first, the departure of Clough seems more painful than his
death. The last three words of this stanza are strangely perfunctory,
It is a sad chronicle of how Thyrsis was sucked in by the strange
disease of modern life, how his restlessness drove him from 'the
shepherds and the silly sheep' (from country to town; from pastoral
tradition to the utterly different style of *Amours de Voyage*, whose
sound is troubled). And then, casually, as if it follows naturally
from all this, 'he is dead'.

And because the sadness of Clough's story lay more in the
troubled sound than in the death, it is a parallel to the poet's
own. Next to Clough's loss lies Arnold's loss: he too has left these
fields.

> *Too rare, too rare grow now my visits here!*
>   *But once I knew each field, each flower, each stick;*
>   *And with the country-folk acquaintance made*
>   *By barn in threshing-time, by new-built rick.*
>   *Here too our shepherd pipes we first assayed.*
>   *Ah me! this many a year*
>   *My pipe is lost, my shepherd's holiday!*
>   *Needs must I lose them, needs with heavy heart*
>   *Into the world and waves of men depart;*
>   *But Thyrsis of his own will went away.*

Here we are still within the pastoral convention: and what it is lamenting is the loss of the pastoral life. The poet is now a towns-man, but a townsman who once felt he belonged in the Oxford countryside. This reminds us that pastoral is an urban genre, but it reminds us in a special way: for the fact that Arnold did not use to be a stranger to these fields gives two special effects to the poem.

First, the immediacy of the descriptions. There are no enamelled meads, no green and gilded snakes in Arnold, but the feel and smell of each rural sight, each rural sound ('Soon will the musk carna-tions break and swell, Soon shall we have gold-dusted snapdragon'). Here the convenient distinction between pastoral poetry and nature poetry seems to break down. His vision of the Thames is pure pastoral, an idyll projected by his need to escape, yet it is the real Thames too, as real as anything in Keats. The two tradi-tions merge in *Thyrsis*.

There is another, even more important, consequence of the fact that Arnold used to belong there: it means that escaping into the idyllic setting is returning to his own youth.

> *Yes, thou art gone! and round me too the night*
> *In ever-nearing circles weaves her shade.*
> *I see her veil draw soft across the day,*
> *I feel her slowly chilling breath invade*
> *The cheek grown thin, the brown hair sprent with grey;*
> *I feel her finger light*
> *Laid pausefully upon life's headlong train;*
> *The foot less prompt to meet the morning dew,*
> *The heart less bounding at emotion new,*
> *And hope, once crush'd, less quick to spring again.*

It is the strange disease of modern life again, but with a change of emphasis. In *The Scholar Gipsy* we fluctuate idly, we have vague resolves, sick hurry, divided aims. It is a description of social disorder and purposelessness, in which we all fluctuate alike. In *Thyrsis* the trouble is more specifically the loss of youth: each detail in this stanza describes not simply modern man but ageing modern man—perhaps even ageing man. The Scholar Gipsy grew old and died during the poem, and the way of life he represents is not inextricably linked with youth; but the Arnold of *Thyrsis* has left his youth on the signal tree, and in catching a glimpse of it again he has made almost explicit one of the great underlying impulses of pastoral, the recapture of the Golden Age in one's own past.

And then, least obvious but most important of all for the actual writing of the poem, there is another loss: that of the pastoral tradition itself. Arnold is a Romantic, and he has made the psychological basis explicit. He begins from his own personal situation, and builds the symbolism in front of us. The two great symbols of the poem, the elm tree and the Scholar Gipsy, are both home made. In stanza three we are told how the first was made:

> *We priz'd it dearly; while it stood, we said,*
> *Our friend, the Scholar-Gipsy, was not dead;*
> *While the tree lived, he in these fields lived on.*

The tree is Arnold's objective correlative for his regaining of hope at the end of the poem—perhaps a rather rhetorical regaining, not as deeply convincing as the earlier melancholy, but all the same it bursts into the poem with the delighted impact of a visual surprise. Arnold can use both these symbols with confidence, because he has been honest with us; he has shown us their roots in his own life. And because he has started from himself, he feels entitled to use other symbols too, that are not home made:

> *Alack, for Corydon no rival now!—*
> *But when Sicilian shepherds lost a mate,*
> *Some good survivor with his flute would go,*
> *Piping a ditty sad for Bion's fate,*
> *And cross the unpermitted ferry's flow,*
> *And relax Pluto's brow,*
> *And make leap up with joy the beauteous head*
> *Of Proserpine, among whose crowned hair*
> *Are flowers, first open'd on Sicilian air,*
> *And flute his friend, like Orpheus, from the dead.*

It is hard to be sure whether this is a stanza of pastoral poetry, or a stanza about it. Telling us what the Sicilian shepherds did, he re-enacts it himself, for he feels he has now earned the right (a right Milton took for granted) to use the convention.

A good deal of this poem, then, is symbolic and indirect in manner: but not the stanzas about the present. When it comes to modern life, Arnold is as explicit here as he was in *The Scholar Gipsy*. When it comes to declaring his loss, showing us a life without Clough, without youth, without Oxfordshire, he speaks directly and in his own person—only for two stanzas now, two weary, death-desiring, embarrassing yet deeply moving stanzas (one of them, 'Yes, thou art gone . . .', has been quoted already). If *The Scholar Gipsy* could carry half a dozen such stanzas, *Thyrsis* can certainly carry two.

'Yes, thou art gone.' A great deal is gone by this point in the poem. Clough is gone, first from these fields, then from this life. The Scholar Gipsy is gone. And finally, it can be no coincidence that these words introduce the poem's two utterly explicit stanzas. The pastoral tradition is gone too. When it comes to laying bare his most personal feelings, Arnold has no confidence in symbol or convention: despite the pressure of his style, the pressure of both classical tradition and Romantic habit, he has to *tell* us, outright.

III

These two stanzas of *Thyrsis*, like the six central stanzas of *The Scholar Gipsy*, are personal in more ways than one. They lay bare the personal defeat, and they confess to the springs of an art. The sense of loss they confess to is the source of all the beauty of Arnold's landscape. In many of his most famous poems this is obvious. The sound of the sea in *Dover Beach* moves Arnold because it is the sound of what we have lost; reading the poem a second time, we hear that loss even in the tranquil rhythm of its opening description. The sad picture of the middle-aged couple in *The Youth of Man* embodies the same emotion:

> *And they see, for a moment,*
> *Stretching out, like the desert,*
> *In its weary unprofitable length*
> *Their faded, ignoble lives.*

There is a border area between direct statement and the objective correlative, and it is occupied by these four lines. For all their explicitness, they are, in a way, objective: they have not the embarrassing directness of the 'piercing untold anguish' a few lines earlier in the poem, for their emotion is contained in the image of the desert, only briefly explicit, but present in the sad unfolding rhythm of the whole sentence. These lines (they make the subsequent stanza seem curiously irrelevant) are the centre of the poem: they tell of hope once crushed, less quick to spring again. They come from the heart of Arnold's nostalgia.

This is the conclusion I must now extract from this short discussion of Arnold's poetry. It is hardly a conclusion, since it has usually been an obvious point which we used in order to point out something else, in style or use of tradition. All readers of Arnold realise that he is the poet of frustration, sadness and resignation. When he is Stoic, it is his reaction to this loss of joy. Nostalgia is primary in his poetry.

IV

As Arnold grew older, his social criticism grew more serious, and his poetry declined. Both as literary and as social critic, he became more and more dissatisfied with nostalgia. *The Scholar Gipsy*, he complained in a letter to Clough, 'at best awakens a pleasing melancholy. But that is not what we want'. What the 'complaining millions of men' want, he thought, 'is something to *animate* and *ennoble* them'. So Arnold's later poetry is not only less frequent than earlier, it has a new, more moral purpose: the melancholy he had such a genius for now has to be replaced, or at least controlled, by Stoic earnestness, classicism and the architectonic power he praised in his 1853 *Preface*. The result is *Merope, Essays in Criticism*, the Professorship of Poetry, *Culture and Anarchy*: the later Arnold.

I don't intend, in this short chapter, to argue the superiority of Arnold's youthful genius over his later sternness, nor to discuss his social criticism systematically. It will emerge (but must emerge in passing) that I am out of sympathy with Arnold the moralist and critic; but in what follows I want to make only one limited point: that for all the change in his outlook, for all his scrupulous attention to the contemporary world in which he lived and was busy, he never lost his nostalgia. It is less obvious (and also less welcome) in the prose, but it is there. To show its presence I shall have to begin with details.

In the course of his attack on Mr Roebuck and the arrogance of *laissez-faire* and self-assurance, Arnold has some remarks to make on national greatness. It is not as easy to measure as Roebuck believes, he asserts, for it does not depend merely on coal. If coal is our criterion, then the present age is certainly our greatest; but if it is replaced by others, then the conclusion may not be so simple.

Greatness is a spiritual condition.... If England were swallowed up by the sea tomorrow, which of the two, a hundred years hence, would most excite the love, interest, and admiration of mankind,—would most, therefore, show the evidence of having possessed greatness,—the England of the last twenty years or the England of Elizabeth, of a time of splendid spiritual effort, but when our coal, and our industrial operations depending on coal, were very little developed.

Mr Roebuck did not stop to think: he accepted unreflectingly the measure of greatness that lay ready to his thoughts. But cannot we make the same complaint of Arnold? 'Vast spiritual effort' is not an easy thing to measure. One could imagine an eccentrically ambitious sociologist devising tests for it, or a patient and modest historian developing a slow sense of an age's spirituality. But any such sense of difficulty is totally absent from this passage. It does not seem to have occurred to Arnold that there is any problem: he simply *knows* that Elizabethan England was a time of vast spiritual effort.

This is not a passing carelessness but an important part of Arnold's thought. We find it again in the essay on 'The Function of Criticism'. The Romantics did not know enough, runs the well-known argument. It was not simply that like Wordsworth they had not read enough books: Shelley and Coleridge had read far more than Pindar, Sophocles and Shakespeare:

True; but in the Greece of Pindar and Sophocles, in the England of Shakespeare, the poet lived in a current of ideas in the highest degree animating and nourishing to the creative power; society was in the fullest measure permeated by fresh thought, intelligent and alive ...

There is no substitute for this, Arnold claims, but if it is absent, then reading can at least help. Thus Goethe, helped by the 'long and widely combined critical effort of Germany' knew more than Wordsworth, who had read too little—even though in Goethe's Germany 'there was no national glow of life and thought there, as in the Athens of Pericles or the England of Elizabeth'.

'Current of ideas', 'national glow'—this is the same thing clearly as the 'vast spiritual effort'. How on earth, we have to ask, does Arnold know? What evidence—indeed, what sort of evidence —would tell us that one age had a national glow and another not?

One suspects that Arnold's evidence is the greatness of the literature itself. Certainly the habit of arguing from the literature to the society that produced it is found in Arnold's followers.

> The age of Dryden was still a great age, though beginning to suffer a certain death of the spirit, as the coarsening of its verse-rhythms shows.

This remark of T. S. Eliot's was singled out by F. R. Leavis in *Education and the University*, as the sort of insight that would lead students to appreciate the complexity of 'summing-up' a century. Yet it is at the same time the sort of remark that has led literary critics to such gross brushing aside of social complexity, to a confident belief that the health of a society can be judged from the quality of its literature. Thus Leavis' essay on 'The Line of Wit', after tracing the connexions between the poetic manners of Jonson, Donne, Carew and Marvell, and contrasting them with the effect of Dryden, moves away from style to the 'dissociation of sensibility', which is linked to 'the great change that came over English civilisation in the seventeenth century'. Leavis' remarks are not meant to be more than a sketch of a possible study, but they have been read with more deference than that—and the direction of their reasoning is clear:

> But that the old fine order, what was referred to above as the 'Court culture', did not survive . . . is apparent even in the best things of Etherege, Sedley, Rochester and the rest.

The key terms here are 'order', 'culture' and 'things'. 'Culture' could refer to poetry only but seems (especially as 'Court culture') to have a wider meaning and to include the way of living and perhaps even the social structure. And 'order' would be a very odd term to use if we were not meant to think of society. Yet in the second half of the sentence, where the evidence for this at least partly social assertion is mentioned, there is no doubt that 'things' means, quite simply, 'poems'. Here is an approach that, with varying degrees of crudity, runs through much of the writing of the *Scrutiny* school: a tendency to argue from the quality of the literature to the nature of the society—and always when they are asserting a decline.

Of course if you define a healthy society as one which produces good poetry, you are as safe as circular arguments ever are. I feel sure that Arnold in 'The Function of Criticism' is going round in just this circle. The purpose of his essay is not to establish but to explain the difference between Sophocles and Shelley, to show why Sophocles did not need criticism and the Romantics did. The one thing that cannot possibly explain a difference is the fact of that difference, so if Arnold is basing his belief on the greatness of Sophocles his mistake is a simple, logical one. But what else can it be based on? On what the great writers say of their society? We may ask, why believe them, but we needn't even ask that: the England of Elizabeth, in its time of vast spiritual effort, produced a literature rich in satire, social denunciation, tears of the muses, contempt for a court that glows like rotten wood, and *laus temporis acti*. As for other kinds of evidence, we need not even speculate what it might be, for that would be to follow where Arnold has not tried to lead.

In an unimportant essay called 'Pagan and Medieval Religious Sentiment' Arnold puts in a good word in passing for the ancient world:

> What in comfort, morals and happiness were the rural population of the Sabine country under Augustus' rule, compared with the rural population of Hertfordshire and Buckinghamshire in the rule of Queen Victoria?

We are given no answer, but we are meant of course to think 'quite as good'. This is the side of Arnold one does not like to sneer at, for it is the Arnold who reminded the Roebucks and the Adderleys that Wragg was in custody. Though you would not know it from this sentence alone, there is a fierce indignation here on behalf of the 'rural population of Hertfordshire and Buckinghamshire'. All the same, why did he have to bring in the Romans? Are we to base our compassion for our own poor on an assertion that earlier ages were better off? It is a shaky foundation, with the economic historians around.

That there is no economic history behind Arnold's remark can be glimpsed from the word 'Sabine'. Why did he choose that, of the regions of Italy? Surely because of Horace: somewhere in Arnold's mind is the Sabine farm on which Horace enjoyed his rural content. It is another reminder that Arnold gets his picture of the past from literature. But in that case, he should write only about past literature, not about the rural population or the national glow.

Arnold's national glow is not the result of evidence and study but of nostalgia—the same nostalgia which informs the poetry. The difference between Arnold the poet and Arnold the critic is at first striking, but there are frequent points of contact when you look:

> We are none of us likely to be lively much longer. My vivacity is but the last sparkle of flame before we are all in the dark, the last glimpse of colour before we all go into the drab—the drab of the earnest, prosaic, practical austerely literal future. Yes the world will soon be the Philistines.

There is a sprightliness of tone here which is not common in Arnold's prose; but the passage is none the less basically serious. If we remove the contrast between poor Arnold who knows what his fate is, and the obtuse Philistine who doesn't, on which the irony of the passage is based, then we get a wholly serious lament for the drabness of those

> *Who fluctuate idly without term or scope,*
> *Of whom each strives, nor knows for what he strives. . . .*

In the same essay (the preface to *Essays in Criticism*) there is a glimpse of Oxford, and of what Arnold values in it:

> And yet, steeped in sentiment as she lies, spreading her gardens to the moonlight, and whispering from her towers the last enchantments of the Middle Age, who will deny that Oxford, by her ineffable charm, keeps ever calling us nearer to the true goal of all of us, to the ideal, to perfection,—to beauty in a word. . . . Adorable dreamer, . . . home of lost causes and forsaken beliefs and unpopular names and impossible loyalties! What example could ever so inspire us to keep down the Philistine in ourselves. . . .

Is this the Oxford which the Scholar Gipsy saw from the hill?

> *And thou has climbed the hill*
> *And gained the white brow of the Cumnor range,*
> *Turned once to watch, while thick the snowflakes fall,*
> *The line of festal lights in Christ-church hall—*
> *Then sought thy straw in some sequestered grange.*

It is the same emotion, certainly; but the use of the symbol has been reversed. The equivalent to the adorable dreamer, the home of lost causes, is the Scholar Gipsy himself: for him, Oxford is the modern world from which he has shut himself out. But not for Arnold: standing next to the Scholar Gipsy on that imaginary hill, he sees *his* Oxford, and in those lit halls they are still debating the forsaken beliefs. Poetically, Arnold is here having his cake and eating it: Oxford evokes to us the magic of the lost past and to the Scholar Gipsy the stern newness he is fleeing, and the picture is enriched with two contrasting clouds of emotion. The effect on our picture of the Scholar Gipsy is of course to make him more distant, more impossibly honest than ever: not even Oxford reaches back into his world. He is—if such a thing were possible—pre-Arcadian.

In the sixth Eclogue of Sannazaro's *Arcadia*, Serrano and Opico condemn the stealing that goes on nowadays and praise the past age in which morals were not depraved. Serrano invites Opico to see how the world is going from bad to worse, and to lament the change *pensando al tempo buon che ogn'or depravasi* (thinking of the good time that grows worse every hour). Opico in reply sings of how his father used to tell him of

> i tempi antichi quando i buoi parlavano, che'l ciel più grazie allor solea producere (those ancient times when the cattle could talk, which the more gracious heaven used then to bring about).

These *tempi antichi* are of course the Golden Age of pastoral convention. Opico describes them in terms of the graciousness of the gods and the occasional occurrence of magic. There was no iron; the gods themselves didn't disdain to lead the flocks to pasture; and

> i vecchi, quando alfin più non uscivano per boschi, o si prendean la morte intrepidi, o con erbe incantate ingiovenivano (the old, when no longer able to make their way through the bushes, either took their own lives courageously, or grew young again by means of magic herbs.)

This age is a country of the mind, not of the past. It is a delicate touch of Sannazaro's that leads Opico to describe how his father used to tell of it. This doubles the loss—even the memory of the Golden Age belongs in the past—and identifies it as having the personal intensity of true nostalgia—for Opico it has become part of his own childhood.

Though nostalgia seldom comes explicitly to the surface in

Arnold's social criticism, it is near the heart of its impulses. His dislike of so much in Victorian England was bound up with a belief that the world had deteriorated, that to find the criterion by which to attack the present, you should look into the past. I do not believe that the 'national glow' he found, when he looked, has a much more substantial existence than the 'tempi antichi' of Sannazaro. But Sannazaro admits what he is doing: by deploying the pastoral convention he identifies the Golden Age as an expression of our nostalgia. In his two great pastoral elegies, Arnold does and doesn't do this: he believes what he's saying, yet the whole form of the poems is an eloquent admission of where it all comes from. Both *Arcadia* and *The Scholar Gipsy* can move us as deeply as we are susceptible to this emotion: one more than the other, perhaps, depending on which style, and which century, we are attuned to. But in Arnold's essays, the scrupulous reader begins to find a demand for the truth of history getting in the way: for a new kind of assertion is being made. This raises new demands, which Arnold does very little to meet.

XIII

CONCLUSION

THE praise of past times is a theme that has recurred throughout the subject-matter of this book; and the original seed that led me to its composition was, as it happens, the wish to discuss man's tendency to idealise the past. When the *laudator temporis acti* sees concentration camps, wars of aggression, racial hatred, and such other wretched triumphs of the twentieth century, the temptation is great to regard them as signs of decline and even collapse, as the end of Western civilisation, the beginning of the thousand-year reign of Satan, or the final exposure of a misled humanism. The past he sees when he speaks like this is a projection of his own nostalgia, an illusion fostered by his need to believe that things were once better. To say this to him, and to dismiss his myth, can easily land us into apparently shrugging off the facts that have goaded him into it. If the wars, the hatreds, the concentration camps of our time are not signs of civilisation's collapse, then they may seem less fearful, less needing denunciation.

One indirect purpose of this book has been to say that this is a false dilemma. In order to denounce the atrocities round us, it is not necessary to jump to conclusions about the past. If men have always tortured one another, that is no reason for condoning torture in our time. We do not need an ideal past to serve as a standard for judging the present—we have our own standards. To base our anger on theories of what once was, is to place it on a frail footing. It gives to the historian who knows more than we do about the Middle Ages, say, the opportunity of shaking our case.

We all yearn nostalgically for childhood, and are often deeply moved, both in life and in poetry, by hearing the sudden note of longing, by finding ourselves suddenly caught in the yearnings of memory. It is here that the tendency to idealise the past finds its true expression. Such nostalgia has produced some of our most moving poetry, and in particular some of poetry's most beautiful moments. Emotionally, the main function of pastoral is as a form for such feelings.

The Golden Age, where pastoral takes place, is not the same as the Good Old Days. For the Golden Age lies outside history: it is a dream, based perhaps on childhood, perhaps (I have had to leave this problem unanswered) on the dream alone. Whereas the Good Old Days, which lie concealed in much social criticism (Arnold has had to serve as a brief example for a whole other book I might have written, had I had competence and space), and which rise to the surface in the grumblings of old men, the *rumores senum severiorum*—these Good Old Days claim to have existed, even at a particular time. The time is often hard to locate, and usually turns out to be one about which the author is ignorant, or might as well be for all the care he bestows on its understanding. As like as not, it is a time when men were already lamenting the good old days.

Because Astraea never really dwelt on earth, the Golden Age has to be seen as a myth only. Then it can retain its power over us, a power it must lose if we tarnish it with verifiable fact, locating it at some specified distance from a present we dislike. The only thing we can specify about the distance is that it is immeasurable because unchangeable. Every generation is equidistant from Arcadia.

INDEX

This index includes only substantive discussions, not
passing references.

Towards End 6 relates the Pastoral
tradition and its break up to the conflict
between the Syncretic view of Pan and
the Puritans

goes a far as poetic analysis can which
has no notion of Religious or platonic conception
Pastoral versus Christianity. Body v Soul
man innocent and man divided but
this begs the question of man
not really at home here, man in
suffering growing pains for another
dimension of being.
Pastoral Poetry as metaphors for the
unknown in terms
of Known, Learner has no mention
of mystical poetry Eg Eliot, Yeats,
St John of the Cross
199-200 good on Milton's sexually so distorted
by graves and Empson
" Perfection and Existence are incompatible "—
if we do not realise we are
evolving for another state of being,
and by suffering, growing pain
come to that nearest perfection which
is obedience to the will
Milton Eden like childhood who are
not metaphorically taken idea of bliss
is doomed because " foxes have holes" etc
and are must be strenuous
quite good on the theology of the
fall that it in the long run
good but that is unorthodox. Prodigal
sons disastrous journey. Blake mills of
satanic experience

Pastoral escapist still going on today.

Nathaniel West "Miss Lonelyhearts

So inclusive is the Nostalgia of the Turn
and so pregnant Nostalgia on the
Image of Better Paralell be more
significant modes of being to Poetry that
almost any work would come under
Leaner Pastoral Umbrella

Revengers Tragedy

Contemptus mundi page 147 & comes
nearer the truth
very intelligent

Rather good on the conflict between the
old gods and Christianity, Syncretist &
Puritan. The spread conflict between the
two in Milton
On the ode he calls Christ Pan but his
myths lament the coming of Xt and
the old gods are driven out. Very
illogical but an Example of the conflict
between humanist (poet) and puritan
— Milton

But in Milton he rather gets off his theme
It is not tied in firmly Enough
With Jonson and Comus he gets off the
theme doesn't really Know where to go
X shifts the bias to old and new Religion
but doesn't really tie up with pastoral
poetry although he has some intesting
things to say.
See 182 for a comment on religious poetry

Religion he thinks of Prelapsarian and Post
Lapsaria Nevein in Platonic terms